The Emerging Europe-East Asia Healthcare ICT Markets

George O. Obikoya

Table of Contents

Executive Summary

With a combined population of over 1.5 billion peoples, nearly a quarter of the world's population, East Asia no doubt, has a potentially huge market for healthcare information and communication technologies. It also has countries with some of the fastest growing economies worldwide. Even the erstwhile Tiger economies of Hong Kong, Taiwan, Singapore and South Korea, have maintained their characteristic impressive growth rates and China has become the second largest world economy in purchasing power parity terms, and not also just its fastest growing key economy, but a major player in sustaining global economic wellbeing. Europe, with a population of almost 730 million and some of the most developed countries in the world also offers significant healthcare ICT market opportunities. The nature and extent of these markets however depend on a variety of factors, some health-related, others not. Many of these factors are common to both regions and indeed, apply to every region and country on the globe. Others are contextual, their dynamics determined by the interplay of socio-demographic, economic, political, and other factors, some of which are internal, and others external to the country or region, all with potential significance for healthcare delivery. This e-book examines the determinants, nature, and scope of the healthcare information and communication technologies markets in these two regions, and the business prospects for software vendors, Telcos operators, and other technology firms of either region in the other.

The e-book also highlights the increasing importance of the health status of any country in its sustainable economic development, and the imperative in view of a variety of constraints, not least fiscal, to pursue with vigor the achievement of the dual healthcare delivery objectives of qualitative health services delivery, cost-effectively and efficiently with which many countries must now live. It analyzes the implications of this imperative for investments in healthcare information and communication technologies, and for market opportunities in these two regions. It also explores the competitive forces that healthcare ICT vendors and operators would encounter in venturing into these emerging markets and the essential requirements for acquiring competitive edge in markets whose emerging dyadic promises prospects and challenges in almost equal measure.

Introduction

Healthcare information and communication technologies are going to play an increasing role in healthcare delivery in the years ahead. This is because of the growing appreciation of the many benefits of a healthy people at both the individual and societal levels. Furthermore, the link between a country's health status and its economy is becoming clearer, a healthy country with better prospects of not just economic growth, but also sustainable economic development. Yet, it is unlikely that any country could afford to keep spending increasing proportions of its economic wealth on health services provision, as is the case increasingly with many countries in our present-day world. It is therefore, important for these countries to seek ways by which they could deliver qualitative health services to their peoples at less costs, in other words, to achieve the dual healthcare delivery objectives, much about which we would discuss in this e-book.

The countries of Europe and East Asia have significant differences regarding the healthcare delivery issues that confront them, although as with other countries of the world, also have those common to them. In addressing these issues, and with a view to determining the most appropriate healthcare information and communication technologies to resolve them successfully, there is need first, to understand fully the issues, and their underlying processes. We would attempt to unravel the interplay of these various issues in the following pages, and to thereof, reveal the true nature and extent of the potential healthcare ICT markets in these two regions. It is unlikely that any healthcare ICT would be able to tap the immense prospects that these markets offer without the firm itself understanding the intricacies of the relevant market drivers and their role in the emerging dyadic relationship between the regions.

As we explore these various issues, would the central underlying significance of healthcare information and communication technologies in contemporary healthcare delivery become apparent, as would the potential massive market opportunities for these technologies across these two important world economic regions, or would they not? Perhaps we should reserve until the end of our exploration of these healthcare ICT markets.

ICT and Contemporary Healthcare Delivery

Information and communications technologies will play an increasingly crucial

role in healthcare delivery to all healthcare consumers in the years ahead. Considering that the elderly are the most intensive users of healthcare services, and that in many countries, particularly in the developed world, we could expect more individuals to become seniors with increasing longevity, these technologies will therefore, be even more important for health services provision.. The appreciation of the value of these technologies to healthcare delivery is not only increasing, there is also keener interest in exp loiting the immense opportunities that these technologies offer. These developments are hardly surprising in view of recent developments in healthcare financing vis-à-vis the quality of healthcare delivery in many of these countries, even the developed ones. Specifically, health spending is soaring in these countries, whereas the quality of services is, some would insist, declining. This is clearly not a desirable state of affairs. On the contrary, every nation, presumably, wants to deliver qualitative healthcare to its citizens without compromising its economic well-being, and this explains in the main the increasing interests in healthcare ICT, technologies evidence shows could enable and indeed, facilitate the achievement of these dual objectives. Healthcare ICT could help improve the quality of healthcare delivery to seniors and everyone else in a variety of ways, but one that this in keeping with the direction in which healthcare seems headed is in facilitating the implementation of the disease prevention paradigm. This paradigm conceptualizes diseases on three levels of prevention, namely, primary, secondary, and tertiary prevention. Primary prevention is preventing diseases from occurring in the first place. Secondary and tertiary prevention are diagnosing and treating diseases early and promptly, and their complications, both in the short and long terms, respectively. Healthcare ICT appropriately deployed could facilitate the achievement of the objectives of any of the variety of initiatives that health systems, regardless of country, or funding model, is implementing and at any of these prevention levels. Progress in medical and technological knowledge is providing the rubric for policy formulation and the development of programs at these prevention levels. These policies and programs would require continuous reappraisal with the emergence of new knowledge further improving the quality of our health services and of healthcare delivery as healthcare ICT implementation helps deliver their goals, and assures that the future of healthcare delivery remains bright. Here then is the reason that we must not only implement these technologies but also do so on a large scale. In order words, we need to continue to promote the widespread adoption and utilization by all healthcare stakeholders of these useful technologies. With regard both, we need to put the necessary policies and mechanisms in place to encourage healthcare providers to purchase and utilize these technologies, as we would likelier reap their benefits for health service provision on a broader scale, the more widespread their diffusion and usage. The health industry seems resistive to their applications in routine patient care, although these technologies have various other uses, in facilitating the processes involved in health service provision as a whole, for examples, in the administrative and financial management domains. There are a number of reasons for this resistance, including lost productivity, costs, even technophobia. Attitudes are thawing though, albeit gradually, which is why we need to focus on change management, training, incentives to buy these technologies, and buy-in issues, among other end-user issues in our efforts to promote the widespread implementation of these technologies. Our efforts must be at once multidimensional and concerted, if we were to make any significant headway, in our quest to promote pervasive healthcare ICT deployment, and utilization in the health, and associated industries. One of the key handicaps to healthcare quality improvement is the pervasive information asymmetry that plagues the health industry, with its roots partly in the paternalistic origins of the medical profession in particular but also of the other health professions. On the other hand, many patients particularly in the developing countries where literacy levels are in general low compared to those in the developed world, also lack the skills to seek medical information, which the often limited institutional and technological infrastructure to do so, compounds. The significance of literacy in limiting knowledge of health issues for health status received research backing recently. A study researchers at the San Francisco VA Medical Center and the University of California, San Francisco conducted showed that lower literacy levels results in poor health and poor access to healthcare for seniors. The findings, published in the May 2006 issue of the Journal of the American Geriatric Society, revealed that persons aged 70 years and above with limited literacy skills are one and one half to two times as likely to have poor health, and poor health care access, versus those with adequate or higher reading ability.

Seniors with limited literacy, as defined in the study, a reading level lower than ninth grade, reported poor overall health, and diabetes one and one half times, and depression, twice more, than other study participants did. One in four of the 2,512 community-dwelling seniors aged 70 to 79 years that participated in the study, which excluded those with dementia or poor physical functioning, had limited literacy, and hence might have problems reading basic health information or instructions on their medication packs and bottles. If coupled with the poor vision that diabetes causes, for example, we clearly have a major problem on our hands. Does this not call for targeted, contextualized, health information dissemination to these and other seniors and for other measures to facilitate their ability to receive, read, or listen to, and hence be able to imbibe and use health information? These are activities that healthcare ICT could enable and facilitate efficiently and cost-effectively, and are indeed, already doing so, and in which they would play an even greater role in the years ahead. The researchers also noted that individuals with a sixth-grade or lower reading level were twice as likely as the ninth -grade and above group to have poor access to health care, which not having a regular doctor or place of care, not receiving a flu shot in the past year, or lacking insurance to cover medication indicated. They also observed that seniors with a seventh- to eighth-grade reading level also had less health care access versus those that had ninth-grade literacy level, although the difference was insignificant on considering confounders. Indeed, for all results the findings held true independently of socioeconomic background and educational levels. Noted Rebecca Sudore, MD, lead author and an assistant adjunct professor of Medicine at the University of California, San Francisco (UCSF), "As a geriatrician, the results of this study break my heart' Elders already have the highest medication and disease burden. Adding limited literacy to the list of problems makes these elders particularly vulnerable to poor outcomes, as we found in our study." There is no doubt that the findings of this study calls for urgent action to rectify this anomaly, lest we would not only be failing to deliver health services to these seniors, even the most basic not to mention qualitative, we would essentially, by our inaction, denying them access to healthcare. Here again, appropriately designed and deployed, multimedia, healthcare ICT could help these seniors, and even connect them with their healthcare providers for effective monitoring and management of their illnesses, without the need to read any health information at all. Again, as Dr. Sudore noted, "Elders with limited literacy have a hard time reading their pill bottles, managing their diseases, filling out needed forms for their care, and being able to navigate through the health care system." She added, "Unfortunately, in this study, we found that the very group of elders who would benefit from having more access to health care actually had worse access. Since the elders in our study were fairly well-functioning, problems accessing care and managing disease are likely to be even worse for frailer elders." Besides providing qualitative services to these seniors therefore, we would, by developing these specialized healthcare ICT, be contributing to our disease prevention, goals, at the primary, and even secondary and tertiary levels, reducing morbidities and mortalities among these seniors, and in effect reducing health spending that we, in effect all payers, would, otherwise have incurred. This study indeed, needs replicating in other countries in order to have a clear idea of the percentage of seniors that have similar problems, which would be valuable information for policy formulation, resource allocation and program planning and execution, among other necessary activities. Besides, we need to know that the reasons why there are these links between literacy, health, and health access, a point the researchers also emphasized, possible reasons including a lack of understanding of healthcare provider instructions, the need for compliance and follow -up with

11

treatment. There could also even be frustration with and resultant distrust of providers and health services in general, for example not being able to receive help completing insurance form s, or those needed to obtain medications. The authors noted that literacy skills are not equivalent to educational levels, hence the need for providers to communicate with and educate their patients in ways they would understand, which underscores the need for the sort of targeted, and contextualized healthcare ICT enabled, health information dissemination mentioned earlier. Indeed, Dr. Sudore advised the need for further research to determine the interventions able to prevent poor health outcomes in these prone seniors, noting the likely benefits of multidisciplinary education programs proven successful in geriatric and low-literacy populations. She also stressed that successful interventions would in the long term save money for taxpayers as "People with limited literacy skills have worse health outcomes, poor access to health care - as our study showed - and are more likely to get their care in the emergency room and to be hospitalized, which has been shown to incur higher health care costs." Should we therefore not be taking a closer look at the varieties of multimedia healthcare ICT-backed interventions that could be efficient and cost-effective in creating the enabling environment for these seniors to receive important health information? Considering that the population of many countries is aging, chances are there would be a significant number of seniors that fall into this category, regardless of their educational, and/or socioeconomic levels, hence the need for attention to ways of addressing these issues successfully. Indeed, there is increasing public awareness on the value of health information reaching the targeted audience. A recent Harris Interactive poll of 2,501 adults reported in the *Wall Street Journal Online* on May 31, 2006 found that over 80% of U.S. adults want the results of federally funded research on health issues and other subjects to be available online gratis to doctors and the public.

Eighty-one percent of respondents strongly/somewhat agreed that access to such information would help individuals living with a chronic illness or disability in " coping with that chronic illness or disability ", 62% that making research results available online free would " help speed up finding potential cures for diseases." Seventeen per cent also strongly/somewhat agreed that scientific journals should publish the information and offer it to paid subscribers, rather than for free online. There is no doubt that such information would reach those that want it and have subscribed to it via the print media, but for those that have access to the Internet, it would doubtless reach them faster, and cheaper, even if only for the journals, key benefits underlying our call for targeted health information dissemination.

Consider a health problem common among seniors for example, constipation, a new study that Boehringer Ingelheim sponsored, conducted on the epidemiology of which, and presented at the Digestive Disease Week congress in Los Angeles in May 20-25, 2006, offers new insights into the incidence of the problem and indicated that sufferers are simply not using the most effective treatments. The epidemiology survey explored duration and frequency of constipation in 13,879 participants from four continents. Its results indicated that 12% of people globally suffer from self-defined constipation, persons in the Americas and Asia Pacific, twice as much as Europeans, 17.3% versus 8.75%, the latter with the least rates. The survey also showed that 25% of people suffering from constipation do not do anything to relieve their symptoms, expecting them to resolve on their own, rather than use a contact laxative, such as Dulcolax®, which is safe and effective even over the long term. Considering that not only is constipation common among seniors, but also could be sufficiently disabling to cause delirium in some case, a life-threatening condition that requires emergency medical treatment and that has a reported mortality rate of about 25%, particularly if left untreated, constipation may not be as benign as it seems. The survey showed that less than 33% of constipation sufferers that treat it use laxatives, despite research evidence that these medications are safe and effective. Indeed, laxative use is lowest in Asia Pacific, despite high constipation rates, 17%, and despite having the highest rates of laxatives use, in the Americas, less than four in ten persons with constipation use them. According to Professor Wald, the lead author of the survey, "Sufferers continue to be highly influenced and misguided by myths surrounding constipation and it is critical to correct and overcome these mistaken beliefs. This survey reveals that on average, 40% of sufferers attempt to treat their constipation by changing their nutrition, despite extensive research showing that in fact diet and lifestyle are not necessarily to blame for the occurrence of constipation and increasing fluid and fiber intake will not definitely provide effective relief from the condition." The Professor added, "The new evidence from the survey has revealed that there is still a considerable unmet need in the treatment of constipation. It is our responsibility to make people aware of, and to offer, the best solutions for constipation, by publicizing the facts and correcting these misunderstandings." Do these observations not underline the need for targeted health information? Constipation could have many adverse consequences besides delirium in the elderly mentioned earlier, such as fecal impaction that could result in intestinal obstruction warranting surgical intervention, which some do not survive; internal, and external hemorrhoids, which could lead to enough blood loss to cause anemia, which if chronic could lead to heart failure; and many others, some potentially fatal. Should we therefore not act, as the Professor suggested? Could healthcare ICT, appropriately deployed not help in debunking these myths and changing attitudes toward this seemingly innocuous, but potentially dangerous health problem? Would we not be contributing to our efforts in achieving the dual objectives mentioned above doing so? There is no doubt that information asymmetry remains the bane of healthcare delivery, but why should we not exploit the opportunities that these technologies offer us in rectifying this perennial problem, particularly as the benefits derivable for adopting these technologies and utilizing them would far outweigh their costs, even if in the long term? A recent U.S study of 104 adults, aged 45 to 64 years, revealed that obese individuals lack awareness, that only 15% of them view themselves as obese, for example. Is this lack of awareness not an invitation to the various health problems that obesity causes or to which it has an association such as increased risk of heart disease, diabetes, high blood pressure, and arthritis? Would someone that does not see himself/herself as obese likely even focus on public health information about the consequences of obesity let alone act on it to reduce his/her weight? Unlike the 15% of participants mentioned above, 71% of individuals w ith normal weight and 73% of those classified as overweight, accurately assessed themselves. According to Kim Truesdale, a nutrition researcher at the University of North Carolina at Chapel Hill who presented the study at a conference in San Francisco "I think part of the disconnect is just the overall image people have when you say 'obesity.'" Is it then a denial issue, or confusion regarding Body Mass Index (BMI), which qualifies some overweight but muscle-bound individuals as having an abnormal BMI and overweight/obese, when in fact they hardly have any fat? Should we not be exploring the reasons for this lack of awareness and debunking the myths behind it? Could appropriately designed, healthcare ICT-enabled, targeted, and contextualized health information dissemination not help us in achieving this goal? Considering recent findings by the Centers for Disease Control and

Prevention (CDC) that 71% of men are overweight and 31%, obese, the figures 62% and 33% for women, respectively, and experts opinion that most Americans are not overweight due to excess muscle, and that over two-thirds of them are fat, is action on this matter not indeed urgent? The role of carbohydrates in our diet has long been controversial, and with overweight/obesity almost of epidemic proportions in many developed and in some developing countries, an important aspect of our primary prevention efforts should be letting the public know about significant research findings regarding carbohydrates and in fact any of our dietary components. Such findings include those of a recent study published in the May 2006 issue of the *American Journal of Clinical Nutrition* that showed that reducing carbohydrate intake could result in lowering of blood fat levels, including of cholesterol levels, even if one were not successful at losing weight. Research evidence now shows that carbohydrates, particularly simple sugars, could lead to unhealthy fat metabolism causing fat to accumulate in the liver, as it does in the thighs and abdomen, fats that ultimately maneuver their way into the blood. Thus reducing fat deposits by reducing carbohydrate intake, would reduce fat levels in the blood, and could improve the ability of the body to break down fats in the blood. The researchers compared three groups of overweight men all of who started out on a standard diet (54% carb intake), for a week. Afterwards the researchers randomly assigned them to those that took the same, 39% and 26% carb for a three-week period. The men then ate a similar diet for another five weeks, but with their calorie intakes cut down to produce weight loss. They went through another four weeks when researchers adjusted their energy intake for weight stabilization. The findings showed that compared to the men on a standard diet, the men with the lowest carbohydrate intake showed reductions in injurious triglycerides and "bad" LDL cholesterol levels, an increase in the ratio of "good" HDL cholesterol to total cholesterol levels, and other benefits to their blood fat profile. The researchers noted these healthy outcomes regardless of the men eating or not eating, less saturated fat, and losing or not losing weight. The authors noted that the 54% carb diet is akin to the normal diet many of Americans consume by adhering to standard dietary recommendations. They recommended that individuals could reduce their carbohydrate intake to a level similar to that used in the study by simply avoiding foods such as sugary foods, white rice, pasta, white bread, which in any case are not essential to a healthy diet. They also noted the need to embark on this or any diet for that matter preferably in consultation with a dietitian to get the right balance. These findings, of course, do not, in any way suggest that it is okay to be overweight, so long as one keeps dietary carb intake low. On the contrary, the adverse consequences on health of overweight/obesity are not in doubt. There is no doubt that the public would benefit from having this information, including seniors many of who not only have weight problems that have resulted in other medical disorders such as diabetes and for whom successful changes in their carbohydrate intake would certainly help reduce morbidities and even mortalities from these medical problems. This would not only improve the quality of life (QOL) of these seniors but would also reduce their medical expenses, saving significant healthcare costs. Are these not enough reasons for us to try to deliver health information to these seniors, or should we expect them to seek it? Even if some of them seek out health information, we should not expect them to be able to keep track all of even the relevant health information, considering what some would call the frenetic pace at which new medical knowledge emerges. Do these issues not speak eloquently to the need for us to embrace and act on the concept of healthcare ICT-backed targeted and contextualized health information dissemination? Health Canada and Health Canada, Eli Lilly on May 25, 2006 released an advisory that Evista, FDA approved to prevent osteoporosis and bone thinning, could increase stroke and mortality risk among some postmenopausal women living with heart conditions. Preliminary research findings of a National Cancer Institute-sponsored study released in April 2006, showed that Evista, aka raloxifene, in generic form, although not approved for breast cancer, is as effective as the breast cancer prevention drug tamoxifen in reducing breast cancer risk for postmenopausal women already prone to the cancer, and its potential for adverse events much less. A different clinical trial with over 10,000 postmenopausal women with heart conditions in 26 countries showed that 2.2 of every 1,000 women that took the medication died of a stroke, versus 1.5 per every 1,000 women taking a placebo, prompting Eli Lilly and Health Canada to recommend that women consult their physicians about the medications. This is clearly information that women ought to know about considering the increased likelihood of osteoporosis in older women, and the chances that many might be using the medication, not mention those that might be using it to prevent breast cancer. Yet, it is highly likely that many might miss the information, if they did not have it delivered to them either by their doctors, or other healthcare professionals, or some way else. What would the implications be for our efforts at primary prevention were large numbers of women not to receive this information? Could this not in fact increase morbidities and mortalities among these women, with significant disease burden for them, their families, and for society? Could we not prevent such adverse implications developing ways by which we could deliver this and other such important health information to women, for example, via healthcare ICT-backed, targeted, and contextualized health information dissemination?

An estimated over 20,000 Canadian women would receive the diagnosis of breast cancer and 5,000 would likely die of it yearly, based on current estimates, according to Canada's Center for Chronic Disease Prevention and Control, which also noted that one in nine women in Canada would develop breast cancer during her lifetime. Breast cancer also occurs in men, although 99% of the condition occurs in women, mostly in women over 50 years old, which is why many experts recommend that women between the ages of 50 and 69 years ought to have a mammogram and clinical examination every one or two years. Despite the alarming breast cancer statistics, a recent study found gaps in knowledge of breast cancer among Ontario women, confirming what we mentioned earlier concerning how the information asymmetry that has for long compromised healthcare delivery persists even today, even in developed countries. The study, an opinion survey showed that women in Ontario have misconceptions about this major health issue regarding for examples, incidence, and risk, signs and symptoms and breast cancer screening practices. The KAP (knowledge, attitude, and Practice) survey is part of Up Front: New Perspectives on Breast Cancer, an all-inclusive inquiry into women's experience with breast cancer, which the Ontario Chapter of the Canadian Breast Cancer Foundation in collaboration with some key breast cancer stakeholders. The Institute for Social Research at York University in the survey, which RE/MAX Ontario-Atlantic Canada and the Princess Margaret Hospital Foundation Breast Centre Women's Committee funded, asked 800 Ontario women not diagnosed with breast cancer questions regarding their knowledge, attitudes, perceptions, and beliefs on breast cancer. Noted Sharon Wood, executive director, Canadian Breast Cancer Foundation - Ontario Chapter, "Significant progress has been made in raising awareness of breast cancer over the past 20 years, but the amount of information can be overwhelming to digest, and there are still some communities where information is limited " . Does this not also speak to the need for targeted health information, which healthcare ICT offers us immense opportunities to conduct and efficiently and cost-effectively? The survey found that 40% of the respondents believe breast cancer is the most important health issue the contemporary woman confronts. Its findings also suggested a need to target women of non-European descent, and those in low -income groups, both the survey found less informed about breast cancer, who would less likely take part in risk reduction behaviors. Considering screening mammography alone could reduce breast cancer mortality rate by 30%, should we not in fact be more vigorous about employing multimedia healthcare ICT to disseminate relevant health information to these and other vulnerable women, for example those over 50 years, with the chances of developing breast cancer known to increase with age, and indeed, to women in general? Should it not be cause for concern that as many over 50% of the women surveyed could name only one symptom of breast cancer, lump in the breast, 11%, unable to name any, this low recognition commoner among less educated women, those with lower incomes, and those born outside Canada? Does this not call for urgent actions to assist women in identifying the signs and symptoms of breast cancer? As Wood rightly noted, "While a lump in the breast is the most commonly-known symptom of breast cancer, it is not the only one". She added, "By knowing the other signs and symptoms of breast cancer and becoming aware what is normal for them, women can be better prepared to recognize changes in their breasts that might be a sign of breast cancer. " Could healthcare ICT properly deployed not help in providing women the necessary information on breast cancer? The survey even showed that many women do not know where to go to have mammograms, and x-ray breast exam that experts

20

recommend women over 50 years have once every two years. Indeed, just 34% of the women surveyed knew the Ontario's target of 50 years for having a mammogram, 45% thought it was 40 years. Cancer Care Ontario, the agency that oversees the Ontario Breast Screening Program (OBSP), actually confirmed that just over 50% of women above 50 years receive screening. There is no doubt about the need to intensify efforts to improve awareness of breast cancer issues among women in Ontario, and in fact, worldwide, and because healthcare ICT could facilitate these efforts, it is absolutely necessary to examine ways by which we could deploy these technologies for this crucial primary prevention purposes. Still on cancer, U.K and U.S researchers recently reported details of a 10-year trial that Cancer Research UK funded and involving 1,410 women in Lancet Oncology. The researchers noted that giving 13 larger doses of radiotherapy was as effective at preventing cancer return as the standard regime of 25 small doses, findings experts believe result in simpler and more effective radiotherapy treatment, improved outcomes with less hospital visits and stays, and significant cost savings for U.K's National Health Service (NHS.) They would also no doubt improve the quality of life (QOL) of patients, save time and money spent traveling to receive treatment, and encourage better compliance with treatment, as patients currently receive radiotherapy once daily, every week day, for five weeks, and only rest at the weekend, a regime quite exhausting for many patients. Further research is under way to determine the effectiveness of this approach versus standard treatment in the long term. These findings also have important implications for resource optimization in the NHS, as there is currently a shortage of people to operate radiotherapy machines, a problem that patients requiring fewer treatments could potentially help ease. This example shows that health information dissemination could also be useful at the secondary prevention level. Would it not be easier to disseminate the information about this and other research findings to the patients that need it, which would also facilitate scheduling therapy appointments considering the limitations in the availability of professionals to handle these radiotherapy machines, thereby reducing wait times, and easing pressure of these professionals? In other words, healthcare ICT could help improve the efficiency of a variety of processes involved in healthcare delivery, some necessary spillovers from the primary implementation purpose, all working in tandem nonetheless more efficiently, to deliver care that is more effective. We could therefore, and this is often the case, be realizing expected secondary, perhaps even unanticipated gains from our investment in these technologies for an initial, specified purpose, in material, via costs savings, and human, via prompt disease diagnosis and treatment, terms. This why conceptualizing healthcare delivery in prevention terms is as heuristic as any could be. We could set out to improve certain processes and along the way not only discover new and potentially cryptic improvable processes, which might have been compromising our achievement of the dual objectives mentioned earlier, but in fact, generate new initiatives that these technologies albeit with a few upgrades here and there could also help accomplish. What's more, the processes become ongoing continuous quality improvement efforts, which would save costs, ultimately, as recent developments in the electronic submissions of health insurance claims in the U.S shows. A recent survey by America's Health Insurance Plans (AHIP) of 25 million claims that a sample of 26 health insurers processed showed that the submission of 75% of all 2006 health claims were electronically, versus 44% in 2002 and only 24% in 1995. According to the report, released in May 2006, healthcare providers submitted 30% of claims within a week in 2006, versus 19% in 2002. While there has been a reduction in lag times for provider-submitted claims, lagging submissions remain a problem, the report revealing that 29% of claims still did not come in until a month or more after the service date, 15%, more than two months or even more. The problems appear to be most prominent with paper claims, 31% of which did not reach insurers often more than 60 days after the service date, a situation that the current shift toward electronic submission would no doubt improve. Insurers are also processing claims automatically, further improving efficiency, 68% of all claims, according to the AHIP survey, 71%, and 41% of electronic and pap er claims, respectively. The report also noted the cost advantages of electronic claims submission, and processing. Thus, with submissions requiring no additional information, the average processing cost for an electronic claim was 85 cents, versus $1.58 for a paper claim, pending claims that need an average of nine more processing days cost $2.05 each on the average to process. Is it any wonder that AHIP President Karen Ignani observed that " These data clearly show the best way to speed claims payment and to further reduce administrative costs is not through costly, new 'prompt pay' mandates, but rather to continue encouraging greater use of electronic claims submission." Does this not underscore the need for us to promote further the widespread diffusion of these technologies among both clinical and non-clinical healthcare stakeholders in our efforts to achieve the dual objectives of delivering qualitative healthcare cost-effectively, and efficiently? Is it not apt that the U.S Congress is enacting legislation to encourage greater use of healthcare ICT, including standardized electronic health records (EHR), with the recent 8-5 vote approval of H.R. 4157, the Health Information Technology Promotion Act, by the House Ways and Means Subcommittee on Health. To underscore the interrelatedness of these various processes, both clinical and non-clinical in making the health system work, or otherwise, could we ask if speeding up such claims not motivate providers to deliver healthcare more efficiently and effectively, or not? A recent study published in the October 12, 2005 issue of the

Journal of the American Medical Association assessed the effects of a pay-for-performance program in a large health plan. The study noted significant quality improvement in a physician group with a quality incentive program (QIP) for one of the three clinical measures studied, versus another without a QIP, the improvements in the other two measures, not significant. Do these findings not suggest that the widespread implementation of healthcare ICT with its prospects for process improvement, could help improve quality, and with clear expectations of incentives in place, either via speeded claims or QIPs, for examples, would this not motivate healthcare providers to invest in and implement these technologies? Incidentally, this study showed that physician groups that performed well, rather than those with most improvement received most of the bonus money in the QIPs for meeting specific targets in clinical quality scores. Indeed, many experts contend that there is a pervasive misalignment of and indeed failure to reward high quality performance in healthcare delivery in the U.S. and call for rewarding excellence adequately, and appropriately, which could no doubt improve healthcare delivery. Could not just paying for delivered services, but going a step further and rewarding the delivery of qualitative healthcare that would move us closer to achieving the dual objectives mentioned earlier, not motivate providers to implement the healthcare ICT that could enable them improve their performance, and indeed enable us to do so? The study examined quality improvements for clinical quality scores on Pap smears, mammography, and hemoglobin testing for diabetics in two groups in PacifiCare Health Systems. The researchers compared PacifiCare s California network, which started a quality incentive program in 2003, with its Pacific Northwest group, in Oregon and Washington that did not, the former given bonuses for meeting the targets. The researchers noted that quality scores for cervical cancer screening improved 5.3% in the pay-for-performance (P4P) group, versus 1.7% in the group without (P4P,) a significant difference, but not so for the other two measures studied, mammography and hemoglobin testing for diabetics, in which both groups improved. Furthermore, the physician groups with performance above the bonus threshold before QIP implementation received 75% of the bonus payments. There is no doubt that P4P could motivate healthcare providers and improve the quality of healthcare delivery, but we must structure it properly. This could be a complex enterprise considering such issues as the involvement of multiple physicians in patient care, let us even say, for a particular disease, such as diabetes, for example, the diabetologist, nephrologist, and cardiologist, even neurologist, depending on the nature and extent of the complications of the disease. Nonetheless, one approach is as in the study above to set clear-cut quality targets based on stipulated criteria at least in the equally clear-cut cases. In other words, we need payment reforms based on a detailed evaluation of a number of clinical and other issues. In addition, we need to provide the public with the results of quality evaluation, and information on pricing, which would make the former more meaningful to the healthcare consumer in taking rational decisions regarding healthcare provider and treatment choices. This way we would be leveling the playing field, literally for consumers and providers to operate efficiently and effectively in the health market. The former would be able to patronize high quality, yet affordable providers, and providers to broaden value propositions employing sophisticated healthcare ICT and other technologies for example to improve quality at competitive prices, hence attract patronage and boost profitability, clearly, a potential win-win situation for all. There is also the need to continue to conduct studies on an ongoing basis to understand further, the various issues, for examples the regulatory, market, technological and clinical factors involved in making the execution of P4P and other payment and incentive systems succeed, or otherwise.

Some might wonder why we tie in costs so much to our discussion on

qualitative healthcare delivery. It is simply because healthcare delivery costs money, regardless of its funding system, and because money is not limitless, we cannot afford to ignore an ever-increasing health spending, as is the case in many countries today, particularly in the developed world. That, as some would argue the increasing health spending is not borne out in a corresponding increase in the quality of services delivered, compounds the problem and would no doubt jar even the most benign among us. For these reasons and many more, we need to accept the fact that the state of affairs with health services in many countries is not sustainable and we need to seek ways to rectify the problems before they assume a life of their own. Consider a *USA Today* analysis of May 25, 2005 for example, which noted that taxpayer liabilities for healthcare and sundry benefits governments promised retirees in future, increased by about $10 trillion in the past two years to $57.8 trillion or about $510,678 per household, Medicare liabilities $263,377 of the total. This is a 20% increase in taxpayer liabilities, 13% more than the inflation rate In other words, governments at various levels need these trillions of dollars to raise enough interest to meet the cost, valued in 2006 dollars, of the promised benefits. Not only must payment on this outstanding tax bill commence in due course, lest the promises made to seniors fail, but also with the costs of retirement programs billed to increase substantially as baby-boomers turn seniors in just five years time and become eligible for Medicare, in fact, for Social Security before then, in 2008. What are the implications of these figures for health spending, not to mention for future tax burden? What would happen to the country's health system if we did not start now to seek ways to achieve the dual objectives mentioned earlier, considering the expected increase in the numbers of seniors, the population segment that utilizes health services the most. Could we do something now that would in fact reduce health service utilization in future, or at least those parts of it, for example, hospitalization rates and stays, responsible in the main for driving health spending sky-high? Could investing now in the appropriate healthcare ICT help us in achieving these goals down the road? Should we not be developing innovative, healthcare ICT-enabled multimedia, and contextualized programs in the different prevention realms that would enable us achieve these dual objectives, and is it not possible to aim these programs also at address seniors' health issues? To underscore the potential impact on loss of benefits to seniors in retirement, consider the results of a survey that the Kaiser Family Foundation released on May 30, 2006. This survey, which examined the impact of the bankruptcies of two steel companies, the LTV Corporation and Bethlehem Steel, on health coverage for the firms' retirees and dependents, noted that it left about 200,000 of them without retiree health coverage in 2002 and 2003. The report also offers a hint into the effect of a tax credit that Congress passed in 2002 aimed at providing provisional support to workers and retirees in "distressed" industries. It found that notwithstanding, almost 75% of respondents had received replacement coverage or a supplement to their Medicare coverage many insisted the loss of benefits significantly disrupted their retirement. Twenty six percent of the 55 to 64 year old respondents said that they use the 2002 Trade Adjustment Act's health insurance tax credit, which funds up to 65% of health insurance costs for eligibles, who also receive refunds from the IRS if they owed less tax than the credit amount. The loss of health coverage meant that for about 50% of retirees 65 years or under,

27

he/she or a spouse had to delay retirement or return to employment, about 25% digging deep into their savings or assets to fund their healthcare costs or premiums. Those uninsured were twice as much likely to go without or postpone needed healthcare on costs grounds. The survey also found that Medicare provided primary coverage for retirees and spouses aged 65 years and above. Medicare HMO or supplemental coverage covers 74% of respondents. However, 51% of all Medicare-eligible respondents without supplemental coverage said that they "often" or "sometimes" were not compliant with prescribed medications due to cost, versus 29% with a supplemental coverage. There is no doubt about the need for seniors not only to have access to care, but not to lack care because of costs. Besides the underlying ethico-moral issues involved in such lack of access to care, and the burden of illness on the seniors and their families, seniors would be less healthy and end up in the ER, perhaps hospitalized, which would in the end cost more to the taxpayer than did they not lack access to healthcare in the first place. The need for seniors to have access to healthcare and the possible consequences of this access lacking as the above scenario shows, also applies to other countries besides the U.S. These examples not only illustrate the need for seniors to have access to care on the one hand, but also not to promote excessive use of hospital services in particular on the other. They also highlight the need for us to design and implement effective services, enabled by healthcare ICT, to deliver health services to seniors at the different levels of the disease prevention paradigm. An example of such efforts is the recent design by the U.S National Institute on Aging (NIA) a part of the National Institute of Health of two easy-to-read booklets on Alzheimer's disease (AD) and memory loss, in which it replaced medical and technical language with plain language, stories, photographs, and other features to facilitate readers' understand of their content. This is the sort of targeted health information that we advocate, in paper form, although these efforts could also be in electronic, documentary-type multimedia formats, for example, which might work better for certain elderly populations. According to Richard J. Hod es, M.D., the NIA director, "Our goal was to produce strong, clear materials to make information about AD and memory loss accessible to everyone, including those with limited literacy skills." He added, "These booklets also are excellent starting points for anyone who needs basic information about AD and memory problems, regardless of reading capability." The NIA produced the booklets after local field-testing, and interviews with care givers and further testing for overall appeal, format, graphic elements, comprehension, cultural appropriateness, and "self-efficacy", which latter measures the individual s appreciation of the significance of acting on emergent signs of AD or serious memory loss, and the incorporation of feedbacks from these and various other sources. As previously noted, part of our efforts to implement disease prevention services involves information dissemination to healthcare providers as well as patients themselves, as the following example regarding stroke shows. German scientists, who presented their findings to the recent European Stroke Congress in Brussels, reported that a rare genetic disorder is the cause of some strokes in young people. The researchers found that 4% of more than 700 stroke patients aged 18 to 55 years also had Fabry disease, strokes occurring ten years earlier in persons with this disease. Although the findings apply to a small number of individuals, it nonetheless revealed a preventable and treatable cause of stroke, Fabry disease, caused by a missing or faulty enzyme that the body requires to process oils, waxes, and fatty acids, which then accumulate to dangerous levels in the eyes, kidneys, nervous system, and cardiovascular system. Persons with the disease could die early due to renal, cardiac, or cerebrovascular complications, which enzyme replacement therapy could slow and prevent, which is why all doctors and healthcare professionals, at least those that treat stroke need to be aware of this disease. Unlike for men and women that do not have Fabry disease for who the average age for having stroke is 48 years, it is 38 and 40 years, for men and women, respectively with the disease. This research underscores the need for screening for Fabry disease in young people. It also suggests that we need to consider it a p robable cause of a cryptogenic stroke in young persons, an important aspect of implementing our disease prevention paradigm, which could reduce the burden of stroke and its complications down the road. Healthcare practitioners in particular should be prime movers in the health-information dissemination efforts to facilitate the screening process, and it would, no doubt be more efficient for them to do so having the appropriate healthcare ICT implemented. We should not only encourage them to implement these technologies, they also need to embrace and use the technologies. In the UK, a recent BBC News survey showed that doctors want a review into the £6.2bn NHS computer project, the ICT upgrade intended to connect 30,000 GPs to nearly 300 hospitals in a major revamping of the NHS ICT network. One important part of this upgrade is the choose and book, which is a system that enables patients to book hospital appointments at a place, date, and time convenient to them from GP surgeries, almost 10m such referrals made annually. Another is the NHS care records service, which is an electronic database of patient medical records for 50 million patients that would give NHS staff nationwide, access to patient information at the point of care (POC). The upgrade also includ es capabilities for electronic prescriptions. With over 325m prescriptions made annually, an electronic version would replace the current paper-based system by 2007. This would enable patients to pick up repeat prescriptions from any pharmacy nationwide. H owever, the survey, which 447 hospital doctors and 340 GPs completed, showed that 50% of the GPs thought that the "choose and book" online booking system was poor/fairly poor. This could be a major setback for the project if nothing happened to understand and rectify the problems the doctors had with the system, other parts of which Ministers incidentally concurred were behind schedule, hence guzzling more than their budgets, the EHR, for example, lagging over two years behind schedule. According to the NHS, the "choose and book system", which it has been promoting, has helped make 400,000 appointments so far, which would no doubt help reduce wait times, and improve accessibility to healthcare. These would in turn reduce morbidities and mortalities, and healthcare costs, which are cogent reasons that it is necessary to address the problems that doctors have with the system urgently. This is more so considering that, as many as four out of five GPs, as the results of the BBC Radio 4's File on Four survey show, had access to the computer system, but 50% said that they hardly or never use it, with only about 20% acknowledging that the system was good/fairly good. Indeed, 85% of the doctors urged an independent expert technical review of the whole scheme to ensure its fundamental viability. Interestingly, when asked if the cost of the upgrade was a good use of NHS resources, almost two-thirds of GPs and hospital doctors did not think so, which is a clear indication of the urgent need to tackle the issue of acceptance of healthcare ICT in the U.K. This issue is not peculiar to the country but pervasive among healthcare professionals in many others, developed and developing. The reasons for this seeming antipathy toward healthcare ICT in the medical professional are legion, but one of the most often mentioned in researches is lost productivity. This however, underscores the need for improvement in the technologies but also the need for training and the learning curve for some of these technologies, particularly for many doctors that are not tech-savvy could indeed be steep, not to mention the costs in time, regardless of prior knowledge or interest in healthcare ICT. Privacy and confidentiality issues also concern many doctors, as do logistics problems for example involved with booking hospital appointments from GPs' surgeries. There is no doubt that there are problems along the road to widespread healthcare ICT implementation, and that of end -user buy is perhaps as crucial, if not more than implementing the technologies themselves. The delay in implementing EHR in the U.K could mean that electronic records might not be deployable in the country until early 2008, which creates immense opportunities to mobilize the appropriate agencies to embark on massive change management exercises for the healthcare professionals. As with any new enterprise, there would also be teething problems, some anticipated, others, not. Solutions to some of these problems would come easy, others would be essentially intractable, at least in the im mediate, possible even in the short term. Nonetheless, we must keep seeking these solutions and moving the enterprise forward, knowing the prospects are real of being able to achieve our dual objectives of qualitative healthcare delivery while simultaneously reducing costs. Reports indicate that software development is one major cause of delay with some of these technologies, for example the EHR in the U.K upgrade project. This is hardly surprising considering the vary nature of software, with millions of codes sometimes required to write and execute for just one product, and sometimes even just an aspect of it, among other inherent problems. There are again, many technical issues involved that could cause such a delay for examples, those regarding verification and validation, or hopefully not, even flawed requirements analysis. Thus, software developers and vendors need to be active partners in our efforts to achieve the dual healthcare delivery goals, as they are major stakeholders in these efforts. Considering that healthcare delivery often involves matters of life and death, there is no room for errors and software must be very near if not perfect. Here we begin to see the interrelationships of various factors in our ability to achieve the dual objectives. This underscores the need for a more widespread campaign to promote the pervasive diffusion of healthcare ICT, not just in the health but also in related industries, for example, the insurance industry. It is also important to promote the use of these technologies in the financial, administrative, and other domains that operate in tandem to ensure the delivery of cost-effective, yet qualitative health services.

With regard the variety of interlocking issues that challenge us in our efforts to achieve the dual goals, let us examine the problems with healthcare ICT implementation in the UK mentioned above a little further. The fact is, there is not much time to waste in implementing these technologies for a number of reasons including for example the state of affairs with pensions in the country, and its possible impact on future health services provision. By 2020, an estimated 26% of the UK population will be over 60 years of age; by 2050, 38%. Millions lack an occupational pension, and many more workers will have to rely solely on the state post-retirement, which would worsen with employers shutting off munificent final salary pension schemes, which helped reduce reliance on the state, and which led to so much frustration, even strike actions, in the early 2000s. The Adair Turner-headed Pensions Commission in 2004 highlighted the shortfalls in the country's retirement provision, with an estimated 11.3 million workers not making any pension contributions. Of those who were, many, pittance. About 12 million persons aged 25 years and over, for example, saved next to nothing, experts noting then that without increasing taxes or retirement ages, pensioners will suffer a 30% decline in relative incomes, borne out by recent events for examples, the planned increase incrementally to 68 years by 2044, and the restoration of the state pension and earnings link. The link would be by 2012, the latest, concerns about this not materializing because of a dispute on its details including funding between the Prime Minister and the Chancellor, now laid to rest with a recent deal announced between them. In addition, in response to the report of the Pensions Commission Government also wants to establish a new savings scheme with automatic enrolment for staff and compulsory employers' contributions. The aging population is at the core of these pensions-problems, with increasing fewer taxpayers of working age to pay everyone's pensions, a demographic zero-sum game slamming pensions everywhere, public and private, the stock market not particularly endearing enough and corporate scandals discouraging enough to boost people's interest in pension schemes. Higher taxes, increased savings, and retirement age are options to tacking these problems but are politically dicey. These issues might have profound impact on the resources available for health spending in the U.K in the near future, or at least make it difficult for it to continue to soar relentlessly as it does currently. These issues underscore the need for urgent steps to curtail health spending while not compromising the quality of healthcare delivery, both that the widespread implementation and utilization of healthcare ICT promises, and could deliver. Within a decade, about 50% of the UK adult population will be aged over 50, yet a recent research conducted for Heyday, a new group in the U.K, to address concerns regarding persons born between 1946 and 1965, shows that 41% of individuals in their 50s have not started actively planning for retirement. Furthermore, even if, as this survey by Heyday, set up by Age Concern, and similar to the American Association of Retired Persons (AARP), of 1,770 persons shows, 48% of these baby-boomers want to work well past the current retirement age of 65 years, ageism stands in their way, as 64% gracefully acknowledged. This is besides the vagaries of the prevailing economic climate, with employers, ever ready to slice the labor force in the event of a downturn in economic growth. In all, the need for sustainability in the U.K health system calls for the necessary steps to achieve the dual objectives mentioned earlier in our discussion. The call in fact applies to all health systems regardless of whether publicly or privately funded. There is no doubt about the role a country's funding structure of its health system in issues such as universality and accessibility, among others, issues germane to the quality of healthcare delivery in the long term, and which healthcare ICT appropriately deployed could help improve the health system's funding structure regardless. These issues also partly explain the differential scorecards the health systems in Canada, the U.K, and the U.S, received recently based on new research findings. According to a recent study published in the May 03, 2006 issue of the Journal of the American Medical Association, white, middle-aged Americans, even the rich, are much less healthy than their English counterparts, the former having higher rates of diabetes, heart disease, strokes, lung disease and cancer, the findings true regardless of income or education level. Yet, the U.S. health care spending is twice, $5,200 per person that of England per citizen in adjusted dollars, the study supporting previously established findings that the U.S. spends more on health care than any other industrialized country, but lags behind in rankings of life expectancy. Too little exercise, excessive stress, the U.S obesity epidemic, and a variety of reasons proffered have not diminished interests in finding explanations for these observations. The researchers, who studied people, aged 55 to 64 years, the average age of the samples the same, even included non-Hispanic whites in the study to eliminate the effect of racial differences. The study found that high-income persons in both countries were healthier than middle-and low-income persons were, but the health status of high-income Americans was similar to that of the low-income English, compounding the mystery. The relative poor showing of the health status of Americans is well known, and according to the World Health Organization (WHO), Americans rank behind not less than twenty other nationals in this regard, but the findings of this study are new and add even newer dimensions to the matter. Could the findings be due to more ethnic-diversity, some ask, given that the health of minorities for a variety of reasons is in general worse than that of whites? However, as noted earlier, the researchers adjusted for this potential ethnic bias. Previous studies have contrasted the U.S. with other countries regarding availability of and access to healthcare services, healthcare expenditures, service utilization, and other parameters, but this is the first to address the prevalence of chronic conditions, incidentally, more prevalent among seniors, and considering the age groups studied, prevalence we should expect they might carry forward into the senior years. Could physical activity be the reason as one of the researchers suggested, although not likely the only one? Some even mentioned financial insecurity, household income increase unknown in all but the top fifth of Americans since the mid -1970s, that of the English improving on the contrary. Were this in fact the case, are the advantages of the English sustainable in the long term considering the pensions crisis mentioned earlier, and in particularly with the necessary measures not taken to reduce spiraling healthcare spending? Does this not speak to the need to eschew delaying the adoption of healthcare ICT that could help reduce healthcare spending while in fact improving the quality of healthcare delivery to the bargain? In a similar vein, would the health status of Americans not improve addressing the process issues that bog down the country's health systems, both clinical and non-clinical, which are the real reasons for its seemingly unwieldy healthcare delivery systems? It is unlikely that the stress of striving for the American dream has more damaging effect on health than that of striving for the English, barring any significant genetic differences in the stress reactions, and considering that, both countries have a social welfare system. Besides, even if the safety net of the U.S were flawed, does it explain why those that have achieved the American dream could only be as healthy as those that presumably have yet to achieve the English dream? Furthermore, does the National Health Service (NHS) in particular considering its many administrative, clinical, including wait times, and financial problems, explain the better health of the high-income English, even if it did that of the low-income? Even if it did, does it explain why Americans with insurance were in such relatively poor health? There is no doubt about the heuristics of exploring the differences in health status revealed in this study utilizing the disease prevention paradigm. We would then be able to see vividly, the natural histories of these chronic health problems and the differences in the processes involved in their evolution, between the two countries, after all, it is not that they exist in one or the other country. This revelation would enable us see all the processes, both clinical and non-clinical, including their determinants and outcomes, the processes and variables constituting the foundation upon which we would formulate the necessary policies within the context of our strategic objectives, that would determine the required healthcare ICT-enabled initiatives we would act on in a change continuum of healthcare quality improvement. Another recent study billed for publication in the July 2006 issu e of the *American Journal of Public Health*, compared the health of Canadians and Americans. The study found that Canadians are healthier, have better access to healthcare, yet spend half of what Americans spend on their health system, $6,000 for every American. They also found that Canadians were 7% likelier to have a regular doctor, 19% less likely to have their health needs go unmet than Americans, who were more than twice as likely to give up go without needed medicines due to cost. With income, age, sex, race and immigrant status taking into consideration, the differences became even more prominent, with Canadians 33% likelier to have a regular doctor and 27%

37

unlikelier to have an unmet health need. The study also showed that Americans had higher rates of almost all serious chronic disease, for examples obesity, diabetes and chronic lung disease, although they smoked cigarettes less. This study's researchers suggest the biggest obstacle to health care in the U.S is cost, responsible for more than seven times more U.S. residents forfeiting needed healthcare compared to Canadians, the uninsured particularly vulnerable, with 30.4% having an unmet health need due to cost. Costs also explain why low income and minority patients fare better in Canada, but could inefficient processes be responsible for the high costs of care in the U.S, or not? Considering that unlike U.S/U.K study, insured Americans and Canadians had about the same rates of disease, and that uninsured Americans worsened the overall figures, does it only have to do with the benefits of access to healthcare? If so, why does this not explain the differences between the health status of the Americans and the English, as noted above? There is no doubt that access to care is crucial and must have a hand these differences, at least on the aggregate, after all the more persons that lack access to care the less health the population would be overall. Yet, even then, it would unlikely explain all the observed differences and it would be in the end a matter of understanding the intricacies of the underlying processes involved largely, with healthcare delivery in either health system. Thus, could the appropriate deployment of healthcare ICT not improve these processes hence improve healthcare delivery and reduce healthcare costs? Would reducing healthcare costs without compromising the quality of healthcare delivery not become possible with the widespread implementation of healthcare ICT, as we have discussed so far? By improving the quality of healthcare delivery, would healthcare ICT not be contributing to making people healthier, and with improved health, would service utilization, in particular hospitalization rates and stays not be less, thus further reducing health spending? Would this not free up scarce resources that could go into other important social programs such as education, or any other for that matter, for example seniors pensions and other benefits as discussed earlier? The study also found that Canadians wait, on average, three times more than Am ericans for medical treatment, which suggests that the country's health system also needs to examine its processes and implement measures to improve them, here again, which appropriately deployed healthcare ICT could help achieve, and cost-effectively too. The point here is that no matter the funding structure of a health system, healthcare delivery is a conglomeration of intricately intertwined processes, which we need to understand in detail for us to determine its flaws and rectify them using the right healthcare ICT, and other suitable solutions. This underscores the need for cautious interpretation of such findings as mentioned above, particularly in order to avoid complacency of the parts of the systems that fared better, and more particularly to appreciate the contextual nature of process evaluation, hence of the applicable quality improvement strategies. Thus, for example, the issue of wait times remains sticky in both Canada and the U.K, and these studies would unlikely change the views of the citizens of these two countries regarding the need to fix these problems. Indeed, in the case of Canada, it has resulted in a landmark Supreme Court ruling in *Chaoulli v. Quebec,* which has rekindled a long-standing debate on the continuing status of the country's cherished Medicare, the publicly funded health system, with some calling for a parallel private health system. In the U.K, it is equally topical, and partly responsible for the various initiatives that have increasingly infused private funding arrangements into the country's publicly funded health system. As we have argued thus far, every health system needs its processes revisited on an ongoing basis, in light of developments such as the "wait times" issues, and even such studies as mentioned above, alth ough it should routinely, periodically, as part of an internal audit effort to ensure continuous quality improvement. Canada and the U.K for examples might be spending less money to obtain better health outcomes than the U.S does but could these latter cou ntries obtain even better outcomes for even lesser health spending, or put differently, could they afford an ever-increasing health expenditure or could they curtail these soaring expenditures yet in fact improve the quality of healthcare delivery? The answer is a resounding yes, provided of course they are willing to decompose and understand the processes involved in the healthcare delivery processes, which by the way are not static, as medical knowledge and disease emergence, patterns and prevalence continually evolve, and embark on a healthcare ICT-based continuous quality improvement efforts. This holds true for any health system in the world. The results of a study published in the May issue of the *Annals of Internal Medicine* are instructive. According to this study, primary care doctors who work in areas with the most medical resources, for examples, hospital beds, laboratory services, and specialists, reported being less satisfied with the quality of care they provide than those working in areas that have less resources did, Medicare spending 58% higher in the former areas. Researchers at Dartmouth Medical School interviewed 6,000 physicians who treat Medicare patients nationwide, and found that 50% of doctors in high-intensity healthcare areas said that they could obtain elective hospital admissions for their patients, versus 64% in low -intensity areas. Doctors in the former were less likely to say that they obtained adequate hospital stays, strong specialist referrals, or high-quality diagnostic imaging services, for patients, and were less likely to say that they were satisfied with their careers. The researchers noted that the increased demand for resources in high-intensity health care areas creates an endless demand-supply cycle, which perhaps explains the dissatisfaction of the doctors in the midst of plenty, literally. Does this not speak to the need to pay attention to processes? Could this not be part-explanation for some of the observations made in the comparative studies mentioned earlier? Does this study not also imply that the increasing health spending does not guarantee service quality? Could we assert that these unhappy doctors would offer the highest quality healthcare? Could we not improve the productivity of these doctors by improving the processes involved in their healthcare delivery activities? According to Lawrence Casalino, professor of health studies at the University of Chicago, "The implications (of the study) are important; it' s not that we need to pour more money into the system , and it' s not that we need more hospital beds and more specialists." In fact, earlier studies conducted in Dartmouth had noted that costlier health care and more services do not improve patient outcomes, and researchers have estimated that 30% of Medicare expenditure is on needless care. Is the U.S Tort system in fact not also fuelling costs nurturing the "defensive Medicine" that results in a lot of the needless care? Are these not some of the reasons health spending in the U.S, and possibly elsewhere is skyrocketing, and could we not prevent this? Could we not make health systems work better via healthcare ICT implementation and utilization? The fact is, we could, and we not only want health systems to work, but to work better all the time. This is the only way some "disruptive disease" such as HIV/AIDS or avian flue would not catch us flat-footed, literally. Countries could also learn form one another regarding measures implemented that seem to be proving effective in not only preventing diseases but also regarding even other non-clinical aspects of the healthcare delivery processes. However, as noted above, the recipient must apply these measures to its health system contextually, which is why the U.K, although introducing private funding arrangements into an essentially publicly funded health system, is not importing the American style of private health system or that of any other country for that matter wholesale.

Efforts to promote the widespread diffusion of healthcare ICT into health systems must continue apace. As noted earlier, changes are occurring in various domains such as demographics, medical knowledge base, and regarding technological innovation that we cannot afford to rest assured that our health systems, in whatever country, is working and needs no improvement. Whereas in fact, health spending is increasing, some would say exponentially in many countries, particularly in the developed world, yet resources are limited, if not in fact dwindling. These combinations call for urgent action to achieve the dual objectives of qualitative healthcare delivery simultaneously reducing health spending. Efforts are indeed afoot in many countries to implement healthcare ICT on a large scale within the health systems, particularly in the developed countries. However, we need to address other important issues besides investing in these technologies, for example, encouraging the end -users, particularly healthcare providers, to embrace, invest in, implement, and utilize these technologies. There is no doubt that there is currently some resistance among these professionals to healthcare ICT implementation and use. The reasons for this resistance are many, cost also being a major one. However, and despite the cost issues that no doubt make it difficult for many providers in small and solo practices to be able to purchase EHR systems, the consensus amongst experts is that these technologies could improve the efficiency and quality of healthcare delivery. Indeed, a recent Commonwealth Fund -supported research to examine the costs and benefits of these technologies, in particular for solo or small group practices, where almost 80% of U.S. doctors operate found the average start-up costs for small group practices with EHRs, were $44,000 per physician, or nurse practitioner, average ongoing costs, $8,400 per physician per annum. As high as they may seem, the researchers also found that the average practice would recoup these costs in less than three years and, after that, profit substantially. The financial benefits averaged $33,000 per physician per annum, savings from two main sources, namely increased coding levels resulting in improved billing, and increased efficiency from reduction in personnel costs, with every practice reporting some savings, ranging from $1,000 to $42,500 per physician, or nurse practitioner per annum. Other benefits such as legibility, better data organization, and easy accessibility to patient records even from home, also improved efficiency. The study, published in the Sept/Oct. 2005 issue of *Health Affairs,* Sept., /Oct. 2005, also observed that many of the doctors worked longer hours initially, and some confronted significant financial risks, such as long payback periods, billing difficulties, loss of data, problems that with time, they typically overcame. The researchers recommend the formulation of policies to provide incentives and support services to assist practices improve the quality of their care by using EHRs. This study clearly supports our assertion thus far of the benefits of healthcare ICT in improving the quality of healthcare delivery, cost-effectively, with all involved deriving some benefits, clinical and/or pecuniary from these technologies, even if in the long term. Indeed, all the practices involved in this study conducted at least some quality improvement (QI) related EHR activities, although just two of them used the EHR systems rigorously to systematically improve chronic and preventive care, and some did not in fact exploit the technologies to the fullest, for example, using p ractice-set reminders or generating reports on provider performance. We should not only encourage healthcare providers to purchase, implement, and use healthcare ICT, emphasizing the numerous benefits of these technologies as the findings in this study showed, we should also encourage the use of these technologies for specific quality improvement efforts, offer incentives for such efforts, and compensate those that do so appropriately. Without such incentives and recompense, deliverable via such payment systems as P4P for example, it would likely be difficult to get providers to commit the time and efforts to learning the use of the many features of the EHR, for example, for quality improvement purposes. We might also minimize costs, time and monetary, to providers offering financial and other support for implementation-related activities such as office do-over, to encourage quality improvement use of the technologies, particularly as EHR software training and installation costs alone on the average were $22,038 per physician, or nurse practitioner, software constituting about one-third of overall costs, according to this study. The U.S Agency for Healthcare Research Quality (AHRQ) has developed a guide, "Pay for Performance: A Decision Guide for Purchasers," released in April 2006 that examines the decisions public and private purchasers of health care services need to make when designing and implementing P4P programs. The guide has 20 questions in four phases, namely, contemplation, design, implementation, and evaluation, and each question reviews the possible options, potential effects, and consequences. It also provides evidence from empirical evaluations and economic theory to help purchasers make informed decisions on P4P implementation, which could be com plex under certain circumstances as mentioned earlier. Such guides would not only facilitate the implementation efforts, but would make the benefits realizable from a P4P more likely achievable, with the quality improvements in healthcare delivery thus engendered helping to move us closer to realizing the dual objectives mentioned earlier. AHRQ developed the guide for public and private healthcare services purchasers, including health plans planning to sponsor a P4P initiative, which AHRQ broadly defined as any type of performance-based provider payment arrangements, including those that target performance on cost measures. There is no doubt that it would serve its intended purposes remarkably, and with consumer-directed health plans gaining increasing currency, according to the a recent study, it would be an invaluable quality improvement tool that would further promote the wider acceptance of consumer-driven healthcare delivery model. The U.S. Government Accountability Office (GAO) report released on May 30, 2006, noted that the number of U.S. residents that enrolled in consumer-directed health plans increased from about three million in January 2005 to about six million by January 2006, the policies typically combined with health savings accounts (HSA). They must also have a minimum deductible of $1,050 for a single person and $2,100 for a family. According to the GAO report, the number of employers offering high-deductible insurance plans to workers rose from 1% in 2004 to roughly 4% in 2005, about 30% of enrollees, previously uninsured. As the consumer-driven healthcare model becomes more widely accepted, the need for the healthcare consumer to have the right information at the right time to take the necessary decisions regarding their health in a rational manner becomes even more urgent. The high-deductible plans have critics no doubt, some for example claiming that it best suits younger, healthier workers, others that employers use it as a ploy to shift costs to employees. Nonetheless, we cannot ignore the facts that not only are many more enrolling in these plans, but also that in the process they are reducing the numbers of the uninsured. The more Americans gain access to healthcare, the healthier the populace would be, as this increasingly discerning population of healthcare consumers demands qualitative healthcare, which would impel healthcare providers to embrace and nurture quality including investing in the means by which to achieve this quality, for example in healthcare ICT, in order to remain competitive. Prices would also fall as competition heats up, making health services even more affordable, and many more Americans able to access health services. It is easy to see how ICT would trigger and sustain a healthcare quality cycle that would enable u s achieve the dual objectives mentioned earlier. In fact, there is increasing research evidence that these technologies do indeed, improve healthcare quality as the following study shows. In May 2006, Mathematica Policy Research, Inc., released the results of a study it carried out for the Centers for Medicare & Medicaid Services via the Delmarva Foundation. The aim of the study was to determine if the use of six specific types of information technology had improved quality of care. The survey involved 650 senior hospital executives asked questions to determine the benefits of EHR capabilities such as e-prescribing and electronic lab orders at their hospitals. The most important benefits of healthcare ICT that respondents reported were more timely clinical information, diagnosis, and treatment, next to which were reduced medical errors and improved patient safety. The researchers concluded that many of the hospital executives felt that healthcare ICT had advanced the quality of care in several important ways, with most hospitals acknowledging improved quality due to the healthcare ICT initiatives that they started. There is though, an urgent need for the establishment of timeliness measures including of health information availability and accessibility, particularly at the point of care (POC), and of diagnosis and treatment, all of which would improve documentation of the benefits derived from implementing these technologies. The need for widespread healthcare ICT implementation in order to obtain more accurate comparative data on quality-related healthcare ICT issues, particularly between different healthcare settings, for example between those accredited by Joint Commission on Accreditation of Healthcare Organizations (JCAHO) and those not and for different health conditions in these settings is pressing. This would enable a deeper understanding of the operational processes that would help us achieve higher quality improvement. The study highlighted the need for healthcare ICT to be efficient in data extraction for quality reporting, and the fact that electronic reminders and prescribing lagged behind other types of healthcare ICT, a situation that needs urgent rectifying considering the values of these features in reducing medical error rates and improving patient safety. There are though, technical implementation hassles one should acknowledge regarding the said features that might be the reason for the lag. However, they are certainly not the only problem, considering that many health jurisdictions do not have the required legislation to enable the use of e-prescribing for example, for reasons such as privacy and confidentiality and problematic certification issues. There would indeed be many issues to deal with right away given this increasing interest in consumer-driven health plans for the scenario described above to materialize, which is to intensify our efforts to promote the widespread diffusion of healthcare ICT. Some would even advocate offering healthcare providers some incentives to adopt these technologies in order to speed this process up. Healthcare ICT no doubt costs money; an estimated $400 billion over five years to build a national health information network (NHIN) for example, according to a study published in the August 02, 2005 issue of the *Annals of Internal Medicine.* The research team led by Rainu Kaushal, M.D., M.P.H., of Brigham and Women's Hospital in Boston, evaluated the status of healthcare ICT within the health system, and projected the costs of a model NHIN, which would have electronic health records (EHRs), secure electronic communication between patients and providers, and electronic claims submissions and eligibility verification capabilities. It would also enable the end - user to view and share test results, and would have computerized physician order entry (CPOE), and electronic prescribing features. Despite the huge costs of such a network, the researchers also noted that the savings that hospitals, physicians, and insurers would derive from improved operational efficiencies could considerably offset, and indeed recoup, the expense. The study observed that a network connecting U.S. health care providers to insurers, pharmacies, home health agencies, and clinical laboratories would cost $156 billion in capital investment over five years and $48 billion in annual operating costs. With capital expenses and operating costs combined, the total cost of a network with the ideal features mentioned earlier would be about $400 billion over five years. This stunningly expensive project would however, by improving communication between physicians, hospitals, pharmacies, labs, and insurers would reduce unnecessary testing, administrative and labor costs, resulting in overall savings to the tune of $77.8 billion annually, according to another stud y published in the January 9, 2005 issue of *Health Affairs*. What we need to continue to do is to present facts such as these to hospital executives, physician groups, and insurers so that they see the value of investing in these technologies, and be rest assured that they could recoup their investments over time. Admittedly, we have not succeeded greatly in so doing thus far, considering the painfully slow pace of healthcare ICT adoption in certain segments of the health industry. Nonetheless, this is essentially work in progress, considering that we have cogent reasons some of which we have discussed in this paper to work fervently toward achieving the dual healthcare delivery objectives mentioned earlier. Experience in the U.S for example indicates that besides some of the country's largest hospital systems, the response to coming up with the initial financial outlay in the healthcare ICT required for the NHIN, has been at best lukewarm, which is why some advocate offering incentives to healthcare providers to invest in these technologies. Considering the potential problems health systems face around the world and in particular in developed countries in view of the anticipated spike in the numbers of seniors in just a few years ahead, this delay in embracing the technologies that could help cushion the adverse effects of these demographic, and other changes, is unmistakably troubling, and could prove exceedingly costly. Many experts do not feel that government should foot the bill in the U.S, but this would likely be the case in countries such as Canada, and the U.K., to a large extent, individual healthcare providers that are self-employed funding their own technologies, albeit perhaps with provincial or other assistance and incentives as is the case in Alberta, for example. In the US, some experts feel that the influence of governments would even be more profound regarding our bid to promote the widespread diffusion of these technologies if they purchased healthcare services from health care providers that have implemented and are using healthcare ICT. There is no doubt that even in the U.S and as is already happening, governments have a critical role to play in funding the fundamental technical infrastructure of such a network, besides their roles in offering incentives to providers to implement these technologies, for example increased recompense via Medicare for healthcare providers that have implemented healthcare ICT. Further, there ought to be even more incentives for those providers that are utilizing these technologies in innovative ways to foster our chances of achieving our disease prevention goals. There is no doubt that providers, health plans and hospitals should have a financial stake in the technologies in their practices. This would ensure that they use them for the purposes for which bought, besides the desire to recoup their investments, not only via broadening their value propositions to their clientele, but also as adherence to quality could attract incentives and rewards as mentioned earlier. Issues such as convincing providers to come up with the initial investment remain potential problems. Further, some might see these technologies as anything but a blessing down the road as improvement in health status might mean less patronage, not to mention the form and standards for a NHIN might change with possible loss of investments, and the price wars that they could trigger in order to remain competitive might make some practices moribund.

These are concerns that we also need to address, in order to reassure these providers, and get them to invest in the technologies, and we might actually also have to offer financial incentives along the way, in addition to providing further evidence of the clinical and financial benefits of these technologies in the long term. It would certainly be likely necessary to prop up smaller, rural, and solo practices by offering assistance with low -interest loans, and direct subsidies, for examples, or linking payments to technology utilization. These measures also apply to other countries such as Canada and the U.K, where providers would still have to purchase their own healthcare ICT. As we have noted all along, the cumulative benefits of healthcare ICT implementation would help us achieve our dual healthcare delivery goals. However, these technologies need to be implemented by all healthcare stakeholders to a greater or lesser extent depending on which stakeholder, and their needs. In other words, we need to promote the implementation and use of these technologies across board, including among healthcare consumers. We need to let the word out about the gains derivable from these technologies to all constituencies. The healthcare consumer would able to communicate with the provider if the former had some rudimentary healthcare ICT capabilities, which are in place in many countries, developed and developing already, for example, the Internet, and even the cell phone. In particular, in order to be able to manage seniors at home, which is possible, and in fact could be more efficient and cost-effective via healthcare ICT, there would have to be some connectivity between the seniors and their healthcare providers. We do not expect all seniors to be able to operate sophisticated technologies, but software vendors and healthcare ICT manufacturers recognize the vast markets and are indeed already developing a variety of assistive technologies tailor-made for seniors that could facilitate the monitoring of seniors health conditions such as diabetes, high blood pressure and many other chronic diseases. We should also be focusing on developing cutting-edge healthcare ICT for operating community and ambulatory, besides domiciliary healthcare delivery in anticipation of the increase in the numbers of seniors in the years ahead. Many doctors are already using a computer with a videoconferencing link to treat their patients living for example in remote and rural areas, many of these patients, elderly. Several doctors in Spain, Italy, and Denmark are now using a telecounselling service that H EALTHOPTIMUM developed in 2005 according to a recent IST Results report. The project, funded under the EC's eTEN programme is helping to trigger the telemedicine deployment across Europe. HEALTH OPTIMUM solutions are Internet-based and work along with a telelaboratory service that enables the remote analysis of patient test samples, with remarkable benefits on healthcare delivery reported where implemented, including doctors saving time, public healthcare systems saving money by obviating the need for hospital visits and stays, and patients receiving improved quality, convenient, and well-coordinated healthcare. Besides saving the patients the trouble of traveling to the hospital to see a specialist, they could see him/her via videoconference with their family doctors in attendance, making for better service coordination, as the family doctor or GP and the specialist could jointly review patient data, including scans and lab investigations, via the telecounselling service. What's more, the results are quantifiable, facilitating quality evaluation and assurance. One trial used this service to connect primary healthcare facilities to hospital neurology departments, enabling the accurate assessment and diagnosis of patients with head injuries, without the need to transfer the patient to a hospital, which essentially exemplifies what we have been discussing that the use of appropriate healthcare ICT could help us achieve the dual objectives mentioned earlier. Indeed, the service in this trial led to almost 80% redu ction in the number of people referred to a specialist facility, with no doubt substantial cost savings, in a situation where previously would mean referring 53% of these patients, but only 11% now were. There was in fact improvement rather than depreciation in the quality of care in this trial because the diagnosis was reliable as the neurologist had access to scans and data from the primary healthcare facility, the patient also prevented from unwarranted and unanticipated risk that could result from moving the patient from place to place. When there is need for such transfers and surgery, the telecounselling system enables doctors to access information about the patient in advance, hence to prepare more swiftly and efficiently for the procedure. The system s telelaboratory analysis capabilities also help facilitate patient management with the potential to save lives. Primary healthcare providers could obtain samples of a patient's blood or urine for examples, remotely, analyze them on the spot, at the patient's home or bedside, and transmit the results to a specialist wirelessly, over a secure Public Key Infrastructure (PKI), the results obtained/sent back within ten minutes in most cases, processes that might have taken days. Does this not underscore the cru cial role that healthcare ICT could play in process improvement and the need for us to promote the widespread implementation and utilization of these technologies? Should other countries and health jurisdiction not employ such technologies by developing their own or collaborating with the HEALTH OPTIMUM project for adaptation and expansion of these valuable technologies, as is the case now in Europe with trials expected in Sweden and Romania, among other countries in the near future? There is no doubt that these technologies will serve the anticipated increased health service needs of the increasingly aging populations in these countries very well. In particular, there would be increasing demand on the health systems of many countries developed or developing, for community/ambulatory and domiciliary health services that such telemedicine technologies would facilitate cost-effectively, as lower tax revenues due to a relative decline in the number of young people entering the labor market results increasingly in budget tightening. We need to brace up for the tasks ahead as changes in the health climate loom. Healthcare ICT could help prepare us adequately for these imminent new times.

Issues in World Healthcare ICT Investments

Changes at the demand and supply sides of healthcare Information and

Communications Technologies (ICT) have been gathering momentum in recent years in most parts of the world and promise to be more vibrant in future. There are a number of reasons for such optimism, and they relate to three major healthcare ICT market players namely, the industry, health care providers, and governments. Six years ago, European ICT investments in the health care sector, was 14 billion Euro, 2% of the 724 billion Euro health care market on the continent, an amount expected to double in 2005, and to continue to increase over the years, driven, in the main by the continuing rapid progress of technological innovation. Experts predicted that some of the developments in the industry that will continue to create opportunities for both new services and business growth would be the shift towards multiple health ICT implementations, and the increasing importance of business process re-engineering in the health sector. Others would be the increasing interest of individuals in acquiring health information, and being actively involved in their treatment, and that of governments around the world in establishing national health information networks. In January 2005 in Prague, at a Microsoft government leaders' forum, members of the European Commission, re-launched "The Lisbon Strategy" aimed at preparing the EU for the challenges of the

twenty first century, first launched in 2000. Significantly, the Commission acknowledged that ICT is crucial to European competitiveness and social cohesion. With half of the productivity growth of modern economies traceable to ICT, investments in ICT being over 40% of EU labor productivity growth in the late 1990s, 90% of all projected innovation in the automobile sector being ICT-driven, and Europe's productivity gap with the USA strongly linked to ICT production, the EU is justifiably paying attention to ICT. Furthermore, Europe lags behind the USA, Japan, and South Korea in ICT diffusion rates. European countries recognize that the most competitive of their members in the global ICT market are also those that have the highest broadband penetration rates. Thus, the EU has been trying to modify its ICT-related regulations in order to promote ICT adoption and the competitiveness of European countries in the industry, particularly in order to exploit the opportunities created by the emergence of new generation mobile phones, wireless technologies, and satellites. The use of the Internet to provide voice telephony (VOIP) and TV also interests the EU. It sees this as critical to the future of communications, including in health, business, and entertainment, and is giving it huge support. However, Europe in general, still has to invest more in ICT, including ICT research in which its investments of 20% of the total R&D budget is much smaller that the 30% average spending by major Organization for Economic Cooperation and Development (OECD) countries. Its hospitals still lag behind those in the U.S in terms of health ICT spending and the sophistication of current IT installations, according to a recent study. The study was a survey of 900 hospital Chief Information Officers (CIOs) in 15 European nations, commissioned by Health Information Network Europe (HINE), a health-IT data service based in Brussels. It revealed that the hospitals spent just 1.8 percent of their total revenues on ICT and most lacked information to help make appropriate decisions on ICT acquisition. However, the study showed a similar pattern of limited ICT diffusion in both Europe and the U.S, with only 2.2 percent of European hospitals and 2.5 percent of U.S hospitals having implemented computerized physician order entry (CPOE) with clinical decision support. The study concluded that the deployment of ICT architecture seems more sophisticated in the U.S. For example, European hospitals have a median of 350 fixed and 20 mobile workstations each and 3.53 staff share one computer, but only 32.2 percent of the mobile workstations are hooked up to a wireless data network, much fewer than in the U.S. This has important implications for the e-health market in Europe, which experts believe has the potential for exponential growth in the future but only if the infrastructure to support ubiquitous data sharing were available. The stage of development of such an infrastructure varies across Europe, some countries obviously more advanced than other countries, with their individual markets being correspondingly busier or otherwise. The U.K budget of $11.2 billion to automate medical records and administration for 52 million patients in the UK is pioneering in Europe, with other European countries now following suit. France and Spain, for examples, are stressing the role of IT in improving patient safety, and most of Europe is considering investing in or already implementing clinical applications such as CPOE and electronic health records (EHR). There is a major shift towards consolidation on the demand side with medical centers merging and implementing "managed care" in the European health ICT market. The trend will increase the complexity of health ICT requirements of these larger entities, a challenge that only firms big enough in size and investment capacity to develop complicated technologies would be able to meet. This means that health ICT firms from the U.S, Canada, and other countries may also to have to merge and become larger to be competitive with the new European mega-firms. The European healthcare ICT market remains open to smaller firms nonetheless, particularly those developing products for niche healthcare ICT markets. Europe is also looking at its financial and regulatory framework for novel technologies, and of standards to harmonize the operations of implemented applications in the industry. Healthcare systems in Europe are not homogenous, although most countries have a socialized healthcare system, with a tinge of private sector involvement. The U.K, for example, which is one of the most active healthcare ICT markets, has been investing steadily in improving its healthcare systems, in particular reducing wait times, the government committing to increase annual spending on healthcare by 7.4% until 2008. The U.K's 28 Strategic Health Authorities, the management arm of the NHS, each of which covers a population of nearly 1.9 million people, oversees eight Primary Care Trusts, two mental health NHS Trusts and eight acute hospital NHS Trusts and has a budget of $2.7 billion, will disburse most of the funds. The situation is quite different in Western Europe where, as governments continue to confront the political conundrum of diverting resources away from welfare programs in order to increase investment and reinforce incentives to seek employment, and to embark on other economic reform programs to salvage their fledgling economies, their commitments to healthcare ICT spending seem disconcertingly shaky. On the other hand, with the renewal of governments' tenure often hinged on their abilities to deliver and to sustain promised welfare programs, it might not be that shaky after all, witness the dramatic swing to the right by Polish voters in the country's parliamentary elections not too long ago. The Dutch ICT sector continues by far to be the fastest growing sector in the country's economy. The country, however, is not experiencing the sort of spectacular growth in the Internet and mobile telephony sectors that drove this growth in years gone by when, in the mid -to late-1990s, the ICT sector contributed over 0.6 percentage point annually to Netherlands s overall GDP growth. This is because the country s subscription to telecommunications technologies such as telephony and the Internet has reached saturation point, contributing to restraints in ICT investments, a significant setback in a country that is one of the most aggressive in Europe concerning deregulation, liberalization, and privatization. The impact of these developments on health ICT spending will certainly play out sooner than later. The opportunities for foreign companies to participate actively in the health ICT sector in European countries depend on many factors other than how much the governments are willing to spend on ICT for their healthcare systems. One such factor is the status of the IT industry in the host country. Consider the case of Ireland. The international IT industry recognizes that country as a major software exporter. Indeed, the OECD Information Technology Outlook 2000 acknowledged Ireland as the largest world software exporter, the country s local software market, also one of its fastest growing business sectors with growth rates of 10 percent yearly lately, with significant involvement of foreign software companies. Indeed, Ireland ranks as the world s most global nation for the third year in a row in 2005, the fourth annual A.T. Kearney/ *Foreign Policy Magazine* Globalization Index™ reported, the country maintaining its economic links and

impressive levels of personal contact with the rest of the world, the recent precarious world economy notwithstanding. Canada ranks sixth in the Index, the US, 7th, and the UK, 12th. The Index showed that global economic integration is alive and well, and seems to have recovered after the slump in the economies of most parts of the world occasioned by the interplay of a variety of factors including increased travel alerts, corporate scandals, and higher airport security levels, some of the recovery IT-driven, particularly by the Internet and mobile phones. The most global countries also appear to be those with people that live longest and healthiest, and where the social, educational, and economic status of women are highest. These countries also have the most equal income distribution patterns, comprehensive political systems, least corruption levels, and protect their environments the most. These are all favorable factors for investments, both local and foreign, hence for economic prosperity. Other European countries also have specific characteristics, knowledge of which may help investors and businesses in Canada and elsewhere to better understand and compete more favorably in Eu ropean markets. Some countries have developed ICT as an economic sector while others hope to use ICT to achieve broader socio-economic development goals. What is common to all these countries is the recognition of the critical role ICT will play in not only the future of their healthcare delivery but also in the overall development of their countries, which will doubtless open up health ICT markets on the continent in the near future. The same optimism holds for the U.S health ICT markets. Experts at the Cambridge, Mass.-based Forrester predicted the U.S. healthcare industry would spend up to $61 billion on health IT systems in 2004, up from almost $55 billion in 2003. A recent report by Scottsdale, Ariz.-based instat/MDR predicted these figures would increase yearly by 6 percent over the next few years, an inevitable trend considering the attention paid to rising medical errors, new legislation such as the Sarbanes-Oxley Act of 2002, and increasing financial support from the government. The U.S ICT market however, also has particular, sometimes little-known characteristics. For example the National Center for Health Statistics for 2000 showed that there were over 1 billion visits to doctors offices and hospital outpatient departments and the figures have been rising ever since. Indeed, total healthcare spending in ambulatory care settings including solo physician settings, group practices, and hospital outpatient units, equals or surpasses that in acute care such as inpatient medical and surgical units, and critical care units, yet health ICT investments in the former remains small compared to the latter. Could this in fact be the reason for the costs differential? Should there and would there not be more healthcare ICT expenditures in this domain considering the increasing shift in emphasis toward community/ambulatory and domiciliary healthcare particularly with increasing longevity, as the population continues to age? The ambulatory EMR market increased from $0.8 billion to $1.2 billion at a yearly rate of 22% between 2003 and 2005. This contrasts with the total healthcare ICT market for acute care in the same period from $39 billion to $45 billion, at a yearly growth rate of only 7%. An optimistic view of the health ICT market would also be valid for most of the other countries in the Western world. Canada's Capital spending on health in particular increased significantly, more than doubling, between 1996 and 2003, a reflection of the country's major investments in high-tech equipment such as MRI and CT scanners, and for a country determined to reform primary care, reduce wait times in hospitals, and focus on population health, among others, such investments are likely to continue. Indeed, Canada plans to infuse approximately $41 billion into its health system over a decade, and in its 2005 health budget planned to add $2.5 billion to the Canada Health Transfer, increasing the base to $19 billion, which itself will increase yearly by six percent, as embodied in the "escalator clause." This increase means that the provinces and territories will have more money to fund their healthcare, including health ICT initiatives. Australia plans to spend $10.1 million over 4 years to improve the nation's infectious diseases surveillance system to enable rapid detection and reporting of infectious diseases, and it has budgeted $29.8 million between 2003 and 2006/7 on its Health Insurance Commission (HIC) Online project. The country continues to invest substantially in a variety of health ICT including the Clinical IT in Aged Care project, launched in June 2002 and one of the "Aged Care eConnect" projects, which also includes "Aged Care Payments Redevelopment," "Ageing and Aged Care Enterprise Architecture," and "ICT Strategic Planning for the Aged Care Sector." The outlook for health ICT in the developing world is quite different, and somewhat guarded. Many of the developing countries are still in the throes of political uncertainties, which at worst repel investors, and inevitably slow down the pace of growth of their economies. Poverty, the result of stalled economic growth creates difficult challenges for these countries; challenges that create a cascade of worsening burden that seems to stick with them perennially and further drags down their economies. Nonetheless, and despite having limited telecommunications and other infrastructures to work with, these countries still manage to implement health ICT somehow or another, and in rather ingenious ways. The markets are expectedly rudimentary and the applications limited to those tailored to their peculiar needs. It is therefore necessary to understand the health priorities of these countries, and the resources they have, in order to appreciate their healthcare ICT needs, and how to meet them. Some Asian and Latin American countries have relatively developed economies, others, "emerging" economies. In many of these countries, there is increasing awareness of the values of health ICT, which is creating burgeoning market opportunities. About 10 percent of total world population, over 620 million peoples, is currently online. The number of Internet users in developing countries is rising, by 40 percent in 2002, and more since then. With the numbers increasing in China, by 75 percent, Brazil by 78.5 percent, India by 136 percent, and even the Middle East, a region regarded as essentially unwired by 116 percent, it is hardly debatable that the ICT market has become global, as has, by extension, its impact on healthcare. An appreciation of the global nature of the current wave of healthcare ICT awareness is evident in the concerted international efforts to deal with outstanding issues hampering ICT diffusion such as security, standards, privacy and confidentiality and a number of others. These efforts, including the deft handling of contentious issues such as net neutrality, will likely result in more healthcare ICT markets opening up globally, further increasing the adoption of and investments in health ICT in healthcare delivery worldwide. With Brazil promoting Open Source software internally, even advocating its adoption in other developing countries, it is uncertain the effect the multiyear partnership and distribution deals for example that announced between Sun Microsystems and Google on October 04, 2005, would have on health ICT investments in these countries, and indeed, in the developed ones. While it may seem like old friends doing business together, considering the long-term ties between several key individuals in both companies, Sun President Jonathan Schwartz was unabashed about declaring the move an evolution of the .Net. Would any alliance that would in the long term, snatch its applications and server revenue by replacing the PC with the Internet as the platform for applications delivery likely amuse Microsoft? Viewed in the context of the issues surrounding newt neutrality for example, the Global health ICT industry indeed, seems about to be even more vibrant.

This vibrancy would also be the direct and indirect results of developments in

a number of different domains both within and outside the health industry. One key domain that would drive developments in the software and the IT industry in general is the medical domain. As medical knowledge progresses and our understanding of the natural histories of diseases improves, coupled with the consequent changes in practice models in different domains, for examples in disease prevention, population health, embodied in ongoing health reform measures, for example in primary care, so would the dynamics of business in the IT industry. In Canada for example, p rojections from recent estimates of the country's gross domestic product (GDP) put the ratio of health expenditure to GDP at 10.1% in 2004, which projections indicate is increasing. Based on 2002 comparative figures, the latest available, Canada at 9.6% is fourth among G8 countries in total health spending as a proportion of GDP, after the U.S (14.6%), Germany (10.9%) and France (9.7%), the UK, Italy, Japan and Russia, next in the order listed. Most of the healthcare budget in Canada services hospitals and drugs, $38.9 billion in 2004, or just below 30% of total health spending, but there is growing emphasis on primary health care and population health. In 2000, Canada's First Ministers concurred that, "improvements to primary health care are crucial to the renewal of health services", in response to which, the Federal Government established the $800 million Primary Health Care Transition Fund (PHCTF) to support, over a six-year period (2000-2006), the provinces and territories in reform ing the primary health care system. There is indeed, interest and fund injection into reforming the healthcare system at the secondary and tertiary levels as well, the Ten-Year Plan to Strengthen Health Care signed on September 16, 2004, by the Prime Minister and all Premiers and Territorial Leaders aimed at the country's priorities for sustaining and reinvigorating the health care system. It provides $41 billion over ten years for actualizing health reforms. Family physicians are vital to Canada's primary health care and population health goals, being customarily, the first doctor and usually, the last the patient sees. Over 50% of Canadian physicians are family physicians, 61% in group -rather, than solo- practices versus 48% of its specialists, many family doctors sharing office space, staff, or equipment, which might be an important consideration for healthcare ICT vendors contemplating developing software and other healthcare ICT for doctors in this market segment, figures also important for resource planning. Variable and indeed, soaring healthcare costs and physician shortage/mal-distribution keep physician-resource policy issues decisively on the health agenda, even long after the Kilshaw report (1995), and all those preceding it, the Barer/Stoddart report (1991,) inclusive. Subsequent reports regarding physician payments, a key issue in these reports, leaned toward capitation or a blended payment system with extra recompense for providing more patient-time and preventive health programs. The weight of opinion was that this would facilitate Canada's realization of its goals of primary care reform including the promotion of equitable, accessible, and quality care, sustainable and effective preventive care, more accountability, improved distribution of physicians, and more predictable health costs. Some may argue that the failed Ontario's HSO program proofs that capitation is suspect, others, highlight its robust outcomes in some European countries for example, Norway, but all will probably concur that fee-for-service is not cost-effective and is hindering primary care reform in the country. There is also consensus that doctors' remuneration model under primary care reform will influence expectations of how they do their job; that fee-for-service may be escalating costs due to doctors providing more services than required; and that other factors beside wages influence the quality of service doctors deliver such as job satisfaction. In response to the reports on physician resource and related policy issues, including the 1997 National Forum on Health report, the federal government has been infusing funds through the $150 million Health Transition Fund and later, the $800 million Primary Health Care Transition Fund into several primary care pilot projects since 1997/98. Many believe a graded rather than a "big-bang" approach to primary care reform is preferable.

The Romanow Commission (2002) gave credence to this incremental approach, criticizing the ad -hoc, short-term, and piece meal, nature of funding for the pilot projects without exploiting their potential for revamping the entire healthcare system. The Commission argued in its 2002 report for targeted funding to stimulate a major breakthrough in implementing primary healthcare reform and of the healthcare system, the Health Council of Canada, which made recommendations, including accelerating healthcare ICT implementation, leading and mobilizing these reform activities. In making its recommendations, the Council, which also acknowledged the difficulty with physicians giving up solo practices for group practices, with multidisciplinary teams providing comprehensive 24/7 year-round practices, underscored the recognition by policy makers of the important role of ICT in healthcare delivery in meeting these challenges. As every province and territory wants to meet the agreed target of 50% of Canadians having round the clock, year-round access to multidisciplinary teams by 2011, there is substantial injection of funds into efforts to achieve this goal, including investing in healthcare ICT, and other measure to speed up reforms. Indeed, the Federal government s $16 billion Health Reform Fund of 2003 also included funds for home and catastrophic drug expenses, and transitioned into the Canada Health Transfer fund in 2004, which reflects the shift in approach from targeted time-limited primary care funding to continuing funding for a variety of initiatives with national objectives, and performance appraisals specified. ICT spending was less than 2% of Canada s overall healthcare spending in 2003 but this also is changing. The Office of Health and the Information Highway announced a new program aimed to support the application of novel technology in healthcare delivery dating back to 2000. The Canada Health Infostructure Partnerships Program (CHIPP), which replaced the Health Infostructure Support Program (HISP), emphasized large implementation models and cross-jurisdictional collaboration. It offers a two-year, shared-cost incentive to promote ICT implementation. CHIPP specifically aimed to support ICT-enabled healthcare delivery applications in telehealth, and EHR. The intention to facilitate information accessibility and sharing remains as germane to high quality healthcare delivery today, as it was back then. For example, in its 2004 budget, the federal government gave the Canadian Health Infostructure Initiative (CHI) an extra $100 million to promote the development and implementation of a pan-Canadian health surveillance system the goal including to integrate present disease-based surveillance systems, and to support infectious disease prevention and protection initiatives. In fact, the federal government has given CHI $1.2 billion since 2001 to collaborate with the provinces and territories to develop Pan-Canadian eHealth solutions for electronic health records, telehealth and health surveillance. Canada has a publicly funded health system, funding via such mechanisms as described above, although there is some private sector involvement too. However, the provinces and territories remain responsible for administering and delivering health care services, guided by the provisions of the Canada Health Act. Estimates for total health expenditure, in current dollars, for 2002 were $114.0 billion, in 2003, $123.0 billion, and in 2004, $130.3 billion, and for total health spending per capita in 2002, $3,635, in 2003, $3,885, and in 2004, were $4,078, the 2004 forecast a 12.2% increase from 2002. There was no significant change in the share of the private sector from 1997 (29.9% of total health expenditure) to 2002 (30.3% of total health expenditure). Indeed, it decreased slightly to 30.1% in 2003 and 2004. Per capita health expenditure varies among the provinces and territories, Manitoba and Alberta expected to spend more per person on health care than any other province, at $4,406 and $4,275, respectively in 2004, Quebec ($3,666) and New Brunswick ($3,865), billed to spend the least during the same period. Health ICT spending also varies across the country, but there is increasing ap preciation of the significant role ICT would play in achieving the agreed primary care reform goals across board. Alberta allotted $2.6 million from its Telehealth Clinical Services Grant Fund to twenty-one new telehealth programs in the province in 2005. The funds were for telehealth initiatives in six health regions, the Alberta Mental Health Board, and the Alberta Cancer Board, offering business opportunities for video-conferencing and other telehealth equipments, as well as specialized medical equipments. The provision of quality patient care and access to services are prominent goals in the province s healthcare plans, on which it spent a total of $7.4 billion in 2003/04, an increase of $529.6 million (7.7 per cent) over 2002/2003. Of this amount, it sp ent $29.0 million on health reform and renewal initiatives such as a 24-hour telephone information services (Health Link Alberta), and on implementing its electronic health record, the continuing direction of the province s health plans consistent with these goals. The province has also established a $66 million Alberta Physician Office System Program in partnership with the Alberta Medical Association, which entitles every of its physician to $7,700 in each of four years to install, undergo training in, and start to use electronic medical records (EMR) in his/her practice. The response of these physicians is so far impressive, again with ample business opportunities open to vendors, courtesy of this program. The EMRs in doctors offices would integrate with the provincial EHR, eventually, also boosting opportunities for businesses in the many technical domains that this would involve in the years ahead. Ontario planned to spend $31.4 billion on healthcare services (including equipment and buildings) in 2004/2005. Nova Scotia is implementing a hospital information system that supports electronic health record (EHR) systems, its installation at Guysborough-Antigonish-Strait Health Authority, billed for commissioning province-wide, by the end of 2005. The province is spending $57 million over five years to support patient care via healthcare ICT, and wants to spend another $45 million on diagnostic, and mobile, equipments between 2003 and 2006. Nova Scotia also belongs to the Health Infostructure Atlantic (HIA), which the Atlantic provinces, namely, Newfoundland, Nova Scotia, New Brunswick, and Prince Edward Island, found in the fall of 1999 to improve cooperation in health information technology and information management activities in the region. The HIA is promoting ICT initiatives with funds such as the $12 million CHIPP (Canada Health Infostructure Partnership Program) provided to implement the HIA Project Portfolio, which along with the $12 - $18 million from Atlantic Canada bring the total project budget to almost $30 million dollars for the HIA Project Portfolio's three initiatives. The initiatives are Common Client Registry, implemented in Prince Edward Island during the CHIPP time frame (July 1, 2001 to December 31, 2002,) Case Management, based in Newfoundland, Nova Scotia, and Prince Edward Island, and Tele-i4, implemented in all the all four provinces; and eight project components. The Tele-i4 project promised to be the largest inter-provincial implementation of Picture Archiving Communication Systems (PACS) equipment in Canada. Nova Scotia's PACS expansion project, a partnership between the Health districts in Nova Scotia, the Department of Health, and Canada Health Infoway, is well under way. On April 18, 2006, Premier Rodney MacDonald noted, "Our plan is to introduce new information technology across the province that will improve the quality of care and access to tests and treatment...the PACS system will mean quicker treatment decisions and the reduction of unnecessary travel for many patients". The Department of Health is investing over $10 million in new equipment as part of the Picture Archive and Communications System (PACS) expansion project, which will replace film -based imaging in the province with speedier, safer, and more efficient processes. According to the Health Minister, Chris d'Entremont, "This technology helps reduce the time a patient has to wait" We are allowing doctors to spend more time with their patients and are providing Nova Scotians with health-care services as close to home as possible." The project started in 2004 at a total cost of $25 million, with Canada Health Infoway contributing $12 million, the remaining $3 million, from the federal medical equipment fund. HIA is quite cognizant of the challenges that standards and interoperability would pose to some of these projects, hence intends to resolve such issues promptly so that the systems could work efficiently across Atlantic Canada, and be able to connect with other systems nationwide eventually. The technical and management issues that this would entail would no doubt present business opportunities for the appropriate ICT firms for some time to come. Newfoundland planned to spend $3 million in 2004/05 to support the implementation of its primary health care programs, many of which will require significant ICT investments. Quebec's $16 billion per annum healthcare budget, about 30 % of the government's overall budget, will increase to $50 billion by 2030 according to experts' projections. The province receives funds from the federal government to fund its healthcare ICT initiatives, for example from Canada Health Infostructure Partnerships Program (CHIPP), which funded several projects on an equal-contribution basis with the province between 2000 and 2002 alone, including CLSC d u futur at the cost of $3 million, and MOXXI at $2.2 million. Saskatchewan invested $2.527 billion in health care in 2003/04, 7.9%, or $184 million more than the year before. During the same period, the province provided $19 million in capital equipment to the Regional Health Authorities to buy CT scanners, surgical, and therapeutic equipment. It gave Yorkton, Moose Jaw, and Swift Current RHAs $2 million for the purchase of CT equipment. The Prairie North Regional Health Authority now has two CT scanners, in North Battleford, and Lloydminster.

The province spent $1.5 million to tackle issues concerning patient safety, which healthcare ICT could no doubt help assure. Its Northern Telehealth Network (NTN) serves the peoples of northern Saskatchewan, the network now established at 17 sites and 15 communities as of March 31, 2004, would have even more portals over time. Saskatchewan also recently commissioned in Regina, a $5 million MRI and interventional radiology suite that the federal and provincial Health dep artments and the Hospitals of Regina Foundation, joint funded, and which is a key initiative in the provinces efforts to reduce wait times. This latter is a problem on which the province, as well as other provinces and territories that have a similar problem, would still likely spend more in the near future in order to eliminate. British Columbia expects to receive $5.4 billion in new federal health funding over the next ten years, or roughly 4% of the expected spending on health services over the same period. The province increased overall funding for the health system to $10.7 billion in 2004/05, including a $123 million increase to $6.2 billion for the province's six health authorities for care and services provision. The province will likely consolidate its $10 million investment in 2004/05 alone to enhance patient safety, much of the money invested in ICT projects. In fact, the province has established an Electronic Health Steering Committee to accelerate the development and implementation of its eHealth, has already started some EHR projects, and the Health Ministry has four all-inclusive ICT priorities for 2005/2006. Planned initiatives to realize these priorities include improving wait list information on the public wait list web site, the Aggregated H ealth Information Project (AHIP), developing a strategic health information management framework, and Bill 73 Technical Compliance, an information security measure with which systems and applications changes must comply to secure personal data within Canad ian shores. The territories are also investing substantially in health ICT, and have been doing so for long, particularly with regard tele-health. Nunavit budgeted $182,244,000 for healthcare and social services in 2003/04, including about $28.8 million allotted for capital. The territory received about $209,000 in 2003-2004 as part of a three-year allocation of $4.4 million from the Primary Health Care Transition Fund Provincial/Territorial Envelope, to assist it in implementing sustainable, large-scale primary health care renewal initiatives, including health ICT projects. Yukon did not sign the Health Care Accord in Ottawa on February 5, 2002 because it did not consider the Canada Transfer (CHST), based on a per capita formula, would meet the healthcare needs of the three northern territories, which all have small populations, large land mass, and high transportation costs. The three northern Premiers met two weeks later with the Prime Minister, who agreed to give the territories $20 million each atop the CHST Funding. Thus, Yukon receives about $10 - $12 million yearly more health care funds, which enabled the territory's overall funding for its main hospital, Whitehorse General Hospital to increase by $5 million in three years to almost $26 million in its 2005/06 budget. The $1.9 million the province received from the federal government's primary health care transition fund (PHCTF) in the same period will fund its healthy living initiatives including healthy eating, active living; provision of health information to the general public, and its health ICT projects, on which the success of these programs would, in the main, depend. Among the ICT initiatives of the Northwest Territories (NWT) is the Informatics Blueprint, which the NWT Joint Leadership Council endorsed in September 2003. The plan includes a number of projects to improve its key health information systems, including a limited pilot electronic health/medical records project at the Yellowknife Health and Social Services Systems (HSS) Authority. All the territories continue to expand the capabilities and coverage of their current telehealth systems.

The projects mentioned above are just a few examples of the intensity of health

ICT investment activities around the country, the overall scale, significantly larger, and continues to grow. There are also ongoing and planned health reforms at other tiers of the health system, as mentioned earlier, many involving substantial health ICT investments. Health ICT investments in Canada remain driven largely by government health reform policies, hardly surprising considering that the country s Medicare is primarily a public health system, but as also earlier noted, with increasing private input. These reforms predicate on a variety of factors some of them medical, for examples, changing disease prevalence and patterns, health indicators, and progress in medical knowledge and the emergence of new treatment and surgical procedures. Non-medical factors such as technological innovation, administrative and management innovations, legislative changes, and costs are also important change drivers. In particular, evidence continues to mount regarding the immense benefits of healthcare ICT in helping us achieve the dual objectives of qualitative healthcare delivery at afford able costs. Consider a recent study for example that appeared in the April 28 2006 edition of BMC Medical Informatics and Decision Making. This study showed that a simple, web-based clinical decision support program, ISABEL, significantly reduces potentially deadly misdiagnoses. This program, designed to offer doctors swiftly, a list of valid differential diagnoses, changed their diagnosis in one-eight of all cases. There is no doubt about the implications of such systems for improved patient care, since accurate diagnosis is the first necessary step for qualitative patient care, not to mention its value in patient safety. A user-friendly program, with the doctor only having to key in the symptoms and other relevant information, which elicits the suggested d iagnoses, it saves time, which the doctor could use for other aspects of the patient s care or for another patient. The program uses data and information from a database of 10,000 illnesses, requires a subscription, and is accessible via the Internet from any computer. Some contend though that its current price of $36,000 plus $750 per physician for a 200-bed hospital might be out of reach for many healthcare providers. Since its initial release in 1991, it has undergone several revisions, based on doctors' feedback, and is now used in many hospitals in the U.S and the U.K. There is no doubt that this healthcare ICT that could also save healthcare costs significantly. By reducing morbidities and no doubt in some instances, mortality, to treating the patient for the wrong condition, such decision support systems (DSS) could besides improving the quality of healthcare delivery also be helping save healthcare costs. Considering the amount countries, spend on prescription medications alone, not to mention that of hospitalization and other costs that could result from such misdiagnosis, the overall benefits of such programs would no doubt offset their initial financial outlays. In its annual report released in May 2006, for example, the Canadian Institute for Health Information (CIHI), noted that Canada's estimated total spending on medications was $24.8 billion in 2005, an 11% increase over 2004. Viewed per capita, the spending was $770 per capita nationwide, Nunavit, and Ontario with the least ($482) and highest ($837) per capita spending on drugs, respectively. The spending on prescription drugs out of the gross total was $20.6 billion. The report noted that drug spending was the fastest growing segment of the country's health system, accounting for 17.5% of all health spending in 2005, and only trails behind hospitals, which walloped an estimated $42.4 billion in 2005, about 30% of total health spending. Do these figures not underscore the benefits of such DSS as ISABEL? Do they in fact not highlight the need for the widespread diffusion of healthcare ICT that could offer immense opportunities to deliver qualitative healthcare and save costs, not to mention lives? Yes, we

73

need to start to consider the non-pecuniary benefits of healthcare ICT and not only think in terms of net present value calculation of costs and benefits or of implementation, and maintenance costs, and discount rates, and inflationary differentials, or even the normative ethics of the proposed technologies. Economic, financial, and philosophic musings apart the need for simplicity is dire in our increasingly complex world, and our urgent need for making our health systems work better. This complexity is evident in how we perceive computer systems, which explains, at least in part, the sometimes-outright fear of these otherwise remarkable devices by many. It is also perhaps what partly makes those empowered to allay this fear use it instead as an excuse to recruit reasons to reject many an ICT proposal, what return on investment the proposal will yield, chief among them. Not that financial consideration is irrelevant, but did we need Katrina to teach us some lessons on opportunity costs, or are we waiting for the 5HN1 virus to teach us some more? Would it not have cost us less had we the appropriate healthcare ICT in place prior to the Hurricane, among other measures, in healthcare costs as it now does? Again, no one would likely argue that it makes no sense to consider the bottom line, even investing in computer systems that will help improve the health system, but what Katrina has taught us all is that making return on investment the overarching reason to invest in or jettison health computer systems might be counterproductive. Take the issue of paper-versus electronic-medical record systems. Many physicians who tried to treat evacuees of Hurricane Katrina could not access the patients' medical records stored in sheaves of paper in GPs' offices and hospitals, now lost, gone with the floods that Katrina caused. Would this have happened if the records were in electronic format, backed up in databases off-site in a secure location, far removed from the wrath of Katrina? Many of the evacuees could not remember what pills they were on, or their dosages, or which medications they previously took interacted ad versely with another. How many lives would access to those records, for example medication history, have saved? It is clear to all that a breakdown in communication contributed significantly to the crisis that followed Hurricane Katrina, including in healthcare delivery. There were children, some of them babies, and ill evacuees, young and the elderly in hospitals in various locations in the U.S, whose relatives did not know where they were. Could accessible electronic health records, which would of course have photo-IDs, have prevented this confused state? Would it not have been possible for anxious parents and relatives to simply check with any hospital and quickly trace the locations of their loved ones? How much would that have also saved in pecuniary terms? How relevant are net present value calculations in these circumstances? The technologies of electronic health record (EHR) systems have been around for decades. Why did Katrina still catch us so flat-footed? Are we prepared to prevent these experiences ever happening again even now, so long after Katrina? Reacting to the difficulties doctors faced accessing evacuees' medical records, Senator Hilary Rodham Clinton (D-N.Y.), co-sponsor of the Wired for Healthcare Quality Act (S. 1418), in a speech to an audience at New York's Memorial Sloan-Kettering Cancer Center, noted that electronic health records could not anymore be "a luxury, it is now a 21st Century necessity." The U.S Senate unanimously passed the bill officially titled a bill to enhance the adoption of a nationwide interoperable health information technology system and to improve the quality and reduce the costs of health care in the United States, which the U.S Senate passed by unanimous consent on Nov 18, 2005. S. 1418 amends the Public Health Service Act (PHSA) to codify the establishment and responsibilities of the entities that the Presidential Executive Order 13335 of April 27, 2004 established within the Office of the Secretary of Health and Human Services (HHS), namely the post of the National Health Information

Technology Coordinator. The Secretary later established the Office of the National Coordinator of Health Information Technology (ONCHIT), and the American Health Information Community (AHIC) to support the adoption of healthcare ICT. S. 1418 would therefore help to promote uniform standards adoption, provide grants to hospitals and other healthcare providers to adopt healthcare ICT, establish a state loan program to help healthcare providers acquire IT, and establish a quality measurement system that will recompense physicians for improvements in healthcare delivery. Furthermore, the bill would authorize appropriation of funding for grants to facilitate the widespread adoption of certain health information technology, including $125 million in 2006, $155 million in 2007, and the required sums for these activities between 2008 and 2010. Congressional Budget Office (CBO) estimates for implementing S. 1418 are $40 million in 2006 and $652 million over the 2006-2010 period, assuming appropriation of the necessary amounts. S. 1418 also would oblige the Agency for Healthcare Research and Quality (AHRQ) to establish a Center for Best Practices to offer technical assistance to support healthcare ICT adoption, and it would extend through 2010 authorization for telemedicine grants. Thus, government healthcare ICT spending in the U.S is gaining momentum, an increasing recognition of the need for embracing these technologies in healthcare delivery in the country. Indeed, there is little doubt that health systems worldwide need information systems that support and facilitate workflow and that capture and make available in real time and at the point of care, life-saving clinical data, and information. EHR meets these needs besides providing a solid foundation for national health information architecture, facilitating the accomplishment of population health programs, of an economically viable health system, and of a progressive state or nationwide health policy, and fostering sustainable economic development. In September 2005, the US federal government implemented a system that enabled doctors to access online, the medication histories of Hurricane Katrina evacuees destroyed or lost in Katrina's wake. This medication data-recovery effort, located at www.katrinahealth.org, comprised 90-days database of prescription drug information covering 150 zip codes in the affected areas, and was available to authorized physicians and independent pharmacists and those in chain stores. It resulted from collaboration between the Department of Health and Human Services (HHS) and some other government departments, and the private sector and pharmacy benefit managers, with business associate agreements under the Health Insurance Portability and Accountability Act (HIPAA). This was to ensure privacy as they exchange data. Although temporary, pilot, and only had medication lists, it could not be difficult to imagine how many lives this effort potentially saved. Further, its speedy development boded well for future interoperability efforts, particularly as not a few yet potent problems have plagued EHR adoption and stalled its progress over the years. Some of these problems are technical, for examples, lack of consensus on standards, hence difficulties with integration and interoperability of disparate systems developed by different vendors. Others relate to costs, with governments and healthcare organizations reluctant to implement often-expensive EHR systems, and physician offices, the electronic medical records systems (EMR) required to work with them. There are also end-user resistance issues, some rooted in technophobia, some in fear of loss of status, even jobs, and others in a lack of iterative assessments of user interfaces during IT design, and in management's ineptitude. There is also the public's legitimate concern for the security, and privacy of patient information, and the seeming lameness of government to legislate or enforce legislation to reassure the public on these crucial issues. It is mandatory to address these issues in order to accelerate EHR diffusion, which would open up immense business opportunities, EHR being an assortment of devices and systems working together in unison, conceptualized technically, or seen in business terms, a value-added array of functions. These functions, which include clinical, administrative, and financial data and information support, the components and functions often in different locations, embody an array of processes that healthcare ICT could help facilitate or modify in other ways. Cost is a major issue in EHR diffusion, which it could potentially and indeed, does hamper. The systems implemented in doctors' offices, often called electronic medical records (EMR) may cost over $10,000, although vendors are starting to develop attractive price options based on the number of functionalities, a move that will encourage EMR diffusion and boost vendors' bottom line. Government regulations are making it a smart option for health organizations to implement EHR, but strapped for cash as most are these days it is a tough call to make. Besides technology costs, they have to struggle with customizing the technology and the costs of change management, including training costs with sometimes steep learning curves, and the costs of office redesign. The CEO focused on return on investment (ROI) bears little blame under these circumstances, although, as Katrina has taught us, the pecuniary benefits of EHR, which can be substantial by the way, may be far less than its priceless less tangible ones. Technology and management both can successfully address the human factors deterring EHR adoption. Technology can help improve the human-computer interface (HCI) whereby end-users access data and information at the point of care or other end-points, hence facilitate decision support, which will foster end-user interest in EHR utilization, particularly among doctors with of course vendors addressing the issue of lost productivity, one of the key reasons doctors shun these technologies, developing more efficient products. Management can allay the fears of some healthcare staff that embracing technology is akin to surrendering their jobs, for example by emphasizing the fact that the human component is integral to computer systems. Involving end -users in proposed health ICT from the start will foster the openness; mutual respect and trust necessary for effective and sustained implementation. Private organizations such as Leapfrog should continue its advocacy for safer health systems, which will maintain EHR in sharp focus in the public eye and in the boardrooms of health organizations. Government initiatives such as the National Health Information Infrastructure (NHII) in the U.S and Canada's nationwide EHR initiative coordinated by Canada Health Infoway should press on with vigor. Vendors should continue to develop innovative and affordable products. Indeed, vendors played major roles in helping Katrina evacuees, for example, SureScripts, which not only provided the technology infrastructure for the medication data-recovery effort mentioned earlier, but also collected data from some pharmacies serving evacuees in other states outside the Gulf Coast that it planned to make available in real-time. Allscripts, which makes clinical software, also helped physicians treating evacuees by offering them free electronic prescribing and interactive personal health records. Others such as Siemens Medical Solutions also helped in other ways. Indeed, we should not restrict our efforts to offer incentives to promote healthcare ICT adoption to doctors. All healthcare stakeholders need to embrace these technologies and we should do whatever we could to encourage them to do so, precisely what Philadelphia's Thomas Jefferson University Hospital is doing currently. The hospital is offering personal health management software gratis to consumers, which would enable them to track personal and family information in a manner akin to utilizing personal accounting software. The individual simply keys in his/her personal profile and health history, disorders, allergies, drugs and their doses, and physician information, and into the software, which enables him/her to file blood -pressure changes, lab results, store images, and physician reports. The user could store insurance information, and the software could automatically remind him/her to schedule/cancel appointments with doctors. The software offers ready accessibility to the user's health information record by doctors at the point of care, whether routine or emergency, and makes it easier for parents for example, to track their children's immunizations and screenings schedules. The software would also be useful for domiciliary care of the aged and chronically ill, and in general empower patients to participate actively in their health affairs, including in the management of their medical and other health problems. Overall, such personal health manager software helps improve the quality of healthcare delivery and the well-being of the user, and would help save healthcare costs significantly. It is also relatively easy to use. The user only needs to install the CD-ROM on a personal computer, and could thereafter input all the information mentioned earlier, following a systematic tutorial that instructs him/her on how to customize the program, which Windows 2000/XP-compatible, and which the user could password - protect for security, and for which he/she could obtain telephone or online technical support. Could this software have made a difference post-Hurricane Katrina, when thousands of evacuees that needed medical attention had no access to their health records except via memory? With the records centrally stored, would they only be ready to print them off this software in the event of a medical emergency? How much could be saving in human and pecuniary terms other hospitals, and healthcare providers offering their patients such software free? Could this in fact not be a value proposition for the healthcare providers that could increase patronage and their bottom line? Would such incentives further encourage the public to know more about and invest more on healthcare ICT that could help improve communication and information sharing with their healthcare providers hence the quality of healthcare delivery, and their health or not? Would these efforts not stimulate efforts by software and healthcare ICT vendors to develop innovative technologies that would fill the process needs of healthcare delivery in different domains, for example, the public, healthcare providers, insurers, and pharmacists, among others? Katrina did teach us a lesson on the importance of automating our health systems, that the benefits derivable from so doing far outweigh the complex calculations of ROI that sometimes cloud our judgment in taking appropriate decisions on EHR and other health ICT implementation. Katrina demonstrated the need to analyze the various obstacles hindering widespread EHR adoption and to apply the results of this analysis toward establishing the necessary parameters for fostering rather than further stalling EH R implementation. It also reminded us of the need for concerted efforts to ensure unfettered health ICT diffusion. Katrina has inculcated in us the need for thoroughness in our preparedness for disasters and for objectivity in our approaches to implementing our disaster prevention and management plans. That we had to wait for Katrina to learn these valuable lessons is somewhat discomfiting, but that it was a necessary epiphany that would improve our disaster preparedness and response initiatives is relieving. What's more, it has galvanized efforts to implement healthcare ICT on a much larger scale as efficient and cost-effective ways to improve the quality of our health systems not just in the U.S., but also across the globe. These developments would no doubt translate into massive healthcare ICT investments creating business opportunities for software and healthcare ICT vendors, and that for improved health for all.

We need to be cognizant of the fact that a multiplicity of factors is at play concerning healthcare ICT investments, though. These factors vary with each country and even with each health jurisdiction in a country. Some experts contend for example that because of centralized management of health services by provincial governments that include price and volume controls, doctors and hospitals would unlikely implement appropriate healthcare ICT. However, the recent release by Canada Health Infoway of an Electronic Health Records Solution (EHRS) Blueprint for Canada, expected to be a business and technical framework that defines approaches to health information sharing "between health services providers (physicians, specialists, nurses, and pharmacists) across care settings (hospitals, emergency rooms, clinics, and homecare settings) and across geographical distances," signals something different. There is little doubt about the need for ongoing efforts to promote healthcare ICT adoption by healthcare professionals and administrators, in order to facilitate the completion of the technical infrastructure that the blueprint aims to achieve. Price controls in healthcare delivery could be problematic, in particular if the prices happened to be too low, as in the first place it leads to shortage, and especially when the product or service is in high demand, such as healthcare is. Shortage in turn could eventually compromise quality, as the limited resources struggle to cope with the increased demand. Worse still, costs even increase, as the healthcare consumer becomes less healthy, and requires even more treatment, including perhaps hospitalizations. To further compound these problems, providers, particularly new providers, either are reluctant to provide services at these reduced costs as witnessed by the current dearth of house calls, nursing home care and obstetrical deliveries, or order unwarranted consultations and labs/treatment to make up for the lowered prices, which is why some reject the fee-for-service remuneration model outright. Primary care doctors would also find treating simple health problems more rewarding financially than complicated ones, if paid the same fixed price per patient visit, the more ill patients ending up in the ER, and in hospitals further increasing healthcare costs. Indeed, Gosden, Forland, and others in *The Cochrane Database of Systematic Reviews* 2006 Issue 2, a reprint of the review first published in 2000, which supported the defects of fee-for-service (FFS) mentioned earlier, highlight these points. The authors set out to evaluate the impact of different methods of payment (capitation, salary, fee for service and mixed systems of payment) on the clinical behavior of primary care physicians (PCPs), revisiting the commonly held view that the method of physicians remuneration could influence their clinical behavior. The authors noted the paucity of information on the effects of different payment systems in achieving the dual policy objectives of cost containment and improved quality of care. As noted above, the authors compared three payment systems, one, capitation, which involves making payments for every patient that received care, in other words, a fixed payment per member per month, which therefore, leaves no incentives for unnecessary treatments, for which the doctor would receive no payment, anyway. Others were salary; and fee for service, with payment made for every item of care given, such as consultation, tests, and procedures. The authors searched numerous databases using specified criteria for the studies they sought. They found that FFS resulted in more primary care visits/contacts, visits to specialists and diagnostic and curative services but less hospital referrals and repeat prescriptions versus capitation, with compliance with a recommended number of visits higher under FFS versus capitation payment. FFS also led to more patients visits, increase in both continuity of care and compliance with a recommended number of visits, but less satisfaction with access to their physician versus salaried payment. The authors concluded that there is some evidence to suggest that the method of payment of primary care physicians influence their behavior, although cautious about generalizing their findings, recommending more

83

studies, in particular regarding the influence salary versus capitation payments on PCP behavior. That in order to achieve our dual objectives of providing qualitative healthcare without creating economic chaos, we cannot afford to have healthcare quality headed for a downward spiral, and costs skyrocketing simultaneously, is hardly debatable. With increasing evidence indicating that implementing and using the appropriate healthcare ICT improve healthcare delivery processes, our efforts to continue to promote the widespread implementation of these technologies must therefore, not only continue, but must intensify. Yet, we could not be so doing not giving doctors and other healthcare professionals that implement these technologies, at not negligible financial costs, any incentives for their efforts. Why would a doctor for example want to provide health advice via e-mail, or the telephone, both technologies with proven potential to facilitate healthcare processes and save healthcare costs? Could e-mails for example not speed up appointments scheduling/cancellation, or bill/payment notification, and even consultations, all of which could help in the treatment process and save travel time for the patient, and free the doctor's time for other patients perhaps with more serious illnesses, with potential significant cost savings? Could telephone cognitive behavior therapy (t-CBT,) for whose efficacy there is supporting research evidence, by helping depressed patients not just reduce morbidities, but prevent some from actually committing suicide? Should we not ensure that the doctors who invest in these technologies at least have a chance to recoup their investments? Does this not also mean active collaboration between these doctors and the health authorities in the jurisdictions they would use them, and among these jurisdictions, nationally, for some sort of understanding and agreement on standards policy to ensure interoperability? Could such collaboration not help doctors in their choice of technologies, which would reduce the chances of misadventures, and minimize financial outlays, encouraging other providers to follow in the path of their colleagues that have had positive experiences with implementing these technologies? Could this not in some way also bring software and healthcare ICT vendors in alignment with developments in the industry, which would modulate pricing an d foster healthy market operations? Some have in fact suggested that Canada adopt members-run, healthcare cooperatives, with information systems implementation factored into doctor's payments, and the healthcare consumers able to patronize doctors with varying degrees of practice automation, or even none at all, paying less the less automated is the practice. Doctors' remuneration and incentive issues demand the attention we have given it thus far considering that doctors are at the forefront of healthcare delivery. In other words, no amount of investments in healthcare ICT would help in the achievement of our dual objectives without being on-board the doctors and other healthcare professionals, and indeed, all the other professional staff involved in the smooth operations of the innumerable processes whose overall outcome is healthcare delivery. In the U.S for example, at least twelve states including Texas, Florida, and California, have recently reported or anticipated physician shortages, and as with any aging population, we should expect an increased prevalence of chronic illnesses, hence service utilization. Even if we were able to reduce service utilization in hospitals through the increased adoption of the appropriate healthcare ICT that would facilitate the management of seniors' health conditions on an ambulatory/domiciliary basis, many would still likely need services for chronic degenerative diseases such as arthritis, even surgical treatment in the hospital. Hence, there is likely to be increased demand for such specialties as orthopedic surgery, and for physiotherapists, and indeed, other experts in other specialties such as Cardiology, Oncology, Urology, Geriatrics, Ophthalmology, and Radiology. There would be increased pressure of medical schools to increase enrollment, and on legislators to increase funding for physician training, as would be changes to immigration policies regarding foreign medical graduates, among other measures that not only promote recruitment but the retention of medical personnel. These issues would clearly bear on the nature and extent healthcare ICT investments, by this segment of healthcare stakeholders, and indeed, significantly too. In other words, even the investments by governments in healthcare ICT would be redundant were healthcare professionals not there to use them, for example, to invest in electronic medical records (EMR) with which they would hook up with a regional or national health information network. Furthermore, physician shortage would lengthen hospital wait times, patients queuing up endlessly to see overworked doctors, working increasingly longer hours, many unable to take vacations in a long time, their frustration compounded by problems referring their patients to the increasingly fewer numbers of specialists. Many of these specialists themselves are delaying retirement because there is no one to replace them in their practices if they did. Some estimates for example, show that one third of the 750,000 active, post-residency physicians in the U.S. are older than 55 years, and likely to retire about when the boomer generation turns seniors, and would need even more medical services provision, doctors retiring estimated at over 20,000 annually by 2020, versus 9,000 in 2000. With 20% of U.S. residents livin g in medically underserved areas, they would likely be even worse hit by the imminent shortages of doctors. Wait times are in fact increasing even in big U.S cities, about three weeks on the average for example for a routine gynecological checkup, or to see a cardiologist, or an orthopedic surgeon, recruiters charging sometimes as much as $30,000 per placement, doctors pay rising according to how high the need for them is. There is even concern about concierge practices, where some doctors restrict their practices to the well off that could afford to pay cash for their steep bills, which could only aggravate the disparities in healthcare delivery between individuals in different income brackets. Incidentally, the shortage of healthcare professionals is not peculiar to the U.S., but is a major issue in many other countries, developed and developing. Some argue that the present situation in the U.S resulted from miscalculation regarding health maintenance organizations (HMOs) that the promise of these organizations reducing the need for doctors by promoting preventive care and reducing tests and procedures did not materialize. Some blame this on the organizations' overly denial of care to patients, which some in fact, allege aimed to buoy their own profits margins. The negative public opinion they garnered resulted in their decline eventually, and the emergence of preferred provider organizations (PPOs), which offered patients more choice of doctors, and facilitated access to care, increasing the demand for doctors. Others also argue that the idea that technology would reduce physician utilization also failed to materialize, due essentially to increased hospitalization utilization as surgeons perform more surgeries for example on healthier, even older patients. Some even contend that the point about doctors' mal-distribution of doctors, and their inefficient utilization, are myths. There is no doubt that these arguments have their merits, but they also have their demerits, and in fact, tend to over-simplify the issues involved in the present state of affairs regarding the shortage of healthcare professionals and what to do about it. To be sure, we are going to need more doctors, as things currently stand, considering the complex issues that have brought matters to this state and the notably long gestational period to produce doctors, not to mention specialists. In other words, doctors are not going to become taxi drivers because of the widespread implementation of healthcare ICT, for example. This is a very important point to make, as this fear of redundancy could be partly responsible for the slowness by some healthcare professionals to embrace these technologies.

However, we need to examine the total picture and not just seek short-term solutions to problems that concern on-going processes that require periodic reappraisals and reforms based on emerging circumstances some of which we are not even in a position to fathom currently. In other words, the reasons for the problems of HMOs are many and variegated. Many HMOs for example started to fail since they became liable for malpractice for negligent determinations post-Senate Bill 386, of 1998, which itself lends credence to claims that some of their denials of coverage and benefits were not flawless, and as some believe, perhaps even belied a covert pecuniary motive. Yet, it is conjectural to suggest that were they able to exploit the immense benefits that healthcare ICT now offer us then, their decisions regarding benefits and coverage could have been more evidence-based and sounder. Even now, no one would deny the fact that we need to curtail soaring healthcare costs, and if indeed, we have identified the relics of the HMOs' heydays as the cause, should we not take measures to rectify them? Does access to care for example necessarily mean access to doctors, or to hospitals? Why should some surgeons relish in operating elderly patients on minor ailments that the surgery often makes no difference to or perhaps worsen, including the individual's quality of life, simply because seniors are now healthier than they were twenty years ago for example, the surgeon sometimes even assuming consent? In other words, are those procedures not creating the enabling environment for the sort of pressure on the health systems, financial, wait times, shortages, which we blame the HMOs for spawning, or at least perpetuating? Recent data from the 2004 CFPC/CMA/RCPSC National Physician Survey in Canada for example showed that doctors spend a significant amount of time on health facility committees and on performing administrative duties. Doctors in community medicine, microbiology and infectious diseases, hematology, emergency medicine and medical oncology, spent the most time, in terms of hours per week on average. Those in ophthalmology, diagnostic radiology, dermatology, rheumatology and family medicine, spent the least. However, as a percentage of the total number of hours all physicians spent on either committee or administrative work, family physicians contributed the largest percentage, 40.3%, followed by psychiatrists, pediatricians, and general internists with 6.2%, 5.2%, and 5.0% respectively. Immunologists and allergists, nuclear medicine specialists, dermatologists, and rheumatologists spent the least with, 0.2%, 0.3%, 0.3%, and 0.4%, respectively. The differences in percentages between ranking by specialty and by the number of hours per week reflect differences in the number of doctors in each specialty in the country.

There is no doubt that these figures exemplify the situation in many other countries, and illustrate the diversity of the possible causes of physician shortages and maldistribution, including the sort of role diffusion that these figures highlight, which have nothing to do with HMOs. In fact, one of the complaints about HMOs is that accountants and non-medical personnel determine which health service to authorize and pay for. By extension, problems such as wait times that such shortages cause do therefore also have varied origins. Should we therefore not be examining the bigger pictures of these issues in order to expose and understand the salient processes that we need to address, with a view to improving? In other words, should we not be conceptualizing healthcare delivery more appropriately as a conglomeration of processes working singly and in tandem to produce an outcome, namely healthcare delivery? Should we not be decomposing these processes in order to improve those that would further result in the exposition of others that would need further decomposition, and improvement, which would lead to a new set of expositions, the cycle continuing ad infinitum, any historical fallacy eschewed? Would this not be a more holistic approach to determining the real problems with any health system in order to be able to solve them successfully? Here is where the issue of technologies comes in. As we noted earlier, implementing the appropriate healthcare technologies could help us achieve the dual objectives of delivering qualitative healthcare and curtail healthcare costs simultaneously, not one or the other. This is a major advantage considering the ever-increasing costs of healthcare delivery, which research evidence even suggests may not be giving us value for the money. In other words, in the U.S. for example, even assuming that HMOs created all the problems with the country s health systems, their successors are not faring much better. Therefore, we need to start to understand the problems with the country s health systems, and indeed, those of other countries, as being flaws in one or more of the processes that culminate in healthcare delivery. We also need to start to acknowledge the fact no health system is perfect and none could ever be, but that we could bring it closer to this elusive goal utilizing rationally, healthcare ICT to improve the processes on an ongoing basis. Thus, as new information emerges for example on disease patterns and prevalence, on novel and effective treatments, on novel, cutting-edge technologies, among other factors known and unknown that could determine the direction of healthcare delivery, old processes become inadequate or even inappropriate for new tasks and to achieve new goals, hence the need for perennial process improvement and quality assurance. Healthcare ICT could in fact not only help us improve processes, the technologies could also help us ensure that processes remain qualitative, pending review, when we set new quality benchmarks, and improve the processes to meet the new yardsticks. Thus, the opportunities for continued healthcare ICT investments and implementation also follow these patterns, in general terms, the specific emphasis on technologies dependent on a host of other factors that are local, linked to regional trade links, and even global in nature. In short, there is little doubt that policy makers would continue to appreciate the significant role that healthcare ICT would play in healthcare delivery and would continue to subscribe to investing in these technologies, as their benefits are too clear and the problems facing health systems worldwide in our contemporary times too serious to ignore. The increasing costs of health services provision for example is no longer a debate subject restricted to academic circles, the public knows about it and is increasingly concerned too. Wou ld it not concern the Canadian public for example recent statistics that suggest that adverse events occur in as many as 30% of medical treatments and that about 24,000 persons die yearly due to medical mishaps? Is it any wonder that a Health Canada-commissioned in its report, *Governance for Patient safety: Lessons from the Non-health Risk-Critical High-Reliability Industries*, recommended the implementation by the health system a new safety-conscious regime much more proactive in averting death and injury that misdiagnosis, surgical mistakes, drug interactions, and other types of medical errors cause? The Commission wants an independent and heavily financed Canadian Patient Safety Agency to be the pivot of this "safety management culture". The commission wants the agency to be able to investigate mishaps and to recommend "useful regulatory or process interventions", to improve safety. Do these not coincide with the points we have been making thus far, about process improvement? Could we not in fact marry efficiency and economic viability with the delivery of safe and qualitative healthcare, which essentially are the elements of our dual objectives, and which we hold that healthcare ICT appropriately deployed could help us achieve? The authors suggested the transformation of the recently established, $8 million Canadian Patient Safety Institute (CPSI) into such as patient safety agency as mentioned earlier, making it independent federal agency and arming it with the resources for in-house analytics. According to the Canadian Adverse Events Study published in the Canadian Medical Association Journal (*CMAJ* 2004; 170:1678-86), 9000 to 24,000 Canadian patients die annually due to an adverse event in hospital and 7.5% of patients admitted to acute care experienced adverse events. Should it be the priority to establish a national regulatory patient safety agency considering that the provinces and territories have jurisdictions over health matters in Canada? On the other hand, should we simply implement measures that would improve patient safety at jurisdictional levels? This brings the concept of decomposition of processes that we mentioned earlier sharply back in focus. Regardless of whether or not there is a federal agency overseeing things, we need to implement the appropriate healthcare ICT and take other measures to improve healthcare delivery processes, and these have to be at the provincial and territorial levels. The federal agency could be an advisory body, with subtle persuasive clout perhaps backed by economic muscle, to ensure the implementation of the recommended guidelines for improving patient safety, for example, the widespread implementation of healthcare ICT and connectivity with Canada Health Infoway networks, at the provincial, and by extension into a national health information network. Implementing these technologies on a large scale as we earlier noted could also help reduce health spending in the provinces and territories, which many consider unsustainable, Medicare expected to guzzle over 50% of total revenues from all sources in 7 of 10 provinces by the year 2022 based on the latest five-year estimates. These estimates would likely even be higher over the years, if we did nothing to reduce health spending, outpacing inflation, total revenues, and economic growth in all provinces, and territories. With the population aging, pressures on the health systems would likely increase further increasing costs, and were we to regard the interest cost of servicing each province and territory's accumulated debt a fixed expense, this would paradoxically cut available total revenues. Furthermore, because we cannot afford to continue to hike taxes indefinitely without irking the people, and probably wrecking the economy, we would have even less funds for healthcare delivery when we most need them. One option would be to ration health services, but would we not be further worsening the wait lists problem, compromising the health of the populace and creating even more need for health services, hence further escalating healthcare costs, and should we be doing that? Should we rather not be seeking ways to prevent the above scenarios materializing, for example, exploring how we could utilize healthcare ICT to help us achieve the dual objectives mentioned above? These issues bring the private v. public health system debate in Canada to the fore, and some suggest there should be a parallel private health system in the country, at the very least, others that patients should have to make co-payments, and yet others scrapping universal healthcare. The point is that regardless of the health system a country adopts, healthcare delivery remains a medley of processes, which if flawed would result in the outcome, also flawed. This is a crucial point we need to understand and appreciate for us to be able to achieve the dual goals mentioned earlier. Policy options are not necessarily rooted in science, and even science does not have all the answers. There is no doubt that health policy must evolve in each country in harmony with the other processes that make the country work. While this suggests the need to take into consideration, other non-health institutional and structural factors peculiar to that country, it does not that these factors must remain static. In other words, it would be necessary to modify the processes in the light of changes that are crucial for the country's continuing existence. Thus, if the country or parts of it would become unviable because of certain current processes, those processes must undergo reappraisals and

93

improvement/replacement. Here is where healthcare ICT comes in with regard to health processes. Put differently, each country has core institutions and structures that have served it well over the ages, and which constitute significant elements of its collective psyche. It also has those that are newer, and less tested. It would be foolhardy therefore to suggest changing the former willy-nilly, or not the latter, despite overwhelming evidence of it not working any longer, or at least not the way it was, and for both vice-versa. In other words, our application of process decomposition, exposition, and further decomposition, in short, of the process cycle to healthcare delivery must eschew the psychological fallacy. The cycle must go on, but not necessarily w holesale. We would need to modify some processes and not others. We would need to improve some processes, leave some alone, and eliminate others, bearing in mind the goals we want to achieve, and not being intimidated to take which action we need to in ord er to achieve these goals, of course realizing that the very survival of the health system is at stake. Determining what to do with processes requires first identifying them, and the role they play in over healthcare delivery. This is not necessarily an easy task, but it is a necessary step in other to solve the problems confronting our health systems wherever in the world. Consider the following study by Bernard Friedman and H. Joanna Jiang of the U.S. Agency for Healthcare Research and Quality (AHRQ) and colleagues[2], on hospital inpatient costs for adults, nonmaternal patients with multiple (more than three) chronic diseases, published in the June 2006 issue of *Medical care Research and Review*. The researchers found that such patients have an unduly large effect on hospital costs yearly, with patients with between two and four chronic conditions accounting for 51% of all hospitalizations for nonmaternal adult patients. The authors noted the need to identify such patients, which could help determine policy formulations on and the development of new services that health plans should

cover and could help in risk adjusting premiums, particularly with such patients'
known difficulties purchasing health insurance coverage at affordable rates. This
study offers an example of the application of the process cycle mentioned above.
Research has identified the problem, which is, the high costs of care for chronic
illnesses among this population. In other words, chronic illnesses lead to high
care costs. High costs of care results in insurers shying away from these
individuals, or requesting them to pay more on premiums, which prompted
some to recommend "community rating," whereby an insurer must charge each
would-be beneficiary the same premium for a given insurance plan, health status
regardless. However, "community rating" means that healthy beneficiaries
subsidize the cost of care for the chronically ill for example, increasing premiums
for the former, reducing them, for the latter. It also offers insurers' financial
incentives to seek healthy rather than ill clients as the former on average would
pay more in premiums than they would generate in claims than the latter,
boosting the firms' bottom line. Would such insurers thus be keen on efforts
aimed to provide high quality service at the least price, our dual goals? This is
the first decomposition process, which as we see, resulted in exposing the new
issues, whose processes need addressing, accordingly. In other words, that
chronic illness leads to high healthcare costs itself involves some processes that
need improving, for example, secondary disease prevention measures that
would facilitate the prompt diagnosis and treatment of diseases, to prevent them
becoming chronic, efforts that the deployment of appropriate healthcare ICT
could not only help achieve but cost-effectively too. Furthermore, they could also
help obviate the need for hospitalization for the illness, if deployed to facilitate
ambulatory/community/domiciliary care for example. What's more, their
appropriate deployment could in fact help prevent the disease from developing
in the first place, in other words, via primary disease prevention. After

95

decomposing the processes, we have an exposition of new issues, and as some of the examples we mentioned above show, do not have to be clinical. Indeed, not all of the processes identified initially, or indeed, processes at any stage of the process cycle, need be clinical, and are indeed, invariably not. Thus, as the exposition consequent upon the first decomposition reveals, insurers are denying the ill coverage or charging them more, and are seeking the healthy preferentially to them, processes that compromise healthcare delivery to the former, and our prospects of achieving our dual healthcare delivery goals.

There are three possible outcome measures in the intermediate processes

leading to our achieving these dual goals involving, namely, the healthy, and the ill beneficiaries, and the insurer. Risk adjustment for example is one way to reduce the adverse effects of community rating incentives insurers have to institute the processes that would support our efforts to achieve the dual goals. Thus risk adjustment would ensure that individuals pay the same premium, health status notwithstanding, but also adjust the premium payments insurers receive to reflect the variations in clients' projected health care costs. In effect, we would then have to decompose these issues to expose the processes involved and that we need to facilitate using the appropriate healthcare ICT in other to implement the risk adjustment process, and the process cycle goes on until we accomplish this goal most cost-effectively. With regard the healthy and ill clients, the former would no longer have to subsidize the latter's healthcare costs, and the latter, to experience discrimination finding coverage or to pay much more for it, with the appropriate healthcare ICT implemented, by the former, to facilitate efforts to continue to improve health and fitness, the latter, to reduce morbidities. In other words, the success of the risk adjustment effort in turn depends on the success of the measures taken regarding the clients, which, as noted above, and just as with the processes involved in the efficient and cost-effective implementation of risk adjustm ent, also would benefit immensely from the deployment of the appropriate healthcare ICT. Again, as with the risk adjustment, we could decompose these measures further to expose even cryptic issues and their processes regarding the clients, and explore opportunities to improve them, if necessary, for example, taking into consideration the many variables involved in the sustenance of health and fitness, and in the resolution, stability, or worsening of illnesses. Thus, we could examine how healthcare ICT could help in improving the processes involved in the operations of these variables. Consider the following the findings of the Youth Risk Behavior Surveillance - United States, 2005, released by the Centers for Disease Control and Prevention (CDC) indicating that more U.S teenagers are turning away from risky behaviors. The report noted that behaviors such as reckless driving, violence, unsafe sex, and alcohol and tobacco use are on the decline among American youth, although not at a fast enough rate, and with differences between racial and ethnic groups still rather high. Thus, more still needs done to speed up this decline, and the development of healthcare ICT-enabled, targeted and contextualized health information dissemination could help achieve this goal among this undeniably technology-savvy segment of the U.S. population. Indeed, such programs create immense opportunities for software and healthcare ICT vendors to develop innovative programs to facilitate the processes involved in implementing these programs. Furthermore, these programs do not have to be public sector-inspired. In other words, is it not time that these companies, not-for-profit organizations, and other private sector organizations, started to develop and market healthcare-oriented health-information dissemination programs targeted at different population segments, inspired by such research findings as mentioned above? With health and fitness going to be increasingly important health issues, and as the report mentioned above suggests would likely be the case even among youths, such products would no doubt feature more on the consumer healthcare ICT markets. The report showed for example an increased use of seatbelt, with just 10% of teens indicating that they rarely or never used a seatbelt in 2005, versus 18% in 2003, and 26% in 1991. Forty three percent of students interviewed reported alcohol use in 2005, compared with 51% in 1991, and compared to 1991, when 54% reported ever having sexual intercourse, 47% did in 2005, when 63% reported using a condom during the last sexual intercourse versus 46% in 1991. Decomposing the findings further, we would need to address issues such as Hispanic or black students being likelier than white students to engage in physical fighting, risky sexual behaviors and to be overweight, and white students likelier to smoke cigarettes and engage in binge drinking. Other issues the report raised, that black students were least likely to use tobacco, alcohol, cocaine and other drugs, compared to white and Hispanic p eers, although likelier to report risky sexual behaviors and sedentary behaviors, for example watching TV three or more hours a day, need addressing. These issues would not only determine the processes to address, but also the technology-based programs to modify these processes, efficiently and cost-effectively. Here we would decompose the issues further to understand the underlying processes involved in the behaviors noted in the different racial and ethnic groups, for example among blacks and Hispanics, violent, sedentary, and risky sexual behaviors, and among whites, the use of tobacco, alcohol, cocaine and other drugs. Only then could we hope to reduce the prevalence of these behaviors even further, and eventually eliminate them. It would also be useful to understand the underlying issues and processes of these behaviors, with a view to reinforcing positive behaviors, and seeking ways to improve negative ones.

Thus, we need to understand why African-Americans reported the highest percentage of eating fruits and vegetables more than five times a day or Hispanic youths reporting higher suicide attempts and use of drugs such as cocaine, heroin and methamphetamines, and the girls, higher rates of feeling sad and hopeless, and of attempting suicide. Such understanding would result in greater exposition that would result in additional decomposition until we arrive at the results we seek. The process cycle we embark upon for example might suggest the need to address some issues on an individual, personalized basis, such as offering Hispanic, and indeed, all youths, healthcare ICT-based avenues to express their feeling and seek answers to questions regarding sex, and drugs, anonymously. It might on the other hand suggest a community approach to addressing certain issues, with the healthcare ICT-based programs developed along these lines, and offered to group participants in community centers, town halls, even the gym, and other appropriate locations. The point here is that we cannot afford to be complacent about health matters of even the seemingly healthy segments of our populations if we were to make our health systems work, regardless of which country. In Canada for example, which runs a publicly-funded health system, the sort of adverse selection described above for privately-funded systems, such as in the U.S., that is the tendency for the ill to likelier seek health insurance, is essentially none-existent as everyone receives healthcare free. However, because there is still some degree of health insurance coverage individuals need, but not obtainable under Medicare, some measure of adverse selection and its consequences for insurance premiums would still occur in the country's health system. Furthermore, even if there were no such adverse selection, moral hazard, both ex-ante- and ex-post-moral hazard, would still exist, the former the tendency of an individual to engage in risky behaviors because he/she does not pay for healthcare, making the insured items more likely to occur. The latter, claims for insured items becoming likelier due for example to reduce premiums could also create costs issues and inordinate pressures on the system, and information asymmetry would worsen both types of moral hazards. In fact, the lack of information by the healthcare consumer, compared to the provider for example on health issues is a perennial problem in the health industry, and one not peculiar to any health system, and needs urgent efforts to remedy, which healthcare ICT could help achieve, appropriately deployed. There is no doubt that suboptimal investment in health capital by individuals due to availability of health insurance would likely result in increased illness rates and disease prevalence, hence increased service utilization of the negative kind, which results in avoidable increases in health spending on curative care. This is why the efforts at decomposition and exposition characteristic of the process cycle described earlier apply to any health system, regardless of the funding model. It is also why the widespread implementation and utilization of healthcare ICT to facilitate the improvement of the processes arrived at due to these efforts also applies to any health system. As we noted earlier, we should not just be interested in treating the ill, we should sustain the health of those that are not, as this, particular with an emphasis on disease prevention, at the primary, secondary, and tertiary levels, is an important aspect of mitigating the implications of the flawed incentives characteristic of the moral hazards described above. In other words, our decomposition/exposition efforts should encompass preventing diseases from occurring in the first place, and diagnosing and treating them promptly, and preventing their sequelae. These issues would be the key drivers of healthcare ICT investments in the future, as it becomes increasingly clearer to health policy makers that these technologies could play a crucial role in the achievement of the dual objectives of qualitative healthcare delivery while simultaneously reducing health spending. Canadians, for example, cherish the Medicare system, and in fact, consider health-care guarantee as most important by far of the Conservative government's five priorities, according to a recent SES Research poll published in the June 2006 edition of Policy Options. According to this poll, 46.9% of Canadians rated the health-care guarantee the most important to them, almost thrice as those that deemed the accountability legislation to clean up government (16.8 per cent), with 14.7% rating the GST as the most important, 10.4%, supporting childcare, the most important, and 9.5%, the crime package. The promised health-care guarantee covers patients for out-of-province or out-of-country medical care rather than have to wait too long, federal, and provincial governments setting wait times benchmarks, for some types of surgery and services in the province. Thus, the expectation of health service provision by Canadians is likely to continue to be high. This makes the need for carrying out the process cycle exercises even more urgent, and this should be for both preventive and curative processes, the exercises, likely to be major determinants of the types and extent of healthcare ICT investments that the country's provinces and territories, which run the health services, would make in the near future. As we noted earlier, the processes that contribute to the evolution of healthcare delivery, are eclectic, some medical, others not, but these processes also coalesce at different junctures in bringing about this outcome. Consider the issue of women not obtaining follow-up mammograms or biopsies. Physicians and insurers for example connected by electronic medical records (EMRs) would enable the identification of those women who did not receive the necessary follow-up care and even create a notification system to ensure they do. This would ensure that women with abnormal mammograms receive the necessary follow-up care, their not so doing otherwise a usual cause delay in diagnosis, which if the lesion turned out to be cancer, would have compromised the chances of a good prognosis. This is another example of how healthcare ICT modified the processes, women not receiving post-mammogram follow -up care, involved in a major health issue, diagnostic delay with implications for disease outcome, with resultant improved outcome, with no doubt about the saving in human and material terms. As we noted earlier, the process cycle is inherently complicated, considering the multiplicity of issues known and unknown involved in the various intermediate processes that result in the outcome, namely healthcare delivery. To be sure, healthcare ICT deployment aims to facilitate the achievement of these processes cost-effectively, and as we saw above, issues are not processes. Issues are the starting research observations or the results of decomposition, and underlying them are processes, which healthcare ICT could help us facilitate if necessary. As we also noted earlier, we should beware of historical fallacies, in interpreting the decomposition and exposition, lest we miss our way completely and incur more costs, and worse still further undermine the quality of service delivery. Some might ask what all these have to do with investments in healthcare ICT, from which, true, this discussion seems, on first glance far removed. However, the issues raised in the discussion constitute the core determinants of present and future healthcare ICT spending. In other words, healthcare ICT investments would increase or decrease, and would vary from country to country, and with health jurisdiction, based on the extent to which each embraces and executes the process cycle.

A new Bill, which U.S. Sen. Sam Brownback, R-Kan., introduced on June 06, 2006, the Independent Health Record Bank Act, for example, exemplifies the new direction healthcare ICT investments would likely go in the years ahead. The Bill, which the Kansas City Business Journal on June 07, 2006, noted the Senator previewed during his April 14, 2006 visit to Cerner Corp. in North Kansas City, provides legal and regulatory guidelines for establishing the banks by nonprofit cooperative institutions akin to member-owned credit unions. Healthcare ICT firms such as Cerner could provide needed technology for the record banks, which would store patients' electronic health records (EHR), creating a nationwide health information network comparable to the countrywide financial system, with individuals able to access their health records the same way they are able to access their bank records using, for example, their ATM card. Patients would also be able to sell their record data on a blinded basis for research and other authorized uses, with proceeds from such sales, tax-free and split equally between the patient and the managing health record bank. The Senator also proposed that the sharing of such proceeds could be with health care providers and payers to encourage them to provide the banks more data and information, and called for investment tax credits for employers to encourage employees to participate in the record-banking system. With this bill, we see how decomposing problems with paper-based medical records including those relating to data accuracy and currency, timely availability, and costs, among others, the issues, led to an exposition, ownership of health information. Further decomposition revealed the various uses to which the record owner could put his/her records, and the processes involved facilitated by the healthcare ICT, EHR. A recent study published by the Center for Studying Health System Change on June 07, 2006 noted that the percentage of doctors with access to healthcare ICT they could use for at least four of five clinical tasks has nearly doubled in the past four years, yet many physicians have hardly started to use such tools. Almost 21% of doctors interviewed in 2004-2005 reported having access to technology for receiving clinical guidelines, accessing patient data, or prescribe drugs, versus 11.4% in 2000-2001. The study also examined inter-provider clinical data/image sharing, and reminder alerts for physicians, for example to contact patients for follow -up lab investigations. The findings showed that almost 17% of respondents in 2004-2005 lacked access to healthcare ICT for any of the five activities studied, and 20% only had the technology for one activity. Yet there is research evidence for the benefits of automating physician activities, including in eliminating paperwork, reducing medical errors, and enhancing patient safety, saving time and money, and overall in improving the quality of care delivery. This underscores the importance the sort of process cycle efforts described for Senator Brownback s Bill earlier. There are reasons common to jurisdictions that doctors and other healthcare providers shun healthcare ICT, for example costs of the technologies and those involved in the time and materials required to change office procedures, lack of national standards, and interoperability issues, and the learning curve involved. Almost 65% of doctors surveyed in 2004-2005 reported that they had healthcare ICT that allows them to obtain clinical guidelines, compared to 52.9% in 2000-2001, most doctors reporting access to healthcare ICT, which is in fact not much more than Internet access, hence incurring minimal costs, to fin d guidelines in both time periods, those to write prescriptions, the least owned. Costs are no doubt involved in many doctors not having the latter but many countries either have legislation prohibiting them, or none permitting them, not to mention other technical issues. This not only highlights the need to decompose health issues but also the fact that many such issues have local flavors and each country or health jurisdiction needs to identify the issues and challenges its health system confronts, and to conduct its process cycle exercises accordingly. It is undeniable that such exercises, which would become increasing unavoidable, would determine the healthcare ICT required to facilitate the processes revealed, hence drive the healthcare ICT that would facilitate or modify them. Put differently, although almost all countries embark on health reforms, as Cassells[3] in a 1995 article in vol.7 of the *Journal of International Development*, observed, health sector reform is not uniform across the globe, with reform packages as diverse as the countries undertaking them. Nonetheless, they all aim to improve health services in a number of ways such as their quality, efficiency, and cost-effectiveness. Furthermore, and regardless of whether the health system is private-type, and seeks non-tax revenue funding sources, or otherwise, such reforms tend to involve reforms in the public sector in general, in particular involving the adoption of the "New Public Management (NPM)" principles, with its emphasis on responsibility, accountability, and performance. Many developed countries including Canada, the U.K, U.S, and France, have implemented aspects of NPM the central theme of which operating the public, including the health system, to a greater or less extent on a market-based and private sector principles, the aim, to enhance efficiency and cost-effectiveness. This underscores the point that the increasing use of the process cycle is inevitable and a natural follow -up to a strategic intent we could no longer ignore, that of achieving the dual objectives of healthcare delivery mentioned above, and governments are investing on healthcare ICT accordingly. In the EU for example, in 2004 the ICT expenditure of general public administration alone (minus verticals such as education, health, and defence, for examples) for EU25 reached € 36.5 billion, the largest markets- the UK, Germany, France, Italy and Spain, respectively. In terms of per capita and/or as a percentage of GDP, ICT expenditure is highest in the Nordic countries, nam ely Denmark, Finland and Sweden, the UK increasingly close to them, another group, France, Germany, Netherlands, Austria, Belgium, way behind, and Italy and Spain, the least budgets. During the same periods, eGovernment expenditure was a total of € 11.9 billion. Experts agree that eGovernment significantly improves public sector labor productivity, resulting in improved services, cost savings, and GDP growth. In fact, estimates indicate that future eGovernment research and pilot programs (2005-2010) could boost EU25 GDP up to 1.54%, or roughly €166 billion. With healthcare ICT underlying the efforts to improve the processes involved in ensuring qualitative performance of the health services, it is safe to expect the pattern and extent of investments in these technologies to flow from the efforts to understand in full, the multiplicity of issues that result in healthcare delivery. It would become increasingly untenable to do otherwise considering the expected further increase in health spending in the developed countries for example that their aging populations would engender. Moreover, with a corresponding reduction in birth rates in many of these countries, or as in the U.S., the changing racial and ethnic demographics, the onus is on us to understand the underlying processes that would improve healthcare delivery to all segments of society, hence the overall health of the citizenry. There is no doubt about the analytic heuristics and the prescriptive viability of the process cycle, although admittedly its practical complexity is also quite evident. Nonetheless, our world is increasingly complex with the variables germane to outcomes legion. Yet, this outcome could be troubling to say the least, for example, increasing healthcare spending with corresponding improvement in healthcare delivery quality, and would worsen with things left as they are. For these and many other reasons, we must face the challenges involved in understanding the real reasons our health systems have poor outcomes, no matter how hard the task. Every healthcare stakeholder must join the efforts to overcome the challenges that face healthcare delivery, as the example of the recent coalition that twenty-two electronics and health care firms formed in the U.S. aimed at developing certification guidelines for healthcare ICT products and lobbying regulatory agencies to implement rules to encourage

106

the use of those products, show. According to a *Wall Street Journal* report, the coalition, christened, Continua Health Alliance would operate as a not-for-profit organization, and includes IBM, Intel, Cisco Systems, Motorola, Samsung Electronics, GE Healthcare, Medtronic, and Philips Electronics. The certification guidelines the coalition develops would meet specified interoperability standards. It would also develop a logo on the products informing on compatibility. The coalition would promote the utilization of monitoring devices for communicating patient data to hospitals and other health providers in domiciliary care. It would also lobby regulatory agencies to facilitate consumer reimbursement from insurers for using monitoring healthcare ICT at home, the more widespread use of which would ease the current and anticipated problem of shortage of health care providers as the population ages, and the prevalence of chronic diseases rises. Commenting on these developments, Joseph Kvedar, vice chair of dermatology at Harvard Medical School and director of the telemedicine division at Partners HealthCare noted, "We've lost the capacity battle already We have to move quickly," highlighting the points we have been making in our discussion thus far. In addition to implementing these technologies, we should also measure their effects in particular around value drivers such as service delivery quality, efficiency, and cost-effectiveness, which would require developing appropriate metrics, both quantitative, for example economic impact, and qualitative, such as consumer satisfaction, for so doing based on the economic and healthcare peculiarities of each country or health jurisdiction. The recent formation of the eHealth Vulnerability Reporting Program (eHVRP) in the U.S. underscores the increasing pace of activities in the healthcare ICT industry that would overall help promote the widespread diffusion of these technologies and encourage their use in addressing issues that the process cycle reveals. A number of key industry executives on June 06 2006 announced the formation of the eHealth Vulnerability Reporting Program (www.ehvrp.org), aimed at enhancing the security of eHealth systems. The program will establish a structure by which eHealth system developers, their clientele, and security firms communicate and share vulnerabilities and assist in how best to mitigate them. The program will set up a means to even proactively, identify, and categorize security vulnerabilities and their severity, evaluation criteria, reporting format and frequency, disclosure measures, and models to implement compensating controls as necessary. These efforts no doubt would make healthcare ICT such as the EHR more secure, foster public confidence in the technologies, and encourage some providers that might have withheld plans to purchase electronic medical records to do so. Indeed, many of these physicians run solo or small group practices that would hardly consider purchasing and implementing costly technologies that they would be concerned about using for fear of litigation. Again, efforts are afoot to help promote these technologies among these groups of doctors as the example of MedPlexus below shows. With a grant from the Centers for Medicare and Medicaid Services, MedPlexus, funded a phased project aimed to speed the adoption of EMR systems among small physician practices. The company, having successfully completed the pilot testing, now is ready to launch the commercial version of its hosted integrated EHR and Practice Management Solution. Six physician practices nationwide participated in the program, implementation, configuration and training conducted remotely, thus minimizing deployment and training costs. MedPlexus provided software and technical support, HP, Tablet PCs and desktop computers, and Siemens hosted the software in massive data centers in Santa Clara, Calif. Company officials assert that the application service provider (ASP), or hosted -model developed in the field for over two years is now ready for marketing. Besides low -cost deployment and maintenance, running the ASP software offers many other advantages, for example, ease of remote access to patient charts, and simple, user-friendly software setup with no need for a server, the integrated EHR-Practice management capability making two-keystroke billing on completion of clinical notes, hence billing at time of service, possible. The company wants to eliminate some of the hindrances to EMR adoption for examples, cost, complexity, time, and lost productivity, and assist doctors to automate their practices at their own pace, in installments or at once. However, the approach underlines the importance of the potential influence of the handling of the issue of net neutrality mentioned earlier on not just future healthcare ICT investments, but indeed, on the prospects of our achieving our dual healthcare delivery goals. This issue also underscores the complexity of the interplay of variables within and outside the health industry that could influence, positively or adversely, the effectiveness and efficiency of healthcare delivery, including healthcare spending. We must therefore, always have a broad perspective of the challenges that confront our health systems, and be prepared to subject them to the process cycle.

References

1. Gosden T, Forland F, Kristiansen IS, Sutton M, Leese B, Giuffrida A, Sergison M, Pedersen L. Capitation, salary, fee-for-service and mixed systems of payment: effects on the behavior of primary care physicians. *The Cochrane Database of Systematic Reviews* 2000, Issue 3. Art. No.: CD002215. DOI: 10.1002/14651858.CD002215.

2. Friedman et al., *Medical Care Research and Review*, June 2006

3. Cassells, A. (1995). Health sector reform: key issues in less developed countries. *Journal of International Development* 7 (3): 329-48.

Developments in the European Healthcare ICT Markets

The economic characteristics of Europe are diverse, even among the twenty-

five member European Union (EU.) Those of France, Germany and Italy, for

examples, whose economies combined represented almost 50% of the EU's Gross

Domestic Product (GDP) in 2003 are quite distinct from that of the U.K, which

bear a closer resemblance to those of the U.S. The divergences in these

economies, and particularly between them and that of the U.S, for example, has

been amplified some would argue since the mid -1970s, by the information and

communications technologies revolution. These economic differences are evident

in the health sectors of the different countries in Europe, which have primary

responsibility for health, even if , there is a collective strategy to handling a

number of public health issues am ong EU member states. One of the European

Commission's stated public health goals is to contribute to the development of

more effective and efficient health systems. The EU will spend €50 million

annually from 2003 to 2008 to improve data collection, information exchange,

and better understanding of the effects on health of EU policies. Also important

to the Commission are strategies for dealing with the effect on health of tobacco, alcohol, drugs, genetic factors, age, and gender, improving mental health, nutrition, and physical activity. The Commission also seeks health parity for all member, although acknowledges that in general, not only does the prevalence of major health problems vary among member states, but also that life expectancy is lower and infant and maternal mortality rates are higher among the new member states. The concept of a single market implies that citizens of member states could travel to, and live and work in any member country, which assumes that they would be able to receive healthcare in these other countries, for which it is necessary for member countries to recognize mutually, social security rights, which the European health insurance card facilitates. EU citizens might in fact be able to travel to another member country specifically to receive healthcare, for example those that live near borders, or that require specialist treatment. These and other issues and challenges that healthcare delivery, pose to the EU have far-reaching policy implications in health and non-health domains, the latter for example including social, the single market, and the environment. However, and more fundamental to tackling these issues is the role of healthcare ICT. Indeed, the EU has, in recent times been focusing on developing the links between the information society and health. It recognizes the critical role of high-speed data links in facilitating communication networks between healthcare professionals across the EU, and patients access to specialists that they may lack in their locale. It is therefore actively promoting e-health programs and funding related research, in its bid to prioritize spending on patient health, part of a larger effort to promote the utilization of information and communication technologies to help people to surmount economic, social, educational, territorial, or disability-related drawbacks. Ministers of 34 European (EU Member States, accession and candidate and EFTA/EEA countries) countries in Riga, Latvia during a recent e-inclusion conference in June 2006 endorsed the Riga Ministerial Declaration, setting the targets on ways to increase the inclusion of disadvantaged ICT users. The E-inclusion targets include reducing by 50%, the gap in internet usage by groups at risk of exclusion, for examples, seniors, people with disabilities, and unemployed persons, increasing broadband coverage in Europe to at least 90%, and making all public websites accessible by 2010, among others. According to Information Society and Media commissioner Viviane Reding "Many Europeans still get too little benefit from information and communication technologies and millions are at risk of being left behind. Enabling all Europeans to participate on equal terms in the information society is not only a social necessity it is a huge economic opportunity for industry. By implementing their Riga und ertakings, European countries will take a big step towards making e-inclusion a reality." Ministers also requested the Commission to tackle urgently, and before the end of 2006, the issues of active ageing and independent living in the information society. There is no doubt that about the implications of the push to achieve these targets in member countries via for examples, actions to promote the adoption of user-recommended best practices, industry-led provision of accessible technology, novel EU research, national e-inclusion plans, and voluntary accord between stakeholders, for immense market opportunities for ICT in general, including health healthcare ICT. An estimated 30% to 40% of Europeans do not benefit from the information society. There are a num ber of reasons for this, including many persons unable to afford access, lacking skills, and motivation, among others, that broadband subscription in Europe increased by 60% in 2005, notwithstanding. In fact, broadband penetration, or "take-up", defined as the number of subscribers per 100 population is still just 13% in the EU, or roughly 25% of households. What s more, differences in access between rural and urban populations not only exist, but also are significant. Understandably, Reding plans to step u p the application of EU telecom rules in the years ahead in order to boost internal market competition, and to attain a broadband penetration of not less than 50% of households by 2010[2]. Just 10% of individuals over 65years in the EU use the Internet, and just about 3% of public web sites fully comply with minimum web accessibility standards. This creates a major accessibility issue for the 15% of persons with disabilities in the E.U., essentially excluding them from full involvement in economic and social life, a percentage that is likely to increase with the population aging were nothing done to rectify the problem. This problem not only aggravates the information asymmetry that has plagued the health industry for long and continues so to do, compromising the health status of those affected, but in fact also undermines the potentials for Europe's labor, goods and services markets, and its overall economic growth and sustainable development. The EU is keen to exploit the opportunities that ICT-enabled job participation creates to involve excluded groups in the job market thereby contributing to Europe's 70% labor-market participation target. This would not only help improve the economy, but would also help improve the overall health of its citizenry, for exam ples by rectifying health information asymmetry and indeed creating veritable treatment portals. Little wonder then that the Ministers in Riga supported robustly the European Commission's plan to prepare for the European e-inclusion initiative announced for 2008 in the "i2010" strategy the Commission adopted on June 01, 2005, and is the digital economy part of the EU's reinvigorated "Lisbon" agenda for jobs and growth. Thus, there is an intricate link between economic and health priorities in the EU whose ramifications would extend far beyond its membership and would not only have a profound influence on future developments in the use of healthcare ICT among its member states, but also would have a domino effect on other countries in Europe. Indeed, the more pervasive deployment of these technologies in healthcare delivery across Europe would be in keeping with the inevitable paradigm shift in health and healthcare that the increasing health spending in many European countries with as some would argue, perhaps s even a decline in the quality of service provision, would engender. Many countries are spending increasing proportions of their Gross Domestic Products (GDP) on health. Their is no doubt this is unsustainable, and that they are going to have to seek ways by which to curtail their health spending while not compromising and in fact improving the quality of healthcare delivery. The need for measures to increase the efficiency and cost-effectiveness of health systems is therefore going to be a central theme in the healthcare delivery strategies of many, if not all European countries. Some of these measures might be difficult political enterprises, particularly those concerning establishing a healthcare market, involving a variety of different providers from the private and voluntary sectors, as a recent report published by the King's Fund, an independent health charity in the U.K, shows3. The Fund urged the British government to declare its commitment to these market reforms, which it patently pursues, lest patients suffer because of these reforms. A working group of senior executives from the NHS and the private and voluntary sectors prepared the report, which noted that the government has shifted towards a supplier market system, with the introduction of new m easures such as payment by results, in which patients could choose where they can have operations, and hospitals receive payment per patient treated. Other such measures include semi-independent foundation hospitals, and significantly more private sector involvement in healthcare delivery. Thus, the funding model of health systems in Europe, where healthcare is in the main publicly funded, is going to undergo some fundamental changes, which even if not seismic, would herald the incremental injection of private sector structures and approaches in the management of health systems. The effects of these reforms would cut right across board as the example of the recent developments in the healthcare software firm, iSoft Group Plc, working on the delayed upgrade of computer systems for the U.K's health system shows. iSoft shares lost about 90% percent of their value since September 2005, in the midst of concerns over delay, which the government has said could extend to two years, to the 6.2 billion pound ($11.42 billion) project to upgrade information technology systems for the U.K's National Health Service (NHS), among other issues. Shares in iSoft, which began 2006 at about 400 pence, closed up 3.1% at 57 pence, valuing the group at about 132 million pounds ($243 million). The shares fell again on June 08, 2006, after the firm announced annual profits would be lower than anticipated due to a change in accounting policy and that it was holding discussions with banks to modify aspects of its banking facilities. Thus, the pressure to deliver the expected goods and services in whatever process that contributes to the health system achieving the dual objectives of qualitative healthcare delivery while curtailing health spending would be substantial in the new dispensation. This is the inevitable and expected consequence, of the process-improvement imperative the achievement of such objectives demands. In its first annual progress report on i2010, Commissioner Reding noted the need for more ambitious plans to exploit the full benefits of information and communication technologies (ICT). Europe is essentially an information society although the penetration of the technologies that facilitate information communication and sharing is far from uniform across the continent. Furthermore, and as the Commissioner noted, there is much more that these technologies offer than currently utilized, even among countries with the largest penetration, and in particular for the delivery of health services. There is indeed, ample room for EU and other European countries to improve access to broadband internet connectivity, facilitate digital content distribution, make radio spectrum available for new applications, and redouble efforts on research and development of novel technologies. These efforts would no doubt contribute in the years ahead to improving the underlying processes of the countries' public services, including the health services. With the emphasis of the i2010 report on speeding these efforts up, there is no doubt that much still need done for European countries, including those in the EU to achieve the dual goals mentioned above. The EU for example has policies to promote competition and investment in the telecom markets, yet Europe continues to be nowhere near its competitors such as the U.S. in ICT research, and the mechanisms to foster cross-border competition, even among EU countries, are sorely lacking. The improvement in economic growth in the EU in 2005, projected to be about 2% in 2006, still falls well below the annual GDP growth of 2.7% in the US in 2000-2005, and could the latter spending twice more on ICT research have played a part in this difference? The growth of the EU's ICT sector is however, above average, and it remains the EU's most inventive and research-intensive sector. It accounts for 25% of the total EU research effort and 5.6% of the GDP from 2000-2003, and produced about 45% of EU productivity gains in 2000-2004. Would this growth continue, and how would it affect the health sector? What would this effect mean for business opportunities for healthcare ICT companies in the near future? EU Member States increasingly consider research and innovation policies as a key priority in their National Reform Programs, and many support efforts to promote the widespread diffusion of ICT., although much more needs done to accelerate in general the implementation of their information society policies and drivers of growth, for examples, convergence of digital network, content and device convergence. However, investments in networks recommenced in 2004 and 2005, and broadband subscriptions increased by 60% in 2005, 60 million or 13% of the EU population included. Telecom and cable operators have new value propositions, for examples, triple-play or web TV, and the new eGovernment

Action Plan, proposed the Commission proposed in April, 2006, which outlines the key role of ICT in making government services more efficient and more responsive, would likely generate momentum in ICT implementation. There is no doubt that not only EU member states but also other countries on the continent need to institute measures for more ICT involvement in their economic development objectives, including in healthcare delivery, which no doubt plays a significant role in any country's economic productivity.

It has been over two decades since the Commission for Worldwide Telecommunications Development (The Maitland Commission, 1984) issued its report, *The Missing Link*, implicating the lack of telephone infrastructure in developing countries as a barrier to economic growth, sparking controversy over the real needs of the developing world. The debate on the need or otherwise for ICT diffusion in developing countries rages on, despite the agreement in September 2000 by world leaders at the United Nations Millennium Summit to adopt eight specific development goals, which many contend ICT diffusion is critical to realizing. The problem centers around this role, which some argue is not a priority now for peoples with more urgent basic survival and health, not to mention infrastructure, needs. With the exponential growth of the Internet is the refocusing of the klieg light on the "digital divide" and the recrudescence of this debate. Most of Europe might not have inadequate energy grids, and massive illiteracy, but nonetheless has differential ICT penetration, significant in some instances. There is indeed, no doubt about the applicability of the essential elements of the report of the G-8's Digital Opportunity Task Force (DOT,) created at its July 2000 Summit, *Digital Opportunities for All: Meeting the Challenge* that was the basis of the Genoa Action Plan adopted at the 2001 G-8 Summit, to

Europe. The report called for increased ICT diffusion as a key ingredient of sustainable economic development, and with the digital divide in Europe between countries and between groups within countries, would the more widespread diffusion of ICT not help foster sustainable development? By enabling the exploitation of the full potential of these technologies hence facilitating the achievement of the dual healthcare delivery goals mentioned earlier, would it not also help improve the overall health of the citizenry thereby further improving productivity and by extension economic growth across the continent? Data from Eurostat, the Statistical Office of the European Communities, reference, STAT/05/143, released on 10/11/2005, showed that 85%and only 13% of students, and the retired, respectively, used the Internet, at least once during the three months prior to the survey, in 2004. The EU25 figures revealed that 85% of students (aged 16 or more in school or university), 60% of employees, 40% of the unemployed and 13% of the retired used the internet during the first quarter of 2004, versus a EU25 average of 47% for individuals aged from 16 to 74 years₄. The divide by employment status was also evident by educational level. Only 25% of individuals with at most lower secondary education used the internet during the first quarter of 2004, 52% and 77% for persons that finished secondary and tertiary education, respectively. These figures reinforce our assertion above of the differential penetration of ICT in Europe, albeit based on a variety of factors such as age, employment status, and educational level widest in Portugal, least in Lithuania, and rural/urban location, among others. This is in spite of the increased availability of ICT in accessibility and costs terms in the past decade on the continent. Experts attribute this digital divide to absent infrastructure or access; and lack of inducement to use these technologies, and of the computer literacy or skills required to participate in the information society. With regard education for instance, there is clearly more

Internet use by the more educated across the continent, although there is no significant link between degree of the digital divide and the overall level of internet penetration. This suggests the need for efforts to improve literacy skills among the less educated if we were to improve internet penetration among them, taking into consideration the differing rates in different countries namely, Portugal (70 percentage points), Slovenia (68 pp), Spain (61 pp), the U.K (59 pp) and Italy (58 pp), with the largest divide. The least divide was in Lithuania (11 pp), Sweden (24 p p), Germany (25 pp), Denmark and Estonia (both 27 pp). Over 50% of the lower educated used the internet only in Sweden (70%), Denmark (64%), Finland (54%) and Germany (51%) during the study period, and the percentage of the higher educated that use who used the internet was less than 50% only in Lithuania (38%) and Greece (48%). The highest internet use among students were in Finland (97%), Sweden and Denmark (both 96%), the least in Greece (55%), Ireland (57%) and Italy (74%). The highest internet use among the employed were in Sweden (86%), Denmark (83%), the Netherlands and Finland (both 82%), the least in Greece (28%), Lithuania and Hungary (both 33%), among the unemployed, ranged from 8% in Lithuania and 10% in Latvia to 86% in Sweden and 76% in the Netherlands. The Netherlands was the only country where over 50% of the retired use the internet, the group that in general least used the internet. In thirteen EU countries, less than 10% of the retired had used the internet, while only in the Netherlands (54%), Sweden (45%), Denmark (34%), and Luxembourg (32%) had over 25% retirees having used the internet. The figures are in keeping with those of internet penetration by age, the percentage of internet users among those aged 16 to 24 years was thrice higher than for those aged 55 to 74 years. These figures could no doubt inform the business focus of ICT firms that develop computer-training software and those involved in imparting computer literacy and skills in general, considering the increasing efforts in the EU, and among other European countries to bridge this digital divide, efforts that would likely manifest in substantial investments in computer literacy programs in the years ahead. Furthermore, and with particular reference to those concerning retirees, the figures highlight the need for even more urgent actions considering the increasing longevity hence the population aging in many of these countries. Some might see the problem that such a drought of internet penetration as one that could become worse before it gets better when the current younger generation among who internet use is commoner, becomes seniors. That might be fair to say, but it does not obviate the need for urgent action considering the health and economic ramifications of not doing so in the interim. A cursory examination of the figures above shows the paucity of internet penetration among retirees even in countries with high penetration based on education, employment, and among students, for example, Sweden, and with less than 10% of retirees using the internet in 13 EU countries, the problem is serious. It is because it means that a large proportion of seniors, the population segment that would increasingly not only be the largest, but also the most intensive users of health services in these countries, do not use the internet, and are out of the most veritable network technologies via which they could benefit from the immense potential of healthcare ICT. The effect of this would be besides compromising their health also that of our ability to utilize these technologies in realizing the dual objectives mentioned earlier. In short, by not taking measures to rectify this anomaly, European countries would be denying their seniors the opportunities for cutting-edge, healthcare ICT-enabled, health services, that could preclude the need for costly trips to the hospital, perhaps even for hospitalization in some cases. It is not difficult to see how much in lost savings in human and material terms that not taking urgent action to understand the reasons for the deficient internet penetration and possibly that of healthcare ICT in general among this population segment and to rectify the problem could cause. Finding the answer to this problem would also doubtless interest healthcare ICT firms, and ind eed, other healthcare stakeholders in Europe and beyond from a variety of business, and healthcare perspectives, some of which might in fact want to commission their own research to do so. The quest to bridge the digital divide is therefore not necessarily restricted to developing countries, and the ICT industry is taking a keen interest in the matter. Intel for example is developing the *Classmate PC,* a sub-$400 notebook for kindergarteners through high school students that will no doubt be useful in emerging nations as well as in the developed world. It will have a 1GB of flash memory rather than a hard drive, in order to be able to withstand accidents better. It will have asset-control software as a threat deterrent, able to disable automatically if out of the classroom for too many days. It will use a special version of Windows that stops children from accessing parent/teacher-censored Internet sites or adding parent/teacher-censored programs, and has software usable during classroom exercises, for example pop -up messages that discourage doing other things on the notebook during classes. This Notebook is part of the ongoing efforts of computer firms to promote Internet penetration in Africa, rural Asia, and Latin America. Even with roughly 1 billion estimated computers hooked onto the Internet by 2010, 5.5 billion persons would still be online. As the European figures show, which indeed applies to countries worldwide, the less money people have, the unlikelier they would have access to the Internet. This is why there is an urgent need for low -cost PC s such as MIT Media Lab founder Nicholas Negroponte s $100 laptops, and Simputer s, although because the current low -cost PCs, unlike the *Classmate PC* are unable to transmit documents between devices, they have limited value in enabling access to the information society. Intel is also developing the *Affordable PC,* for this market, a nonupgradeable desktop with 128MB or 256MB of memory, a 40GB drive, optical drive and two USB slots. It uses either Linux or Windows and costs, with monitor, between $220 and $300. It has a mobile Celeron chip, which being low - powered enables the PC maker to reduce the computer's size. It is also able to withstand outside temperatures above 45 Celsius (113 Fahrenheit). This is a crucial feature considering the plan to sell the PCs in combination with pay-as-you-go and credit programs to which many developing countries have subscribed, which would facilitate the purchase of these machines by the poor. Owners could set the PCs up in say village stalls and sell computer access time, raking up money to pay off the PC over time. Intel might even create a special processor for emerging markets if sales volumes reach between 50 million and 100 million for example, further making the computers m ore versatile. These low-cost computers although would serve emerging markets more, would no doubt serve just as well many of the less financially endowed populations in Europe, where even countries such as Portugal, were until recently classified as emerging economies. As previously noted, there are complex, sometimes cryptic links between the economy and health. In the EU, the notion of the common market is increasingly becoming reality with restrictions on the movement of labor easing across the borders of member states. The resulting cross-border migration would inevitably put the health systems of host countries under fiscal strain were no measures taken to account for such developments, including the ability of all residents, including the immigrants to participate in the information society, including in the utilization of healthcare ICT for the delivery of efficient and cost-effective health services. The fiscal strain might be sufficient in the medium and long terms to knock a hole in the economies of these host countries, which many would argue the influx of foreign labor has already compromised, although figures for the U.K for example, shows otherwise. To underscore the significance of the issue of labor mobility, the European Commission tagged 2006 the European Year for mobility of workers, with the aim of increasing awareness and understanding of the benefits of both working abroad and in a new occupation. With current figures indicating that, very few Europeans work outside their countries, about 1.5% for the last three decades, seasonal workers, quite many at certain times in the agriculture or the hotel sectors, excluded, and in nine EU countries, 40% of workers not changing jobs for a decade, almost 50% in several countries, there indeed, seems to be labor inertia. However, the EU determined to take measures to address some of the legal, administrative, and linguistic obstacles to worker mobility, and raise awareness of the benefits of such mobility, dedicated €4.3 million of the year's €6million budget, to mobility awareness raising projects alone. With these measure, coupled with the recent introduction of the European Health Card, and the directive on the portability of pension rights, among other recent developments, the inertia might be about to turn into a surge. Job-to-job mobility figures are more impressive than those for cross-border mobility are, with about 8% of workers changing jobs yearly. Thus, there is a dual labor market in Europe, a small mobile and a large static labor market, a proportion that the EU hopes to reverse, and which if it succeeded in doing would have major implications for healthcare delivery in the EU, in particular in quality and costs terms. The EU needs to start to explore the full ramifications of these potential developments, including on the continent's ICT, including healthcare ICT, industry. This is more so with the end on May 01, 2006, of the two-year transition period when we expect the EU-15, the old, and the strongest and richest EU countries, to lift the restrictions on access to their labor markets by workers from Eastern Europe, although just seven of the EU-15 countries have so far opted to open their borders. In an effort to convince, skeptic states, the Commission issued a report on 8 February 2006, highlighting the positive effects on employment opportunities, of EU enlargement, especially with reference to the UK, Ireland, and Sweden, which had not applied restrictions after May 2004, namely, high economic growth, and decreased and increased unemployment, and employment, respectively. Four more countries have opted to lift restrictions, namely Spain, Portugal, Finland and Greece, five, Belgium, Denmark, France, Luxembourg, the Netherlands to apply be more flexible, for instance partially removing restrictions in some sectors, but three, Austria, Germany and Italy, have actually increased restrictions for another three years. The community law (Article 39 of the EC Treaty) guarantees free movement of individuals, also an essential aspect of European citizenship. These community rules on free movement of workers are also applicable to member states of the European Economic Area, which is to Iceland, Liechtenstein, and Norway, the relevant rights, which systems for the co-ordination of social security schemes, and to ensure the mutual recognition of diplomas, complement. While, according to the Commission's February 2006 report, very few citizens from the new member (EU-10) states were in fact moving to the EU-15 countries, those moving, less than 1% of the working age population in all old EU member countries save Austria (1.4%) and Ireland (3.8%). Should we not expect these figures to change with the expiration of the 2+3+2-year arrangement, the "transitional measures that the Ascension Treaty permits, which make it mandatory for members to declare their stand on maintaining restrictions on or opening up their labor markets in May 2006, and again in May 2009 and May 2011? What would be the effect of the likely cross-border labor surge on the host countries' health and social services? Should these countries not already begin to seek answers to these questions? Even now, countries such as the U.K are already feeling the financial burden of women coming to the U.K to have babies in National Health Service (NHS) hospitals. This practice costs some Trusts over £500,000 annually, with some suggesting that the authorities request that anyone coming to the U.K as a visitor must show a certificate of medical insurance. Indeed, patients from outside the EU must normally prove they can pay for medical treatment but expectant mothers receive the status of emergencies, with NHS expecting to claim the treatment fees back, most if not all of which they may never recover. Women cannot normally, fly if they were over 34 weeks pregnant, but with 6-month visitor visas, many do, not declaring their pregnancy. With six million individuals visiting the UK on such visas annually and currently no obligation for them to have travel or medical insurance, the voices of those callin g for policy change is becoming louder. It is unlikely that health tourism is peculiar to the U.K, and is one that points to the potential increases in the healthcare budgets of many countries in Europe with increased labor mobility, particularly with workers coming in from non-EU countries in Europe. Should European countries, particularly those likelier recipients of this labor influx not already be seeking ways to maintain if not improve the quality of healthcare delivery while not compromising their economies? Considering that the widespread diffusion and utilization of healthcare ICT could help achieve these dual objectives, should they and would they not increase investments in these technologies, and promote the exploitation by healthcare providers of the immense opportunities they offer?

Besides seasonal workers, about 600,000 cross-border workers commute daily

between EU countries, which did not go into the current cross-border labor mobility of 1.5% mentioned earlier. The push by the Commission in its "Year" efforts would ostensibly help achieve the Lisbon objective of more and better jobs. Yet the main reasons many countries still maintaining restrictions give for so doing is because of the unemployment problems that they have. There seems therefore to be still significant obstacles to Europe achieving a genuine labor market. Thus, while we are examining the possible consequences for health service provision and health spending of the influx of workers into some countries, should we not also be looking at the reasons for example, that almost 50 % of Belgian, Italian or French workers have remained on the same job for a decade, 25%, in the U.K., and Ireland? Should we in fact not also be examining the effect of labor movement on healthcare delivery in the countries losing their workforce? What would this mean in terms of retirement benefits, the survivability of the companies they work for, the costs of health service provision in their health jurisdictions, both local and national, and on employment/unemployment down the road, including the possible influx of migrant labor then? Furthermore, 25 % of the European workers have had only one employer, age group regardless, and the average European worker spends 50% more time on a job than the average U.S w orker. What would increased job mobility mean for Europeans overall? What role is the diversity of the European citizenry, for example, play in the hindering the mobility of labor, and how could we tackle successfully these challenges, and in fact turn diversity into an asset that would not only foster the mobility of labor, but attenuate its potential adverse consequences on say, healthcare delivery quality and costs? What role could healthcare ICT appropriately deployed play in facilitating positive outcomes regarding these issues? Should there not be the healthcare variations of projects such as the IST-funded SEEMseed which is giving the European Commission's goal of establishing a Single European Electronic Market (SEEM) a major boost up, with 1,400 exp erts and other stakeholders from all over Europe and beyond coming together to identify challenges and recommend solutions, for example? The goal of the SEEMseed initiative is to "seed the development and implementation of the SEEM concept to create a virtual space where individuals and companies of any size can come together to do business without technological or linguistic restrictions," project coordinator María José Núñez observed. In July 2006, a roadmap is expected out on how to actualize SEEM from a business, technological, and regulatory perspective. There is no doubt that the implementation and use of healthcare ICT would face similar challenges. The many small, largely sector or area-specific electronic marketplaces that have emerged on the internet over the years remain highly patchy and do not meet the SEEM goal of providing any firm anywhere in Europe with effortless, secure and reliable access to clients, suppliers and partners. We could say pretty much the same thing for the current state of healthcare ICT use on the continent, health jurisdictions operating essentially in "silos" communication and information sharing among networks deficient if not altogether non-existent. Interoperability and standards issues, including commercial software model and open standards, are ongoing challenges that also promise business immense opportunities akin to how 2G paved the way for the mass-market adoption of mobile telephony. The open standards model obviates cost issues, at least to some extent, that could potentially increase healthcare ICT penetration. On the other hand, many would argue that the commercial software model creates jobs, has a positive influence on taxes, and creates business opportunities for commercial software partners, building a formidable small and medium enterprise base that could engender significant economic growth. It is also arguable that commercial software vendors have ample technical backing that ensures all-inclusive security testing and software reliability, crucial attributes in the often mission-critical healthcare milieu. Just as barriers to interoperability between the systems used that different firms use need overcoming, so do they in the health sector, among healthcare providers, and between them and patients, and other healthcare stakeholders.

Similarly, just as the need for new electronic market solutions to provide access in various languages and be straightforward and inexpensive, perhaps offered gratis, would facilitate e-commerce, so would novel healthcare ICT solutions, the exchange of patient data and information. This information exchange constitutes the essential core of the benefits, and guarantees of the exploitation of the full potential of these technologies to help us achieve the dual healthcare delivery goals mentioned earlier. The development around a registry of businesses in the sector, and a repository of data related to business processes of the demand - driven electronic market model that emerged from SEEMseed s talks, whose real-life testing in a multilingual prototype for the waste management sector involved industrial firms, transporters and waste processors, exemplify the process approach contemporary consumer-driven healthcare also requires. As Núñez noted, "A company in Spain that needs to dispose of hazardous materials could easily find a waste processor in France who can solve their problem, for example They could also negotiate the contract and carry out other processes online," many of the processes, clinical and non-clinical that together resu lt in healthcare delivery also involve networked transactions. Again, just as the prototype mentioned above revealed, regulatory and business challenges also confront the operations of health systems that need identifying and addressing for health systems, also as with a continent-wide SEEM, to function effectively, with information communication and sharing at a variety of levels, seamless. Again, the coordinator's observation that "Virtually all regulations are geared toward paper transactions There is little legislation to support e-business models," apply to current health systems in many if not most countries in Europe, including those in the EU. There is also the issue of reliance, which in the health sector is a major challenge in the acceptance by the public and healthcare providers alike of any electronic healthcare system, as the operations of such a system would involve the exchange of private and confidential patient health information. With the public no longer in the dark regarding issues such as hacking and identity theft, much efforts need put into securing this trust and confidence for e-health systems to work. The potential for business opportunities in the software and healthcare ICT networking, and security sectors is immense and would likely be ongoing, even increase as the implementation of electronic health records (EHR) systems become more pervasive, and persons and organizations intent on malicious activities not only continue but also step up their activities, as they seem to do to date. Measures such as the Council of Europe s cybercrime treaty, and EU initiated e-security initiatives should also help curb the menace of cybercrooks in the healthcare ICT industry, with the active collaboration of software and healthcare ICT vendors and developers, both law enforcement and technical counteroffensives, essential to so doing. There is likely to be growth in ICT business opportunities in general, including in the health sector. However, in order to appreciate fully the dynamics of this projected growth, we need to decompose the facts. What for example, do the prevailing forecasts that EU new member states will account for the most part of Europe s growth in ICT in the next few years portend for the interplay of factors, including labor mobility crucial to the creation of business opportunities for healthcare ICT in Europe? Would it be enough to be an EU member, with the benefits of open internal markets, for ICT markets to develop competitively in member states vis-à-vis other European countries, and the rest of the world? What would be the implications of developments in the health sector for these countries competitive power in the ICT sector? Would the opportunities for economic growth to which a buoyant healthcare ICT would contribute create further opportunities for improved healthcare delivery that would in turn spawn further increased economic productivity? The answers to these questions would reveal the more salient determinants of the future of healthcare ICT in Europe. The new member states for example, would need to catch up with the "older" countries in Western Europe in strengthening their institutional capacities to improve their economies. Hence, ICT investments would likely increase as these technologies could help the countries facilitate e-government or local government projects, and the competitiveness of their small and medium enterprises, broadening the potential platform for economic growth. They could also help them improve the efficiency and effectiveness of their health services, thereby fostering cost-effective, qualitative healthcare delivery. However, with almost 25% of the peoples in these countries computer illiterate, there is a significant gap in ICT penetration between the 'old' and 'new' EU member states that could hamper efforts at achieving the dual healthcare delivery objectives mentioned earlier, particularly crucial in these countries with fledgling economies. Efforts to bridge this digital divide and boost the economy of these countries would need to go beyond improving computer literacy. They would also need to deregulate the ICT industry, and take other measures to facilitate ICT diffusion, for example, making broadband more available, and actively promote the diffusion of computers and mobile and wireless technologies, the 1997 "Tiger Leap" push by Estonia, which helped improve ICT penetration in the country remarkably one example of such measures. There is no doubt that these measures also apply to many European countries outside the EU. The contributions of healthcare ICT to these efforts, such as the development of inexpensive PCs, mentioned earlier, would also help in this regard. The Lisbon strategy aims to make the EU the world's number one knowledge-based economy. Thus, following the Lisbon Council agreement by EU heads of states and government in 2000, European leaders intend to promote the pervasive access to cutting-edge information and communication technologies, including the internet, television, and the telephone. It is therefore imperative that it bridges the digital divide were it to achieve this goal, achieving which would also facilitate realizing the dual healthcare delivery goals. However, not doing so could not just compromise the achievement of these healthcare delivery goals, but also the abilities of firms, particularly small and medium enterprises that are the bedrock of economic growth to compete successfully in prospective money-spinning markets in the EU-15 and in the new member states, jeopardizing sustainable economic development in both. As previously noted therefore, a key driver of healthcare ICT business in the EU and indeed, the rest of Europe would be efforts to bridge the digital divide created by whatever reason, for examples, age, education, costs, digital literacy, social exclusion, gender, rural/remote location, or disability, among others. That the success of two previous EU attempts at e-inclusion is questionable, considering that member states were not obliged to abide by the plan, and they only have legal obligations to provisions of the new regulatory framework for electronic communications relating to universal access and users' rights, could hamper e-inclusion. Thus, adherence to other provisions of the framework, for examples those regarding prices and general accessibility of services, is also important for e-inclusion efforts to succeed. This is more so that EU' s enlargement on 1 May 2004 has widened the digital divide with peoples in the ten new member states having on average lower income levels and lower ICT penetration rates than the older member states do. Indeed, there are wider income, rural, educational and age disparities in the former than in the latter. With a June 2003 survey in the former showing that 11% of households had no idea what the internet was, and 23% not knowing how to use the computer, the potential for the use of healthcare ICT, and indeed, ICT in general in these countries to achieve stated health service delivery and economic development goals is seriously restricted. Internet and broadband access in the business community in some of the new member states are impressive, for example, in Estonia, where businesses have the same connectivity rates to high-speed networks (2Mbps - two megabits per second) as the U.K, France, and Germanys, the "Tiger Leap" mentioned earlier likely to be a key factor here. Nonetheless they still need some catching-up to do regarding more refined e-business applications for examples, online procurement and supply chain integration that typically need back-office re-organization, where business opportunities will increasingly open up in a variety of economic sectors in these countries, including in the health industry. With regard the latter, and as previously noted, both clinical and non-clinical processes result in healthcare delivery, both equally important in the quality and cost-effectiveness of the transactions involved in these processes. The e-Business W@tch survey carried out in November 2003 across 26 EU, EEA and Acceding Countries gave Slovenia, and the Czech Republic firms, superior marks among the new EU members, those in Poland or Hungary, not as high but still at comparable levels as the older member states. It showed that just 19% of Polish firms ordered some of their goods and services on-line, versus 46% in older member states, Hungary, Slovakia, and Latvia, even lower adoption rates for e-procurement, one of the most costs saving of e-business forms. It also showed differential ICT adoption based on company size and industry sector, smaller firms with less adoption, and manufacturing more adoption than consumer-oriented services, such as the health industry, which points to the growth areas in future ICT business opportunities among these countries.

E-Europe's efforts to reduce the digital divide, term ed e-inclusion policies have social, regional, and technological dimensions. The social aspects involving the role of advanced technologies in changing society and the economy to improve the quality of life and work conditions. Achieving this objective requires pervasive ICT diffusion, and utilization, the latter requiring the skills and interest in doing so, which suggest the likely role that change management would play in the years ahead in the overall efforts to ensure the inclusion of all EU citizens in the information society. Indeed, the e-inclusion goals of e-Europe 2005 include tackling these issues via a variety of education and culture initiatives, which among others foster "e-learning", cognizant of the corresponding need for fair and affordable access to these technologies, and that for the correct balance between copyright protection and, information availability. These initiatives bear particular relevance for healthcare delivery considering the perennial information asymmetry in the healthcare industry that continues to threaten the achievement of the dual healthcare delivery. Indeed, the EU emphasizes the need for access to these technologies by those at high risk of exclusion from the information society such as disabled and older people, with various "e-accessibility" initiatives ongoing to ensure that these high-risk individuals gain ready access to ICT and to valuable information, including health information. This is another potential avenue of business opportunities for software and ICT vendors, particularly in the health industry, which could develop innovative products to facilitate e-inclusion, for these citizens. The consumer healthcare ICT sector is indeed, going to offer lucrative business opportunities for the development of devices that would help the disabled and seniors leave higher quality lives, despite their illnesses. Seniors, for example, who would constitute a sizeable proportion of the population of not just EU member states but other European countries, are major health services users. Their inclusion in the information society would increase our chances of using healthcare ICT for ambulatory/community/domiciliary service provision, which besides being more cost-effective, would afford the seniors the opportunity of their ailments treated and monitored at home, among their loved ones, likely increasing their quality of life. This would also save hospitalization costs, and on the aggregate would reduce health spending, without compromising healthcare quality, in other words, enabling us to achieve the dual healthcare delivery objectives. The same applies to the disabled and indeed to everyone else in particular those that have chronic illnesses, many which are not only preventable, for example, via eliminating information asymmetry, but are manageable cost-effectively and efficiently at home using appropriately-deployed healthcare ICT. Thus, not only would the markets for assisted technologies for the disabled and the elderly continue to expand among EU states, and in many countries outside the EU, so would those of ICT in general. This is more so, at least in the EU, with the strong emphasis on the provision of ICT services on multiple devices or platforms besides the PC, such as digital TV, satellite, and third generation mobile phones, among others. The trend is likely to spill over into the other European countries, many of which have even worse economies, hence tighter health budgets, and coupled with less developed health systems, for which the need to achieve the dual objectives is more urgent. Among these countries, again, though, efforts to bridge the digital divide in their respective societies must precede any expectation of the benefits of healthcare ICT. It is no surprise therefore that another important aspect of the e-Europe 2005 is regional, with a focus on ground-breaking programs to cover remote and under-served areas, satellite communications key in bridging the regional facets of the digital divide, and give under-served areas high-speed (broadband) internet connections. This would no doubt, create immense business opportunities particularly in the new EU member states, The Commission has also established the European Regional Development Fund (ERDF), which latter bankrolls ideas and their testing laboratories for regions. ERDF essentially offers the enabling milieu for innovative, perhaps high financial-risk experiments to tackle the challenges of the contemporary economy, including reducing the digital divide. That the Commission allowed member states to use structural funds for broadband deployment underscores its resolve to speed up widespread ICT diffusion in all regions, facilitating access where it could not count on market forces to do so. This is not indicative of its loss of faith in the competitive process-far from it. In fact, among its e-inclusion measures are establishing the appropriate immigration policies to increase the pool of technical expertise required to effect e-inclusion, outsourcing of ICT-related services to low-wage countries also on the table. It also plans to recognize ICT skills certification across board by EU governments, and other relevant bodies. Outsourcing in particular is increasingly attractive even in health services provision. However, with countries such as the Philippines, and China, Vietnam, and other Asian countries in the fray, competition is likely to be stiffer for India, which has customarily being the main beneficiary of outsourcing, in both non-medical and medical fields. In fact, countries in Eastern Europe, such as the Czech Republic, Poland, and Hungary, are becoming preferred countries for British and U.S firms for example, seeking to outsource their secretarial, and call-centre tasks to countries with an inexpensive but skilled workforce. In facilitating its social and regional e-inclusion goals, the EU supports ICT multi-platform access and convergence via eEurope, and the regulatory framework for electronic communications, including a variety of projects in the "Information Society Technologies (IST)" research and development program, from many of which have emerged ideas and devices invaluable not e-inclusion in disparate sectors including health and healthcare delivery. Thus, the multi-platform and convergent approach offers the opportunities to exploit maximally, the benefits that one or more interoperable ICT offers, including for healthcare delivery, including disparate utilization needs and patterns, making access to the information society possible via not just the PC, but also digital broadcasting, third generation mobiles and other types of wireless access. In healthcare delivery, this creates the enabling environment for targeted, and contextualized, healthcare ICT-enabled information dissemination, for example, and for the use of these different technologies for the treatment and monitoring of a variety of health problems. In other words, this approach enables the achievement of the dual healthcare delivery objectives mentioned earlier by offering efficient and cost-effective means to provide a variety of health services. Using the disease prevention paradigm for example, we are able to offer primary prevention services such as the targeted information dissemination mentioned above wherein we could initiate programs that could help prevent diseases occurring in the first place. This approach also enables us to design and deliver secondary and tertiary prevention programs, essentially with the former, the early diagnosis and prompt treatment of diseases, and the latter, the effective treatment of diseases, including instituting the necessary rehabilitation programs, in order to prevent the sequelae of diseases including the onset or worsening of chronic, debilitating complications. These measures would cumulatively, improve the quality of healthcare delivery and save costs, hence enable us achieve the dual objectives. It is clear from our discussion thus far not only that there are undeniable links between health and the economy, but that the measures we take to improve one would influence the status of the other, and the corollary is true, that is our inaction in one could severely hurt the other. There is no doubt for example of the need to reduce medical errors, which could save many lives. Effective collaboration between health authorities, patient advocacy groups, software and healthcare ICT vendors, and other healthcare stakeholders including employers would facilitate the development and the most effective use of healthcare ICT for meeting a variety of health services delivery needs including ensuring patient safety. The EU also adopts a patient-centered approach to healthcare delivery. As Viviane Reding noted, "The European approach to eHealth should be about: spending euros on patients not on paperwork!...For example, electronic medical records can help doctors to diagnose illness and prescribe treatments more accurately, thus reducing medical errors. It also means cutting down paperwork to improve efficiency. Electronic patient referrals in Denmark are saving €1 million a year and could rise to €3.5 million a year, if all referrals were sent electronically." She was speaking ahead of the third European Ministerial conference on eHealth held in Tromso (May 23/24, 2005) that the Commission, Luxembourg Presidency and the Norwegian government jointly organized to debate ways to realize the potential of "eHealth". Consider the potential long-term savings by these and other countries if they implemented these technologies, resources they could plough into other sectors of the economy, to further enhance economic d evelopment, not to mention the improved quality of care, and of the overall health of their citizenry and the benefits on economic productivity that could arise thereof. Is it therefore unlikely that more European governments, both within and outside the EU would invest more in these technologies in the years ahead? In Europe, fully functioning health information networks connecting hospitals with general practitioners, pharmacies, administration and finance departments, and patients' homes abound. Indeed, more than 80% of European primary care physicians have Internet connectivity and many practices have gone paperless, and with more electronic transactions comes more time to devote to patient care, with the potential to further improve the quality of healthcare delivery. Speaking recently on May 10, 2006 in Malaga, Spain, at the eHealth: Connected Health for Europe Conference, Reding itemized her priorities for the years ahead, namely, ICT for independent living, Proactive and personalized care, and Interop erability and the ehealth Action Plan. Is it any surprise that an aging society demands plans to use ICT to assist the elderly in living qualitatively, including regarding their health, and could we not save substantially on health spending by so doing? With seniors being heavy users of health services, would healthcare costs not further increase with more of them using the services were nothing done to curtail costs, such as deploying appropriate healthcare ICT in service provision for these seniors? Again as Reding noted, most people aged over 50 years today are on medication for some type of long-term medical problem, for examples, high blood pressure or joint, muscle and bone disease, with roughly four in ten of them with noticeable degree of activity limitation, and a third seniors approximately consult a doctor more than once every month. Even if medications are not as expensive in Europe as they are in the U.S, they still constitute a significant portion of health spending in virtually all European countries. Also in comparison with the U.S., malpractice suits are less common, not as expensive, and are typically more unsurprising in outcome and costs. Yet, they are important cost drivers in the health system in Europe as well, considering that doctors are wont to practice defensively in order to avert these suits, a practice that increases healthcare costs. Costs rise because of unwarranted orders of lab tests and avoidance of untested medications for examples that could have cured an illness whose avoidance would do the reverse increasing morbidities, even mortality, and with sometimes-significant cost implications. The plan to focus more on proactive and personalized also underscores the increasingly important role that healthcare ICT would play in healthcare care in European countries, in a pervasive atmosphere of patient-centered healthcare delivery. As we noted earlier, these technologies are invaluable in facilitating disease prevention programs at various levels, for example in providing the necessary health information to the public that could significantly reduce the prevalence and distribution of diseases. In fact, the EU now has its online health information portal Health-EU Portal[6], where the public could access a variety of current and accurate health information. It conforms to standards in keeping with the Riga Ministerial Declaration, in which 34 European countries have expressed their strong commitment to promoting an inclusive and barrier-free Information Society that fosters social and economic inclusion. With over 20% of European citizens having some type of heart disease, which also cause 45% of all deaths, the EU's MyHeart[7] project, which is developing wearable and portable systems to enable individuals with heart diseases live a normal life and reduce their risk of developing heart attacks is apt. It is also an example of the value of healthcare ICT in secondary and tertiary prevention. Cardiovascular diseases (CVD) cost Europe billions of Euros annually. The MyHeart project aims to empower the individual to fight cardio-vascular diseases by preventive lifestyle and early diagnosis. The effort begins by acquiring knowledge on an individual's actual health status via continuous vital signs monitoring incorporating system solutions into functional clothes with integrated textile sensors. The researchers process in situ the combination of functional clothes and integrated electronics. The process would involve making diagnoses, detecting trends, and taking action, feedback devices enabling interaction with the user and with healthcare professionals. MyHeart would be able to help CVD patients through personalized guidelines and feedback mechanisms, market for the product potentially immense, besides reducing costs to EU of these conditions. The consortium involved in its development comprises 34 partners from 11 countries including industries, research institutes, academia, and medical hospitals, representing a variety of interests ranging from textile research, to electronic design, and to home-based applications and medicine.

140

Collaboration in healthcare delivery is no doubt an important approach toward improving the quality of healthcare delivery and reducing its costs. However, such collaboration could be difficult if not impossible under certain circumstances, for example, in the communication and sharing of patient information electronically with the technologies involved disparate and not interoperable. As with many other health systems across the globe, those in Europe also have fragmented electronic records, which hinder the full exploitation of the opportunities that healthcare ICT offer in achieving our dual healthcare delivery objectives. After 15 years and five hundred million euros of financial investments by both the Member States and the European Commission into eHealth, the need for interoperability of these systems could not be more urgent. EU member states, having defined and consolidated their respective roadmaps and eHealth priorities, must now seek ways for the sort of integration that ramifications of the efforts at e-inclusion are bound to engender, such as increased mobility of labor among member states and the need to access an individual's health information far away from home. Thus, efforts at interoperability are not just a national affair, but involve cross border, collaboration, between EU nations, on the one hand, and between them, and other European countries, and indeed, other countries around the world in establishing common standards that would facilitate interoperability, on the other. The recent international conference on eHealth held in Malaga, Spain, in May 2006, is an indication of the keenness in Europe and indeed, worldwide, of the crucial role that healthcare ICT would play in healthcare delivery in future. The fourth annual European Conference on eHealth essentially agreed on the need for "moving from strategies to applications," which would be the theme of the next conference in Berlin in April 2007. "Interoperability" was a key issue discussed at this year's conference, the goal to facilitate access to patient health information by healthcare providers worldwide. Delegates made a commitment to collaborate in working toward an all-inclusive eHealth program not only for the EU, but also across the globe, with several countries in fact, agreeing to establish initiatives to maximize the benefits of existing and emerging technologies, in the march toward building global healthcare economies. Over 90% of family doctors in the three Scandinavian countries and Holland reportedly use EHR, although they also confront interoperability issues, their EHR essentially in silos. Nonetheless, other European, and indeed, many other countries elsewhere lag behind these countries in their e-Health diffusion efforts. There is no doubt that we would see increasing investments in these technologies in Europe over the next few years, but the challenge to make them interoperable remains. The benefits of eHealth interoperability for improvement in the quality of healthcare delivery and in reducing health spending are legion, and efforts at ensuring it would no doubt create immense opportunities for business among the relevant software and healthcare ICT developers, and other professionals, and vendors in the near future.

Just as efforts are afoot in the EU to improve healthcare delivery, individual member countries still have the ultimate responsibility for delivering qualitative healthcare in their domains and for cooperating with the EU in its efforts to improve health services among member states. Health systems across the EU and the rest of Europe are not uniform either in funding or in approach. There is a general tendency among European countries for health services to rely on public funding, for example, but many also have private sector involvement to a more or less extent. There are also significant differences in the organization of service delivery. These differences are significant determinants of the nature and extent of healthcare ICT investments, hence the magnitude of the m arkets for these technologies in different European countries. Consider for example, the plan in the U.K by the Barnet, Enfield, and Haringey Mental Health NHS Trust to reorganize services so that GPs would see patients with mild to moderate mental health problems. This decision if taken, would give GPs greater responsibility for about 3,000 persons with mental health problems, who would normally have had referrals to specialist teams. A team of dedicated specialists, including psychiatrists, psychologists and social workers, would in turn support the GPs. Psychiatrists would see patients with severe or long-term mental health illnesses deemed at risk without extensive care, for example, those suicidal, and as with current practice, referred to the community mental health teams. With this model, the Trust would likely scrabble back £1.8 million from efficiency savings and the more you treat individuals in the secondary sector mental health trust, the more stigmatized they likely are. Some have questioned the availability of the required staffing and resources within the GP sector to do the job, and if this defect would not result in more patients relapsing and healthcare costs further increasing. These are genuine concerns, but which the appropriate deployment of healthcare ICT could help ameliorate, and besides, even if there were adequate staffing, there still would need to be adequate and timely communication between the different professionals for the plan to succeed. The proposal typifies the trend in the U.K towards ambulatory/community/domiciliary care as opposed to hospital care a shift in the app roach to care that makes the need for the widespread diffusion of healthcare ICT even more imperative and urgent. There is therefore likely to continue to be more healthcare ICT investments in the U.K health systems in the years ahead. The issue is however, not that simple. As with other developed countries, the U.K essentially has an aging population. True, it would be more cost-effective to treat patients outside the hospital, and with a rapidly aging population, developing services to treat seniors at home and in the community is even more urgent if the country, which funds its health services with tax revenues, were not to run into financial crises, with the costs of healthcare escalating relentlessly. To compound the issue, there is also a trend toward early retirement, threatening tax revenues, and by increasing pension and other benefits, healthcare delivery quality too. These developments could either speed up healthcare ICT spending if the government acted promptly to prevent the downward spiral that could possibly result from the lack of such action, which itself, by siphoning funds into escalating healthcare costs might further compromise the ability to fund the very technologies that could have prevented this spiral in the first place. Evidently, the present U.K government is doing the former, albeit with lukewarm support from, if not outright resistance by the very professionals that need to utilize these technologies in order for the achievement of the dual objectives to materialize, the healthcare professionals. This highlights the complexities of the issues involved in the direction of healthcare ICT markets not just in the U.K but also in other European countries, and indeed, other countries worldwide. The U.K Health Minister, Lord Warner, recently announced plans to expedite the implementation of the electronic patient record. He was speaking at the British Medical Association's Local Medical Committee Conference. Lord Warner mentioned a number of initiatives to accelerate progress on the electronic patient record, termed the NHS Care Records Service. The first is to determine a date in early 2007 to start pilots for the uploading of patient information onto the summary care record, which would enable the transfer of patient records on changing GPs. There is also the establishment of a new taskforce to develop a detailed implementation plan for stepping up delivery of the electronic medical record, which will comprise clinical and laypersons, chaired by one of the latter. The task force will produce a detailed action plan by the end of 2006, drawing on the experience of the U.S. Veterans' Administration Department, which has an operational EHR system. Deputy Chief Medical Officer, Professor Martin Marshall will work with the taskforce. The National Clinical Leads will also participate actively 'selling' the concept of EHR to healthcare professionals, which would complement a public information campaign to explain the patient benefits and implications of the shift away from paper to electronic record s, building on previous and ongoing efforts in this direction. According to Lord Warner, "We cannot carry on with the cumbersome, outdated and I would say sometimes dangerous paper-based system. It is critical we make the transition to electronic records and the sooner the better for patients and doctors alike." How true. The Minister added, "I understand fully the concerns and reservations some doctors have about electronic patient records. We will fully consult with all professional interests and patients on the nature of the summary record and the confidentiality safeguards. But now is the time for leadership in this area and by that I mean clinical leadership as well." NHS Connecting for Health, the agency responsible for provision of IT services to the NHS and delivery of the National Program for IT, no doubt is up to the task, but we must all support its efforts in order for this crucial phase of the development of health services in the U.K to succeed. It is doubtful that any government would continue to invest significant sums of money in technologies that the supposed end -users would shun. This means that part of the efforts to promote healthcare ICT diffusion, which by the way should involve the software and healthcare ICT companies that seek market shares, should be winning "hearts and minds" in the health sector, in particular among healthcare professionals. Some might even advocate legislation that would mandate the use of these technologies in the overall public interest but again, while laws are part of our existence, there is need for discretion in promulgating

145

laws that might not only be difficult to enforce, for example, compelling doctors to buy healthcare ICT, but might backfire, the doctors not using them, anyway. The fact is that the health system in the U.K as elsewhere has not collapsed, and in fact seems to be doing well compared to that in the U.S for example according to recent studies, but the question is how enduring this performance is, and even now, at what costs. There is no doubt about the fact that the U.K health system is not perfect. In fact, no health system is, or could ever be. This might sound strange, but considering that change is inevitable, we could only ignore changes at our peril, as not only might they signal the need for changes in our practice, as they often do, we should in fact anticipate change by reviewing our practice periodically. This is in order that we could modify it as necessary, which by meeting the demands of the change, is inherently an improvement in our practice, as not doing so could even render it moribund. In other words, the process is ad infinitum. Faced with the twin issue of population aging and early retirement for example, should the U.K government not review its processes, not just regarding pensions, but also healthcare delivery? Is it any surprises then, that some are calling for promoting better employment opportunities for seniors? There is no doubt about the need for reform of old -age pensions and early retirement schemes. Some wonder, however, if these measures would be adequate to increase employment rates for seniors significantly or to reduce the future risk of labor shortages. There is no doubt that the approach to this issue would involve the concerted efforts of both the public and private sectors to adjust wage-setting practices to ageing employees. There is also the need to examine the degree other welfare schemes facilitate early retirement, and to tackle issues that tend to exclude seniors from the workforce such age discrimination, unsuitable work environments, and deficient skills. These issues underscore the need for example for e-inclusion, and are potential triggers for

ICT investments including assisted technologies that could make it easier for seniors to keep working, at least those that want to. To underline the importance of these issues, the Organization for Economic Co-operation and Development (OECD) is even urging the U.K to do more to encourage older individuals to work longer9, to help offset the negative impact of population ageing on economic growth and public finances and could help alleviate future labor shortages. In a report on *Ageing and Employment Policies,* the OECD surveyed the main barriers to employment confronting seniors, evaluated the adequacy and effectiveness of existing measures to overcome these barriers, and made policy recommendations for further action by the UK government, employers, trade unions, and seniors themselves. The report noted that, versus many other OECD countries, the U.K has not been complacent about dealing with these barriers. It also noted that the government has attempted to eliminate deterrents to continue working embedded in public and occupational pension arrangements, and to change employer attitudes via its *Age Positive* campaign and *Code of Practice on Age Diversity in Employment.* It commended the *New Deal 50 plus* and *Experience Works* are unique initiatives among OECD countries, in terms of active labor market programs. The report also acknowledged other government initiatives, for examples, the Employer Training Pilots, and a number of lifelong learning initiatives and skill-improvement programs open to help all workers, even older ones, and the contributions of the private sector in addressing these issues. It noted that the recent strong performance of the UK economy, the percentage of persons aged between 50 and 64 years that work being higher in the UK than the averages of both the EU and the entire OECD area, partly reflected these measures. However, the report also pointed out that these percentages are still lower than in Denmark, Iceland, Japan, New Zealand, Norway, Sweden, Switzerland, and the United States, hence the U.K could do even more to improve employment prospects among older workers. That the share of older men who participate in the labor market is at 72%, still around 7 percentage points lower than in the mid -1980s, and that many older workers withdraw from the labor market well in advance of the State Pension Age suggest trends that could potential have adverse consequences for healthcare delivery in the U.K. With the decline in the level of private pension provision and in the average public pension vis-à-vis the income of those in work, individuals might not be saving sufficiently for retirement, which could compromise the quality of life, with a backlash on overall health status. These concerns have some advocating increasing the state pension age in keeping with increasing life expectancy. These developments also further support the need for a paradigm shift in the approach to health service delivery with emphasis on maintaining its quality while reducing its costs, both of which the appropriate deployment of healthcare ICT could help achieve. There is also room for the involvement of older women in the labor market, their increased participation, a positive policy reaction to the challenges to economic prosperity that ageing societies create. With an increase from 27% to less than 50% in the ratio of persons 65 years and above to those between 20 and 64 years in 2050, there is a real chance of available labor in the country standing still over the next 50 years, without a sizeable increase in labor force involvement, in particular among older persons. The resulting increased dearth of labor and a marked deceleration in economic growth could severely compromise healthcare delivery, which would further reduce economic productivity, plunging the country into a dangerous vicious cycle. It is therefore in the interests all to pursue options that could prevent this scenario, one being support by all healthcare stakeholders for government's efforts to implement electronic health records systems and other healthcare ICT initiatives on which it is currently expending significant financial resources, and likely would even more in future. Since government is not and cannot be the sole employer of labor, the private sector should also be actively involved in promoting not just the use of healthcare ICT among healthcare professionals, but also the utilization of these technologies in particular for primary prevention programs among their workers and the public. This is in addition to encouraging older persons to work and remain at work. By simply promoting the dissemination of current and accurate health information to its w orkers for example, utilizing any of a variety of multimedia healthcare ICT it might have a company could be helping save itself and the NHS significant funds in lost productivity due to illness and the costs of treating a chronic illness, respectively as the following example shows. Scientists now believe that testing for levels of the protein, retinol-binding protein 4 (RBP4,) may help identify insulin resistance and associated cardiovascular risk factors, hence determine persons at risk of diabetes, including people with normal body weight and normal blood glucose, but a strong family history of diabetes, before its symptoms even become apparent. Increased levels of this protein in the blood may be a marker of imminent type 2 diabetes and for therapeutic improvement, according to the findings of a study published in the June 15, 2006 issue of the *New England Journal of Medicine.* Besides offering identified individuals to step up preventive measures such as losing weight, and commencing physical exercises, medications to cut RBP4 levels may also help reduce the risk of full-blown disease[10]. Would a company that provides such information to its employees and actually supports them in commencing those preventive measures via contextualized healthcare ICT-enabled programs, not benefit immensely from doing so, both in terms of having a healthy workforce many of who would likely appreciate its efforts thus enhancing loyalty and dedication to service, and in costs savings. This example also highlights the need for targeted and contextualized health information in general, even for those

149

unemployed or retired. The mobility of labor among EU countries might help ease the potential labor shortage in the U.K., which as mentioned earlier appears to have benefited from not applying restrictions after May 2004. The country however, risks negating the economic gains from this measure if its healthcare spending, including on the workforce flowing into the country, if it failed to rationalize resource utilization, something that the appropriate deployment of healthcare ICT could facilitate. It is also pertinent to note that the ability to achieve the dual healthcare delivery objectives mentioned earlier under these circumstances would not depend alone on what the U.K government does even in terms of putting the necessary healthcare ICT in place. This is because realizing the full benefits derivable from the implementation of these technologies is contingent upon their use in full, by healthcare providers and other health stakeholders, whose activities result in the many processes that ultimately result in healthcare delivery. Put differently, the NHS would still be incurring avoidable costs if it had no efficient and cost-effective means to communicate and share patient data and information, with say the immigrant worker from say Slovakia, an EU state, who took ill while working in England, and the treatment of whose condition such lack of communication might compromise. This is not to mention the costs implications for one from a non-EU member state, who would not have the European health insurance card, launched in June 2004 to replace the previous EU health insurance document, the E111, and which over 30 million Europeans adopted in its first year. To further underscore the fluidity of the potential influence of the mobility of labor on the health status of the U.K, SMER, the social-democrat party of Robert Fico, which won the Slovak elections held on 7 June 2006, promised in its campaign to roll back some of the neo-liberal reforms of the current government led by Mikulas Dzurinda. The ramifications of Fico's promise would be significant for the

150

country, which has made significant progress since joining the EU compared to other East European countries, if he is able to form the coalition he would need to rule. Such ramifications might include reversing the privatization, even if not fully, of health services by the present government, which could stifle funding, reduce investments in healthcare ICT, and compromise the quality of healthcare delivery, and the momentum of economic growth in the country. These developments might in fact make it even more difficult for the sort of collaboration mentioned earlier between healthcare providers in the U.K and in Slovakia on the management of the Slovak on say even a temporary visit or work permit that suddenly developed a life threatening illness in the U.K. The cost implications of this scenario for the U.K would be much worse for were it another individual, perhaps not even a worker, say on a six-month visit to the U.K, who required emergency treatment in the U.K during the period with no insurance cover from which the NHS could redeem the costs of treating this individual. Incidentally, this individual might have insurance cover in his or her country that it is just the lack of effective communication that stalls NHS chances of redeeming its costs, which itself highlights the need for other countries and regional blocks to pursue the sort of e-inclusion policies that the EU is, all health stakeholders, including the insurance industry, involved. This would not only provide access to health information that could save lives, but would facilitate the retrieval of costs incurred by individuals outside their countries, or even health jurisdictions, which would help in the sustenance of cross-border healthcare provision without adverse consequences for the health budgets of the host countries, or its healthcare providers.

N o doubt, taxes and public expenditure have surpassed economic growth in

the U.K with the public spending to GDP ratio at 44% in 2004 versus 40% in the late 1990s, not surprisingly the increases attributed in the main to publicly funded provision of healthcare and education. It is important for the country to keep the balance between market flexibility and tax pressures in order for its welfare program expansion to thrive. In so doing, efficiency is also pivotal, with the need to have quality assurance measures in place for the periodic process review mentioned earlier, crucial to process quality improvement. Payment by results and incentives to healthcare providers would help inspire adherence to quality standards, as would the infusion of some measure of private sector participation in healthcare delivery, which would trigger competition. These measures would also invariably result in more widespread diffusion of healthcare ICT, technologies that research evidence indicates facilitates process improvement in healthcare delivery, particularly as they then offer competitive advantage to service providers with more sophisticated value propositions. There is also little doubt that by chipping in to the costs of service provision, in some instances, for example, the use of private hospital facilities, there would be more discrete service use with the potential for costs saving while not necessarily compromising healthcare delivery. U.K s total health spending was 7.7% of GDP in 2002, versus the latest available average of 8.6% in OECD countries. It is also lower than those of the U.S, Switzerland and Germany, 15%, 11.5% and 11.1%, respectively in 2003.U.K also spent just below the OECD average in terms of total health spending per capita, with 2231 USD in 2002 (adjusted for purchasing power parity), versus the latest OECD average of 2307 USD. Nonetheless, between 1998 and 2002, the country s health spending per capita increased in real terms by 5.7% per year on average, above the OECD average growth rate of 4.5% per year, only behind Ireland among the EU-15 countries. The public sector continues to be the main source of health funding in the U.K, as with its European counterparts, 83% of health spending in 2002, above the average of 72% for OECD countries, least in the U.S and Mexico, 44% and 46%, respectively. There is no doubt about the country's commitment to increase public health spending, its percentage of public spending up from about 80% in 1998, the increase mostly on health. Other European countries such as Denmark, Norway and Sweden, also spend a significant portion of their public expenditures on health. With its health spending increasing, and its population of healthcare professionals, 2.2 practicing physicians per 1 000 population, below the OECD average of 2.9, in 2003, the latest figures, although an increase from 1998 at 1.9 doctors per 1 000 population, the country needs to seek ways to ensure qualitative healthcare delivery. However, it also cannot afford to keep spending more and more of its GDP on health services provision. Besides increasing the number of professionals, it should also therefore, be keen to improve its healthcare delivery processes, for example, promoting the widespread implementation and use of healthcare ICT. As with most OECD countries, there is a reduction in the number of hospital beds per capita in the U.K, over the past decade, a decline that coincided with a reduction of average length of stays in hospitals and an increase in the number of surgical procedures performed on a same-day (or ambulatory) basis. This is in keeping with the paradigm shift in healthcare delivery mentioned earlier. This trend would in time spread to other European countries, including those in the EU, with all countries, and health systems increasingly striving to deliver qualitative health services, efficiently, and cost-effectively, developments that would open up the healthcare ICT markets, considerably. The underlying reason for this assertion is the irrefutable link that we mentioned earlier between health and the economy. We have exemplified the typical problems facing health systems in Europe with that of the UK, and the interplay of certain economic parameters with health, both currently, and regarding its likely future direction, and in particular, with the role that healthcare ICT would play in how these forces play out, exposed in the process. Indeed, we also examined how the outcome of their interactions in turn would determine, significantly, the nature and extent of the healthcare ICT markets in Europe. Because of the similarities in the economic systems, in Europe, it is relatively safe to extrapolate our observations with the U.K to other European countries, in particular, those in the EU, and even those outside it. This is not to pretend that these health systems have no differences at all. Indeed, they do. The differences are, however, marginal compared to their similarities, not least in their funding systems, which is pivotal to the organization of health services. In fact, the differences center more on details of health services delivery than their underlyin g health economics principles. Yet, there are significant emerging economic factors that would no doubt influence these health systems, for example, the position of these countries on labor mobility, employment of seniors, and the nature and extent of private sector involvement in healthcare delivery to varying extents. Thus, as we noted with the U.K, France is also embarking on a drive to get older people back to work, French Prime Minister Dominique de Villepin intend on labor market reforms, with new schemes for older workers, in an attempt to increase employment rates among seniors. Although his youth employment program "CPE" failed, the Prime Minister has launched a plan to bring up employment rates among seniors from now 38 % among those 55-64 years to 50 % by 2010, in keeping with the EU Lisbon strategy. France also has an aging population and as with many other EU countries, is under pressure due to demographic change, soaring social expenses,

154

and a labor market that need reforming, were it to remain competitive, not just in Europe, but worldwide. The proposed scheme would enable firms to offer jobless workers over 56 years of age short-term contracts (" CDD senior "), and no more legal for them to send workers into early retirement, before 65 years. The plan, slated to start in 2007 will also enable individuals with low pensions to supplement them with other income and workers over 60 years to receive a pension bonus, in some instances. Three unions (CFDT, CFTC, and CGC) and the French employers federation Medef have already approved the plan, which underscores the point we made earlier regarding the similarities between European countries on the problems that could have a profound effect on their health systems, and their investments in healthcare ICT. The functional arrangements of health services is no doubt different between the U.K and France, but both health systems remain largely funded from tax revenues, and both have some measure of private sector involvement. Depending on the flow of funds or otherwise from the sources, health systems in either could thrive or confront serious problems that could compromise its integrity, and possibly its survival as we know it. Governments in these and other countries therefore all confront the same issue namely that of achieving the dual objectives of healthcare delivery, namely delivering qualitative healthcare while simultaneously reducing health spending. In any case, and regardless of the funding system, resources are limited, and it makes intuitive sense, even if they were not to be frugal, although not at the expense of quality. Furthermore, considering the chances of the need for a major overhaul of the processes involved in healthcare delivery based on our continuous quality assessment exercises, even without health pending soaring, we might need a significant cash injection into the health system, for which our prior rational health spending would stand us in good stead. There has been much controversy over the future of Europe s social model, one of whose pillars is the public funding of health services. The emphasis of the EU for example on growth, employment, and deregulation policies, some contend threaten this social model. These policies no doubt, have their pros and cons and influence health policies being crucial to the economy, but the achievement of the dual objectives of qualitative healthcare delivery while simultaneously reducing health spending is no longer an option, it is imperative, healthcare ICT the final arbiter in the outcome of the interplay of health and the economy.

References

1. Available at: http://europa.eu/pol/health/overview_en.htm

Accessed on June 14, 2006

2. Available at:

http://europa.eu.int/rapid/pressReleasesAction.do?reference=IP/06/769&format=

HTML&aged=0&language=EN

Accessed on June 14, 2006

3. Singh, D. Clarify role of NHS market or patients may suffer, says King s Fund

BMJ 2006; 332:1353 (10 June)

4. Available at:

http://europa.eu.int/rapid/pressReleasesAction.do?reference=STAT/05/143&form

at=HTML&aged=0&language=EN&guiLanguage=en

Accessed on June 15, 2006

5. Available at: http://ec.europa.eu/enterprise/library/enterprise-europe/news-

updates/2004/20040225.htm

Accessed on June 17, 2006

6. Available at: http://ec.europa.eu/health-eu/index_en.htm

Accessed on June 17, 2006

7. Available at:

http://cordis.europa.eu/fetch?CALLER=PROJ_IST&ACTION=D&RCN=71193

Accessed on June 17, 2006

8. Available at:

http://www.thisishertfordshire.co.uk/news/roundup/display.var.796432.0.gps_co

uld_take_on_mental_health_patients.php

Accessed on June 18, 2006

9. Available at: http://www.oecd.org/dataoecd/45/59/33764039.pdf

Accessed on June 18, 2006

10. Graham, T.E, Yang Q., Blüher, M., et.al. Retinol-Binding Protein 4 and Insulin
Resistance in Lean, Obese, and Diabetic Subjects. *NEJM*, Volume 354:2552-2563,
June 15, 2006, Number 24

An Overview of Healthcare ICT Market Trends in Asia

Business process out-sourcing and increased private sector participation in

government initiatives offer potential business opportu nities for European and North American firms, and in turn the Philippines to strengthen its economy. Observers at the three-day ICT and tourism business conference and exhibits, the InTourPreneur 2006 that opened on June 21, 2006 in Cebu City, noted that p ublic-private sector partnerships would increasingly be of interest just as business process outsourcing (BPO). Participants from the U.K. in particular noted that public-private partnerships (PPPs) have transformed developments such as schools, hospitals and military organizations in the U.K, and could do much the same in the Philippines. Participants also noted the significance of information and communications technology (ICT) and telecommunications infrastructure, in particular, broadband, in developing the country's BPO and tourism industries and, indeed, its economy. The conference, focused on a number of issues, including health and wellness, typifies the increasing scope of business opportunities in healthcare ICT, and in fact, ICT in general, of not just the Philippines, but also the whole of Asia. Many Asian countries already have a well-developed ICT industry, but just as many face the challenge of increasing the awareness of various sectors of their economies, including the health industry, of the applications of these technologies for their own benefits. The fifth Association of Southeast Asian Nations (ASEAN) Health Ministers Meeting held in April 2000 in Yogyakarta, Indonesia adopted a vision of "Healthy ASEAN 2020". This vision is that by 2020, "health shall be at the centre of development and ASEAN cooperation in health shall be strengthened to ensure that our peoples are healthy in mind and body, and living in harmony in safe environments". The ASEAN region, established on 8 August 1967 in Bangkok, and comprising Brunei Darussalam, Cambodia, Indonesia, Laos, Malaysia, Myanmar, Philippines, Singapore, Thailand, and Vietnam, with a population of about 500 million, a combined gross domestic product of US$737 billion, and a total trade of US$ 720 billion, is a key Asian geo-economic group. Asia is the largest continent, in size and population, with over 60% of the world's human population. The continent also has several multilateral economic forums besides ASEAN, for examples, the ASEAN -plus-three group formed following the Asian economic crisis comprising China, Japan, and South Korea, and the Asia-Pacific Economic Cooperation forum (APEC), even proposed ones, such as the South Asia Free Trade Agreement. Significantly, China, a rapidly rising global economic power, is not in ASEAN. In fact, unlike Europe, Asia there is more tendency, for bilateralism than multilateralism, in both economics and political alignments, both based on their different historical pathways. Yet, Asia has some of the most successful world economies such as that of Japan, the second richest country in the world. Furthermore, there is little agreement on what constitutes Asia, and depending on the platform of the discussion, that is whether it is among geologists, politicians, an d even linguists, this could vary remarkably. Thus, some would make the distinction between East Asia (the Orient), South Asia (British India), and the Middle East (Arabia and Persia), others even further into Northern, Central, Western, Southern, Southeastern, Southern, Eastern, and Southeastern Asia. Some would include Turkey, the Middle East, or Russia, but others would not. Some would even restrict its definition to the Asia-Pacific region, which excludes the Middle East or Russia, but includes Pacific Ocean islands, some of which some would consider under parts of Australasia or Oceania. Furthermore, and unlike Europe for examine that has relatively homogenous antecedents, there are significant historical and cultural differences among Asian countries that have important influences on healthcare delivery concepts and approaches. They also have different socio-economic circumstances, and have different priorities and financial capabilities, hence adopt different approaches to tackling their problems inclu ding those pertaining to healthcare delivery. It would therefore be difficult an enterprise to generalize about the status of not just the health industry but also the healthcare ICT market in Asia. Nonetheless, there is no doubt about the continent offering immense business opportunities for healthcare ICT, and about the numerous developments in the economies of these countries, in particular, which would be crucial to the nature and extent of these markets in the near future. There is also no doubt that these countries collaborate in a number of ways in the ICT, including the healthcare ICT domain that has significant implications for investments in these technologies, hence for market opportunities. The Asia-Pacific Development Information program (APDIP) for example, is a regional organization that collaborates with the governments of member states to aid national and regional institutions in Asia-Pacific to improve ICT access, knowledge-sharing, networking, and management, and the applications of these

161

technologies for social and economic development. APDIP also helps to mobilize awareness and support for ICT, to build capacities via consultation for national and regional e-policy formulation, and by providing technical assistance, their implementation in achieving relevant development goals, including bridging economic, social, and digital divides in more inventive and effective ways. The organization aims to promote equity, including in healthcare delivery, stressing the need to contextualize technology applications deployment, and enhance regional and national public-private partnerships in achieving development goals. APDIP covers both ASEAN and non-ASEAN, Asian countries, and is actively involved in a variety of ICT and other projects in these countries. For example, it awarded a grant in November 2004 to Centre for Health Informatics and Learning, Gadjah Mada University to improve the detection and management of Dengue Hemorrhagic Fever (DHF) cases, and the prevention and control of dengue transmission, a Web-based Integrated DHF Surveillance System in the community, the Sleman District, Yogyakarta, Indonesia. Billed to start in January 2005, the project confronts DHF, the foremost cause of hospitalization and death among children in Indonesia and in other developing countries in which the disease is endemic, and where in most cases, incidentally, case detection and management, disease surveillance, and community-based control of the transmission of the disease are underdeveloped or lacking completely. This means that healthcare and other personnel are invariably unprepared to prevent let alone manage DHF outbreaks, a defect that an integrated web-based geographic information system (GIS) and decision support system (DSS), developed through action research (soft system) methods, involving the local government, community members, health care and public health personnel, would rectify. The researchers planned to utilize open-source database management system (mysql) and web application (PHP) to facilitate the integrated GIS and DSS to make DHF surveillance activities more effective. The web-based surveillance system will be the tool to enhance intensive efforts to reduce the incidence of DHF drastically with continuous evaluation of how effective the DHF con trol is, also conducted, the system not only serving as a model of DHF control method in other endemic areas, but also applied in the efforts to control other communicable diseases. This project illustrates one key area of need in many Asian countries regarding healthcare ICT, that of controlling communicable diseases. Because these diseases are prevalent, there is a huge market for healthcare ICT that could facilitate their prevention and could help in the preparedness and response to their outbreaks in many Asian countries. Besides those used in the project mentioned above, technologies that could help disseminate information on measures to take to prevent these communicable diseases would also continue to attract significant investments. In other words, health education for disease prevention, and indeed, also for health promotion are public health activities that healthcare ICT could facilitate cost-effectively and efficiently, hence offer significant market opportunities for healthcare information and communications technologies in many of these countries. Additionally, in many Asian countries, such information needs to reach persons living in remote areas, with hardly accessible terrain. Tele-health technologies also have a huge market in these countries, where they would double as both disease prevention/health promotion, and treatment portals. The above project also highlights an important aspect of healthcare ICT in many Asian countries, the issue of open standards. Indeed, there was a regional conference on "The Key to an Open ICT Ecosystem," held in Bangkok, Thailand, 2-4 May 2006, organized by the National Electronics and Computer Technology Center (NECTEC), in collaboration with Software Industry Promotion Agency (SIPA), Ministry of Information and Communication Technology, and major ICT industry players in the country, IBM, Intel, Oracle, and Cisco, and APDIP. Among the reasons for interests in open standards and open architectures, include the facilitation of interoperability and improvement of system value, and by fostering competition, access, and control, the promotion in the long term, of national economic growth and development. In Thailand, there is in fact a Committee on Open Standards established by the National Electronics and Computer Technology Center (NECTEC), itself operating under the auspices of the National Science and Technology Development Agency, Ministry of Science and Technology, Thailand. The Committee aims to promote awareness and utilization of open standards in order to realize an Open ICT Ecosystem, which in turn would help nurture the efficiency, originality, lucidity, and growth, crucial to the development and implementation, in collaboration with partners within and outside the country, of open and interoperable ICT system s. The goal of the conference mentioned above is to promote this concept of Open ICT Ecosystem, by increasing awareness and understanding of the significance of open standards, in Thailand and other Asian countries. It also aimed to explore avenues for collaboration on promotion and implementation of open standards in the Asian region, in a variety of domains such as e-government, e-learning, information exchange, Internet, and e-commerce, many of these domains, for example information exchange, with direct and indirect implications for the application of these technologies in healthcare delivery. There is likely to be continuing interests in not just the widespread diffusion of these technologies, particularly on costs grounds relative to "commercial" softw are, but also in ensuring their interoperability, hence both with notable chances for business opportunities in many Asian countries in the years ahead. There are certainly disparities in the economies of Asian countries that would influence healthcare ICT investments and orientation or otherwise to such technologies as open source technologies. In gross domestic product (GDP-PPP) terms, the People's Republic of China has the largest economy on the continent, and along with that of India, the fastest growing in recent times, both with an average annual growth rate of over 7%. China's economy is only second in size to that of the United States worldwide, followed by those of Japan, and India, in descending order. Japan has the largest economy in Asia and the second largest in the world in exchange rates terms (nominal GDP), after the USA, although experts predict that China will overtake Japan in currency terms to become the largest nominal GDP in Asia in the next ten or so years. There are a number of other strong economies in the Pacific Rim, for examples South Korea, Taiwan, Hong Kong, and Singapore whereas there are other Asian countries, for example East Timor, which has the smallest economy, whose economies are struggling to keep afloat. The circumstances surrounding the current state of the economies of Asian countries are multifaceted, and include among others forces of past and recent history. The saga is indeed still unfolding with for example, China and India, now the main sources of cheap labor as the East Asian Tiger economies (South Korea, Taiwan, Hong Kong and Singapore) continue to struggle to overcome in full, the devastation of the 1997 Asia financial crisis, and as they lose their erstwhile competitive advantage. Besides the state of the economy being a critical determinant of the state of health of the nation, and the nature and extent of healthcare ICT investments, the technological prowess of some of these countries, for example, Japan, and South Korea, is also an important factor in this regard. However, they are not the only factors. In fact, important challenges the region confronts in the near future both in the health and non-health domains, such as unstable oil prices, how gradual or otherwise global external payment imbalances pans out, the effect of increased interest rates and the ominous prospects of the avian influenza becoming a human pandemic, are also critical determinants. In the long term, how successful many of these countries are in improving education, bridging the digital divide, reducing poverty, and in fostering trade liberalization, would also play a significant role in the magnitude of their healthcare ICT markets, and in the health status of their citizens.

Both these short and long-term factors would be significant not just for the

health of these countries, but also for their economic growth, and sustainability. Consider the issue of bird flu virus for example. A World Health Organization (WHO) inquiry showed that the virus mutated in an Indonesian family cluster but experts insisted on June 23, 2006 after a closed meeting in Jakarta that this did not make it easier for the H5N1 virus to hop between humans, which would increase the likelihood of a human pandemic. According to the WHO the virus that infected eight members of a family in May 2006, seven of who died as a result, seems to have slightly mutated in a 10-year-old boy, thought to have passed the virus to his father, the first evidence for human-to-human transmission of the virus. Furthermore, the strain seemed to have died with the father and did not pass outside the family, WHO emphasizing that viruses are always to some extent changing and that there was no real cause for alarm. The three-day session followed Indonesia's call for international assistance in checking the virus, which has killed 39 individuals in the country. There have been concerns that the virus mutating into a form that could spread from human to human, although until now, most human cases have emanated from contact with infected birds. Bird flu has killed no less than 130 people worldwide since it started killing Asian poultry stocks in late 2003. Even without being transmissible from human to human, there is need for action to stop the transmission of the virus from poultry to humans, the achievement of which goal would involve the deployment of the relevant healthcare ICT in facilitating a variety of processes. Such processes range from those pertaining to health education and disease prevention, to surveillance activities regarding the movement of migratory birds, for example, or the incidence of cases of the disease. Yet, it is important for efforts at promoting education, reducing poverty, and bridging the digital divide for examples to complement these disease prevention and other health-based efforts, all of which could benefit from the use of the appropriate information technologies. In order words, the efforts by many Asian countries to contain, even prevent the virus would be multidimensional, and would involve the intensive implementation of not just healthcare ICT, but ICT in general. The degree to which these countries would invest in the technologies would depend on the availability of the financial resources required to do so. However, this does not necessarily imply that those cou ntries with more buoyant economies would invest more in these technologies. Other factors such as the availability of funding for specific projects by international donors or lenders would determine the availability or otherwise of the resources needed for implementing these technologies. The current level of a country's technological infrastructure could also mean the need for less intensive investments in these technologies, as would the perception of the need for particular technologies, for example, whether or not Singapore would invest as much in Tele-health technologies as Indonesia. There is, however, no doubt about the significance of the link between a country's healthcare delivery and economy, and the important role that this link would play in the opening up of healthcare ICT markets in the country. Because the link, in one direction, the effect of the economy on health, does not have to be direct, for example, with health declining even with increased health spending, assuming that the latter indicates roughly, economic buoyancy, it is important to understand its precise status in any particular country. This is necessary in order to begin to analyze and to hope to establish the specific dynamics of factors that determine this status. It is important to understand for example why the health status of the country' s citizens is declining despite increased health spending, in order to know what to do to reverse this situation. It is also important to understand how a country with limited financial resources could still ensure the delivery of qualitative health services to its peoples without crippling its budget. A closer scrutiny of the factors that determine these situations would require the decomposition of the processes involved, which would expose newer processes that would need decomposing, the resulting exposition, also leading to further decomposition, the exercise continuing ad infinitum. This decomposition/exposition, or process cycle, assumes that a multiplicity of interacting systems, themselves comprising processes result eventually in an outcome, barring any psychological fallacy, and in this case qualitative healthcare delivery, and even in the most prosperous Asian countries, which should preferably be cost-effectively. The second assumption is that these systems and their respective processes are not always determinable. It might be possible for example for one country to budget for the year, but even in a year, within which it could fail to operate, and usually governments overrun the budget, due say to unforeseen circumstances. With the variety of such circumstances regarding healthcare delivery innumerable, the accompanying changes are bound to render the status quo inadequate, if not useless, say for example, with the emergence quite suddenly, of an epidemic of a strange virus, or a new technique for treating skull fractures. In other words, engaging in the process cycle exercise is not fancy, but imperative, if we were to ensure the survival of a country' s health system, and as is the case with the link in the opposite direction, the effect of health on the economy, which is always direct, that of the economy of the country at that. In other words, the decline in the health of a country's citizens would in time compromise that country's economy. It is for these reasons that even the most buoyant Asian economies would need to ensure the delivery of qualitative healthcare services to its peoples and at affordable costs, since even these countries do not have inexhaustible financial resources. In short, all countries would have to explore avenues via which they could achieve these dual healthcare delivery objectives. With evidence to show that, the deployment of appropriate healthcare ICT could facilitate/modify healthcare delivery processes, thereby enabling the delivery of qualitative healthcare, and could do so cost-effectively, these technologies, no doubt offer opportunities to achieve the dual objectives. Preliminary results, announced in June 2006, at the annual meeting of Premier Inc. healthcare alliance for member hospitals in Orlando, Fla., of a joint government-private sector pay-for-performance project in the U.S for example, suggest that improving patient care could save money1. The results showed that care improvements participating hospitals realized in only two areas, pneumonia treatment and coronary artery bypass graft procedures, among the most common ailments for Medicare and Medicaid populations could save the U.S about $925 million. The findings also showed that care improvements countrywide could reduce mortality by 3,000 per year, and both complications and readmissions by 6,000 and result in 500,000 fewer inpatient days, with the results extrapolated to all U.S. facilities, with undeniably substantial costs savings. The p roject, a three-year demonstration approved by the Centers for Medicare & Medicaid Services (CMS) and called the Hospital Quality Incentive Demonstration, involved about 260 hospitals affiliated with the Premier Inc. healthcare alliance. Noted Richard A. N orling, president and CEO of Premier, "We re trying to improve quality among 28 process indicators and eight quality indicators The goal of the project (which is in its third year) is to create a rising tide of improvement across hospitals." Clinical data collected in the first year establish a baseline for performance, with data collection and monitoring of hospital progress toward implementing a range of evidence-based care protocols, still ongoing. Hospitals performing in the top 20% of all facilities in documented adherence to care protocols would be eligible for extra payment from Medicare, which has so far paid $8.85 million in first-year incentive payments to 123 facilities. On the other hand, hospitals that do not meet the first-year baseline of performance would have their Medicare payments reduced, although none has met this faith thus far, after two years of the study, which itself suggests the potency of the approach in inspiring commitment by healthcare professionals and others involved in health services provision to service quality. Indeed, the study has led to striking improvements in care for pneumonia and heart failure, two of the five focus conditions that the project aims to improve, which project could no doubt help improve the care of other diseases, and healthcare service provision in general. The project utilizes data from about 77,000 patients in Premier's Perspective data warehouse, a national clinical database that over 500 hospitals in the U.S. use for benchmarking and quality assurance. Incidentally, CMS is seeking validation of the Premier data by an independent analyst, a measure of the importance that it attaches to the project, which is a potential testbed for some type of a Medicare value-based purchasing system, an approach for which it has a mandate to formulate a plan by the FY 2009, under the Deficit Reduction Act. In fact, CMS wants to modify and expand the project to decide best practices for other diseases besides meeting this target. With the chances of healthcare ICT facilitating the processes that result in qualitative healthcare delivery, would there not in fact be increasing pressure on every health system, regardless of a nation's economic prosperity, to consider adopting these technologies, with supporting findings such as these? Would countries, not just in Asia, but worldwide not invest more in these technologies and promote their widespread diffusion in order to be able to exploit their immense benefits in enabling the realization of the dual healthcare delivery objectives mentioned above? However, as previously noted, we need to engage in elucidating the process cycle in order to be able to do this, and this engagement does not have to be at any particular level. Thus, the issues we would have to decompose and analyze at the national level would be different from those at the international level, although they would likely interface at some point, regarding a particular country, or even a geo-economic or other groups of countries. Let us illustrate this point again using the example of the avian flu. At the national level, it would be important for example to consider the role that education would play in reducing the risks of the transmission of the virus not just from poultry to humans but from one person to another. This would no doubt be an important determinant of the types of healthcare ICT we would focus on, as would those that could help with tracking disease outbreak and documenting treatment and the response to that received. On the other hand, international concerns would include not just securing financial, technical, and humanitarian assistance, but also cross-border tracking of migratory birds, and disease outbreaks, all of which the deployment of the appropriate technologies could help facilitate. Similarly, there would be different concerns even within the country, at local levels all of which we need to decompose in order to ensure that we utilize the most appropriate means to address the issues involved. According to the World Bank for example, there is a funding shortfall to fight bird flu in Indonesia, which had estimated it needed US$900 million for its campaign against the virus, US$50 million needed just for initial "capacity building," over the next three years, according to some experts, but with donors pledging only US$100 million. Could healthcare ICT not help in facilitating the capacity building for example, and other processes necessary in the country's preventive and preparedness efforts against this virus? Perhaps this would make the need for additional process improvement stark enough for the pledged funds to start flowing into the country. Incidentally, ICT is becoming increasingly versatile with novel and valuable applications in improving healthcare delivery processes, for example, 3G and Internet technologies enabling the sort of multiple video conferences that emergencies such as coordinating efforts on prompt response to disease outbreak for example warrant. These technologies enable several persons to communicate simultaneously with, including seeing, one another in disparate locations, and five taking calls using 3G and Internet technology. Incidentally, access technology would unlikely define broadband in the region in future with carriers likely to use both wired and wireless technologies, perhaps even concurrently, due to costs, regulatory, infrastructure, and market characteristics, among other reasons. Some of these new technologies are not just faster than current systems, due to higher compression, but also utilizing identical broadband allowance results in clearer audio and sharper images. Furthermore, these technologies, in 3G mobile phones, combine two of the most sought after communication features in contemporary times, mobility, and vision, making it possible to make conference calls between two or more persons anywhere, anytime, without the need to be within the four walls of a room/office. Indeed, the video conferencing market in Asia, particularly in Asia Pacific, is rapidly growing, projected to grow in the latter at about 20% per annum. It is necessary for healthcare ICT implementation and use to be pervasive in any country for the realization of the full benefits of these technologies in achieving the dual healthcare delivery objectives mentioned earlier. Some countries in Asia, for examples Singapore and

South Korea, have more ICT penetration and connectivity than do others, which would make the use of these technologies in the dissemination of health education easier. South Korea for example has equipped virtually all classrooms in its schools with computers with universal Internet access. Nonetheless, the country still faces challenges such as affordability of Internet access and of computer hardware/software, and improving more-widespread access to the Internet, particularly by persons living in remote and rural areas. This underscores the point we made earlier that we should not expect any health system to be perfect and the need for ongoing quality improvement efforts, which would necessitate process improvement on a continuous basis. Indeed, a clearer understanding of the role of various issues in hampering progress with regard healthcare delivery could only facilitate modifying the underlying processes that determine these issues, hence the chances of their inhibiting effects removed. Because these issues could be any of a variety of health and non-health related issues, this should reflect in our approaches to highlighting relevant issues, for examples, as it is with many countries in Asia, digital rights management, and copyright issues, or some technical or even ethico-legal issues, but also we must examine issues in all relevant domains. Some Asian countries such as Bangladesh, Cambodia, Maldives, and the Pacific Islands, have restricted ICT and other necessary infrastructures and ICT penetration, and lack the financial resources to accomplish pervasive healthcare ICT diffusion. Issues such as affordability, computer literacy, and access are just as important as those of a country's national policies on healthcare ICT and the political will to invest in these technologies to improve healthcare delivery are. It is important for these countries to recognize the importance of healthcare ICT directly or otherwise in helping improve healthcare delivery to their peoples and in improving their prosperity. Indeed, countries, developing and developed, and in particular the latter, in Asia, and elsewhere ought to start to conceptualize ICT and their applications in healthcare delivery within the context of sustainable development. This would likely promote the will to invest in these technologies, particularly also to foster the implementation of the United Nations (UN) Millennium Development Goals by 2015, from which many developing countries stand to gain immensely, and whose realization, the widespread penetration of ICT in these countries would facilitate. These investments would have to start with developing the ICT infrastructures in these countries, which could be incremental, starting with those crucial to the achievement of the most important issues that they want to tackle. This again, is why it is important for these countries to engage in the process cycle, with its tendency to reveal additional issues, and their processes that need addressed. This exercise is also crucial to policy formulation, which would facilitate resource allocation and optimal resource utilization. Software and healthcare ICT vendors and carriers would also need to understand and follow developments on these issues in order to plan their product development and marketing strategies for these countries, and indeed, to make projections on the direction, nature, and scale of their healthcare ICT markets. This issue of the contextualization of healthcare ICT investments is one that applies also to the developed countries of Asia, whose ICT needs differ in some respects from those of the developing countries in the region. This is not to say for example, that Japan has no need for tele-health, and Indonesia, or India, does. These latter two countries sure need such technologies for health to reach their citizens living in far-flung areas. However, Japan could use them also not just for the same reasons, but in particular to provide qualitative and affordable health services to their seniors on an ambulatory/community/domiciliary basis. Thus, these technologies would serve two distinct albeit related purposes in the two countries, an appreciation of which would be important to the prospective healthcare ICT supplier to these countries, for example, besides the health authorities that would invest in the technologies. Yet, even the disparities in the economies and ICT infrastructures of these countries do not mean that they have nothing in common as far as healthcare ICT goes. Far from this, it is becoming increasingly clear that the health status of one country in a remote corner of the world could significantly influence that of another, and indeed, the global health status. That some countries in Asia have not experienced an incidence of avian flu for example does not mean that they should not invest in the collaborative efforts, including in the necessary surveillance technologies that could help prevent the spread of this virus across countries. These investments, which, with its "human-to-human" transmission quite possible, as noted earlier, could indeed, help prevent a potential pandemic of avian flu that might spare no country. In other words, we are likely to see increasing investments in surveillance and other healthcare information technologies, right across Asia, in the years ahead, a process that the recent evidence of the possible mutation of the H5N1 virus into a form that could hop from person to person, would most invariably speed up. As also noted earlier, though, the extent of investments in these technologies would vary not just with the most urgent needs of a country, but also its budget, among others. Tele-health as we have noted plays a key access role in healthcare delivery to persons living remote/rural areas, facilitating access to care via diagnosis, treatment, and monitoring, and in fact also in health education and disease prevention, offering expedient and location independent access to scarce professional expertise, among others. The increased prospects of more use of these technologies would likely open markets in the wired and wireless domains. However, markets would likely open up for other healthcare ICT as well, for example, those pertaining to electronic health records (EHR), or elements of it. In general, besides the likely fast tracking of investments in technologies that could help with the preparedness and response to an outbreak of avian flu, but also to disasters in general, natural and manmade, with their healthcare delivery implications, healthcare of various types would increasingly feature in healthcare delivery in the region. Asia has had its fair share of both types of disasters, yet they continue earthquakes, tsunamis, typhoons, floods, and many more, with the displacement of sometimes millions of peoples, many injured and ill, into refugee camps, the risk of disease outbreaks always looming. Implementing tele-health systems in disasters could no doubt help save many lives, both in the preparedness and response phases.

Just as changing disease patterns and natural or manmade disasters would have

great significance for health policies in Asia, so would the economies of the countries in the region. In relation to the latter, the inherent, and emerging market forces, for example the preference for Asians in general for products rather than services, and the increasing influence of outsourcing on the shift towards services would also be key issues in the future of the healthcare ICT in the region. There would still be a huge market for products, if the rate at which individuals subscribe to cell phones, 10 million per month in the Asia pacific alone, which also has thriving broadband markets and almost 90% of global 3G, were any indication of the market status. There is therefore likely to be increasing market opportunities in ICT in general, but also in consumer healthcare ICT, in which the region is in fact a sort of trailblazer considering that there are already cell phones in South Korea, for example, capable of checking blood alcohol and sugar levels. Monitoring these levels could in the former case, help prevent accidents, and in the latter, control diabetes, in both instances helping to save lives. As we mentioned earlier, the analysis of issues relating to healthcare delivery via the process cycle exercise would lead to a fuller understanding of these issues, and more accurate evaluations of the technology solutions that would modify/facilitate the underlying processes in order to obtain the desired results. Thus, with more such exercises would be an increased tendency towards investing in the relevant solutions. Asian countries that embrace this approach would be able to develop the appropriate healthcare ICT strategy, and formulate the necessary, resulting in the work plans for which software and healthcare ICT vendors would have to develop solutions. There would therefore also be, as components that would be necessary in actualizing the developed strategy, the need for services such as change or knowledge management, among others. As is already happening, IT outsou rcing firms in Asia, in India, the Philippines, and Vietnam, for examples, becoming larger, and more global, the increased competition that results would likely force prices down. There would also be increasing markets for interactive, rather than broadcast, content, as this becomes increasingly the preferences of mobile and broadband subscribers. Besides the implications of these preferences for larger gaming markets, they would also likely increase the messaging markets, both of which apply to the health industry. In other words, there are in fact already "brain games" on the market aimed at keeping seniors cognitively actively, thereby helping to improve their memory functions, which could perhaps help some individuals with some forms of dementia. There is also increasing usage of text messaging in healthcare delivery, for example, as conduits for targeted health information delivery, or for communication between health consumers and their doctors, including the transmission of lab results investigations, which could lead to faster treatment and enhance the chances of treatment response, reducing morbidities, and even mortalities, and saving healthcare costs. No doubt, such use of text messaging would likely also increase in many Asian countries. There is also likely to be an increase in mobile commerce market in Asia, not just in the more sophisticated markets such as South Korea, but right across the region, with novel technologies that enable electronic cash, b2b, b2c, and a variety of internet transactions, emerging from countries such as India, Vietnam, or the Philippines. The rate at which countries such as China, and India, and indeed, many of the developing economies in the region add new mobile and broadband subscribers attests to this development, experts predicting the investments in ICT, in particular in 3G infrastructure even likely to supplant those in the U.S and Europe in the near future. This development is also in consonance with developments in mobile data, which would occur in tandem with those of 3G, which latter would continue to compete with 2G series services but not on cutting-edge features but on price, relevance, and worth. There are regulatory concerns in many parts of Asia that would limit the use of certain information and communications technologies in healthcare delivery for example, Voice over IP (VoIP), but things might improve over time and the markets for these technologies thus might also increase. VoIP could facilitate the delivery of health services, cost-effectively and efficiently, including telephone consultation, or even telephone cognitive behavior therapy (t-CBT). Unlike in the consumer end however, there seem to be greater prospects for these technologies in the enterprise domain, and hospitals, and larger healthcare establishments could use them to reduce networking costs. The convergence of fixed and mobile telephony and of voice and data, is well under way in Asia with experts predicting almost 1.3 mobile phones for every fixed line phone by the end of 2005, and that fixed line carriers would have to think hard about not also embracing wireless services. These developments would no doubt influence the nature and pace of healthcare ICT investments in the region, the growth in the sales of hardware and software according to experts predict would recover from the recent decline to over 7% in 2005, although outsourcing, put at US$50bn in world business, would remain the chief market driver. India, and less so, China, the Philippines, and Vietnam, would be the main markets. Some have cautioned on the effect of the increasing subscription rates to mobile and broadband services in Asia on carrier revenues, particular the recouping of the significant investments involved in operating next-generation services that commoditization, a real possibility with low-priced voice and broadband access in the region, might compromise. This concern highlights the need for engaging in the process cycle mentioned earlier, as with particular reference to healthcare delivery, this might be an indication for broadening value propositions by 3G operators that that would increase options for revenue generation, for example, offering services besides access and messaging that would facilitate the processes involved in healthcare delivery. In other w ords, the underlying value of health information technologies is in their applicability to problem solving, and it is possible to recognize the problems that need solving, if only we would adopt the process cycle, and decompose current issues and problems. Again, here is another instance of the tight link between health and the economy. Thus, the directions that 3G operators for example decide on with regard this issue could be crucial not only in determining the nature and magnitude of these aspects of the healthcare ICT markets, but also in our ability to achieve the dual healthcare delivery objectives mentioned earlier. The need for software and healthcare ICT vendors and service providers to innovate and create more value for their clients would also characterize the process outsourcing markets in which other Asian countries that have the expertise and offer perhaps lower labor costs would challenge the dominance of countries such as India in this market. This would augur well for the healthcare industry, where more outsourcing would likely occur, both within Asia and globally, and the competition that ensues would engender higher value outsourcing, which would benefit the health industry also besides the likely lowered pricing, and enhance the chances of achieving the dual objectives in the countries utilizing the services. According to expert estimates, Asia's volume of the multi-trillion world market for software, hardware, and ICT services is increasing, about 25% in 2005, most on account of its established ICT markets, particularly in Japan, whose telecom revenues alone makes up more than 30% of Asia's almost $300bn mobile, fixed and Internet services market in 2004. However, the south East Asian markets are also developing at a fast rate, particularly those in India and China, the acquisition rates of computers, and the subscription rates, almost 80% of the total monthly new subscribers in the region. These developments would benefit healthcare delivery particularly in the poorer Asian nations, where the need for ICT diffusion not just to bridge the digital divide is more urgent, but also where the need for health services to reach individuals living in remote areas is even more urgent. However, the question is whether Asian telecoms carriers would be eager to continue to invest on network infrastructure considering concerns about commoditization, and the need to minimize costs, hence slash capital expenditures (capex,) among others, despite the increasing market diffusion of these technologies. Some are indeed, cutting capex, although others continue to build more infrastructures, in older generation technologies, whose falling prices incidentally reduce the worth of their investments. With carriers' increasing drive toward 3G, we could expect more in cap ex. Thus, the Asian markets remain poised to feed the rising demand for home entertainment technologies that seem insatiable in the U.S., so will the region's chip market experience increasing growth, in particular with the rate of growth of the markets for mobile telephone and other mobile devices. The consumer electronics rather than business devices, the main drivers of the chip markets, which Japan by far dominates in the region, and to which, that is consumer electronics, the health industry ought to explore in developing novel programs that facilitate healthcare delivery. Indeed, the current wave of mobile multimedia devices would be significant in ensuring that health systems in the region not only deliver qualitative health services, but that they do so cost-effectively, in the years ahead, as services such as consultation, with healthcare professionals at different levels, for examples doctors, counselors, social workers, and psychologists, become more commonplace, and treatment too. Individuals, for example, depressed persons, would be able to seek advice on matters anonymously via these devices, making it possible to, perhaps even prevent imminent suicide, and persons could book and change appointments with health service providers, or even make telephone payments for services they rendered. These services would clearly prevent needless clinic visits, saving time and money, yet with the required services delivered qualitatively, and the technologies utilized would not be expensive. Many Asian countries would likely increasingly embrace these technologies in health services provision, which not only underlines the need to continue to promote their widespread adoption, but also that in ensuring their affordability, and utilization, the achievement of both of which would in turn facilitate that of the dual healthcare delivery goals in these countries. The more pervasive the adoption and use of these technologies, the larger their markets would be. In other words, rather than reduce capex for the reasons m entioned above, carriers and vendors really ought to encourage even greater adoption of these technologies, as they could then follow this stage with the next one, which is devising healthcare delivery solutions that the healthcare consumer effect, using the devices and technologies that they have purchased. The carriers and vendors could modify these technologies, to offer these solutions to healthcare

181

problems that the healthcare consumer need solved and for which they would find the solutions valuable. In other words, rather than become commodities, these technologies could form the " templates " for the development of novel healthcare solutions. Business devices manufacturers could also adopt a similar strategy, their products tailored to fill demand vacuu ms in the consumer-oriented markets. This approach also highlights the need for the process cycle exercise in addressing healthcare delivery issues, which would reveal some of the processes that need addressing, and for which healthcare ICT solutions need developing. Such a decomposition and exposition exercise is crucial were we to fully elucidate the issues that result in healthcare delivery, both those that foster, and hinder it, both, which we need to manipulate for the purpose of improving healthcare d elivery, on an ongoing basis. With one of the issues involved in healthcare delivery being the timely availability of patient information, at the point of care (POC), there is no doubt that there are manifest opportunities for chip makers in Asia, and elsewhere in engineering novel chip technologies that would meet this challenge. As noted earlier, applying the process cycle to such an issue would reveal even cryptic processes, and issues, with their processes, and so on that would facilitate decision making on such new chip development projects. There is no doubt for example that newer and faster chips might be necessary the more sophisticated the value propositions healthcare consumers expect from their healthcare providers. This could emerge for example from a process cycle analysis revealing that patients not just want to receive text messages about lab results or treatment change, or any other information relevant to their healthcare but also want to see their doctors, and perhaps their psychologist on the same screen and sort of video-conference with them. The product with poor streaming sound quality and fuzzier image for example would stand no chance with another with hi-fi sound and sharper image quality.

The demand for services would not likely only be coming from the healthcare consumer in some of these Asian countries, for example in those with highly-developed technology infrastructure, but also from pressure to deliver qualitative services cost-effectively, anyway, as would the case in all the countries, considering as we noted earlier, the limitation in resources that all countries have. The prediction by the Semiconductor Industry Association that Asia's markets will grow by less than 2% in 2005, and Japan's by virtually nil, might change in the near future as Asian countries confront the developments in the healthcare sector that would also play key roles in the direction of the ICT industry including that of healthcare ICT. These developments would of course depend largely on the peculiarities of the healthcare needs of the respective countries, including the prevalence and patterns of diseases, health indicators, demographic characteristics, the availability or otherwise of healthcare professionals, the level of healthcare and technology infrastructure, and ethico-legal and regulatory issues. Others include the status of education and computer literacy, the stat of the country's economy, and its political will to implement change. Nonetheless, every Asian country would be impelled to promote the widespread adoption and utilization of healthcare ICT in the years as none would likely not appreciate the need to achieve the dual healthcare delivery objectives mentioned earlier, and those that fail to do so, likely to discover that they would have to sooner than later. Let us briefly consider the issue of the avian flu once again. Should any country not revisit the issue considering the WHO report mentioned above regarding the prospects of the virus hopping from human to human, for example? According to estimates by the U.S Centers for Disease Control and Prevention (CDC), a medium-level pandemic could undeniable cause roughly 90,000 deaths, over 700,000 hospitalizations and between 20 to 40 million outpatient visits and affect up to 25% of the population.

With 191 diagnosed with bird flu and 108 deaths, since 2003 according to the World Health Organization, there is no doubt about the virulence of this organism, even when transmitted from birds to humans. However, could it even be more so, transmitted from human to human, with seven members of one family dead, the eight killed by the initial bird to human transmission, as the WHO report mentioned earlier shows? Should countries therefore not start to prepare for an imminent pandemic, or in case one occurs? There is no doubt about the need not to create panic but at the same time, we need to prepare adequately to prevent and tackle this menace. Indeed, such preparations should not just be by healthcare authorities but by everyone, including private sector businesses. Considering the relationship between the economy and health that we mentioned earlier, every business should measure the possible effect the flu would have on the business in all operational domains, and how to handle supply disruption, labor force shortages, maintaining communication lines, reducing cash-flow, ensuring back-up services, and maintaining contact with staff to monitor the progress of their illnesses. It would also be necessary to maintain practice runs to assess the effectiveness of the plans, and determine their flaws with a view to rectifying them before a pandemic hits. These measures also apply to any organization, the details and other considerations specific for each organization, including healthcare organizations such as hospitals, and physicians' practices. They also exemplify the points we made earlier about the need for the process cycle in elucidating issues that foster or hinder healthcare delivery. By decomposing the issues raised above, each organization would be able to figure out the processes involved in realizing them, hence be able to determine the most appropriate healthcare ICT to deploy in facilitating them. This also highlights the point that each country and the systems within it, be they public or private-sector-based, would need to determine its healthcare ICT needs, at some point or another, and in fact, the sooner that they do, the better. This is not to say that the funding system of a health system does not influence its operations. In fact, the increased costs of providing free or almost free healthcare in some Asian countries, and as some would argue, their negative consequences for the quality of healthcare delivery in these countries is well known. Yet, even countries that do not provide free health also could end up with poor quality healthcare delivery, as some in fact do. These issues underscore the need for process improvement that we have emphasized in our discussion thus far. In other words, no health system is perfect or could ever be in Asia, or elsewhere in the world, the imperfection in one country, worse than in another based on a variety of issues peculiar to each country. What is common to all countries is that they could improve the quality of the health services that they provide their peoples even cost-effectively, or put differently without wrecking their budgets, implementing the appropriate healthcare ICT. Perhaps we should add that the urgency attending to the issues involved demand would of course be even higher in countries that the issues they contend with tend to be quite acute, for example, the need to prevent the emergence and spread of infectious diseases, or arresting an epidemic of obesity. Other countries might have to deal with different issues for examples, reducing hospital wait times, or curtailing soaring health spending, or improving access to care. Whatever the issues are, each country, whether in Asia or Europe needs to conduct process cycle analysis on the identified issues, accordingly, whereof the need for particular healthcare ICT technologies or solutions would emerge, which would modify the issues, improving those that need improving, or indeed, eliminating those that are redundant but obstructing progress. Conducting such exercise on an ongoing basis would make the health system better, facilitate optimization of resource allocation and utilization, reduce wastage, and ensure its survivability.

A s we noted earlier, the combination of mobility and TV is a major trend in Asia, and one Telco's are probably going to agonize over considering the prolific entrepreneurial climate that the increasingly widespread interest in the Internet Protocol (IP) is generating in the region, and indeed, elsewhere. "Niche TVs" seem to be the order of the day, with anyone with a couple of thousand dollars to secure bandwidth now able to produce and transmit TV programs on any subject of his/her fancy, ranging from country living to "auto drifting." With the increasing diffusion of high-speed broadband, entire TV channels, available not only on the internet, but also via TV and mobile, are springing up in numbers. IPTV uses the internet protocol, also used to deliver web and voice content on surfing and with internet telephony, respectively. It is able to transmit, seamlessly, video from the content producer to home TV either via a cable TV provider or directly via set-top box, the system not only clearer yet cheaper than satellite transmission, but also capable of real time broadcasting into any Java™ capable device with a player or special software unnecessary thus rendering streaming media old -fashioned. These developments would no doubt influence healthcare delivery in the near future, as healthcare providers and entrepreneurs establish TV stations using IP technology narrowcasting, or slivercasting, to deliver targeted and contextualized health information and other services globally. There are though outstanding technical issues that might give Telco's and other big industry players an edge in what would likely be a huge market in Asia, for example buffering and frame dropouts, even with streaming speed under control, and other practical problems particularly regarding streaming into mobile phones and set-top boxes with broadband connections. Indeed, some experts predicted growth in the Asia-Pacific market for IP video services to be almost 80% yearly, an over US$4 billion market in the next decade, Asian Telco TV subscribers almost 50% of all global subscribers by the end of that period. In other words, Asia promises immense IPTV market opportunities in the years ahead, including in healthcare delivery, for businesses with creative value propositions based on an exploration of the needs of the countries to which they want to market their products and services. As mentioned above, even for these companies it is best to base this exploration on a process cycle analysis of the factors at play in the particular country s health system, conducted in-house or using expert consultants. IPTV penetration would vary in different Asian countries, due among others to existing technology infrastructure. It would be as diffused as cable in Hong Kong for example, available in roughly a third of digital households in the next four to five years, the digitalization of cable and satellite responsible in the m ain if IPTV did not in fact overtake the latter in popularity. In fact, IPTV might overtake Digital Terrestrial TV (DTT) and satellite over time, in Asia, considering its adoption rates in places such as Hong Kong, where PCCW, a major IPTV provider has more than half a million subscribers, although its penetration in others, even in Japan, Taiwan, and South Korea hovers around 5%. This is testimony to the huge potential market openings in many countries in Asia, even those with advanced technology base. IPTV providers would also need to consider, based on the market, broadening their service offerings for examples with HDTV, among others, to secure competitive edge. PCCW for example provides HDTV and Video-on-Demand (VOD) services via its DSL network, its broadband TV services. Technologies that could accelerate purchaser programming while reducing costs, enable flawless voice, data, and video blending, and provide first-rate content that would increase subscription, and offer TV services to current voice and data subscribers and package inexpensive digital TV programs, are some of what IPTV providers that hope to capture sizeable market shares would need to do in Asia. It would be a Herculean task to veer millions of Asian clients from their current analogue terrestrial TV without such moves. The network infrastructures that DSL and FTTH providers, in Japan, for example, need in order to compete with cable and satellite effectively, and that would enable foraying into the multi-location TV and HDTV markets wou ld be crucial determinants of the future of these technologies in general, but also with regard their possible applications in the health industry. Firms that expect to make any major inroad into these markets would need to invest in these technologies, which would no doubt also facilitate their incursions into the analogue terrestrial, TV domain, for example. Broadcasting, rather than streaming programs over the Internet is indeed, a major market driver, with opportunities for Telco s, broadcasters, broadband, and content providers, device manufacturers, and software providers, among others in Asia, in fact on the rise. Health systems in the region would not only be important players in the eventual size of the markets, but also in its future evolution in p articular of the value propositions that would facilitate the achievement of the healthcare delivery objectives. We would likely see the increasing applications of IPTV for example in services such as ambulatory/domiciliary monitoring, security and video p hones, and indeed a variety of personalized interactive services, which could improve domiciliary healthcare service provision, particularly in countries in aging populations, with the potential to reduce healthcare spending significantly. Firms need to stress customer self-service, offering exclusive services that utilize the distinctive IPTV characteristics to produce a client experience dissimilar and superior to that cable and satellite currently offer. In other words, it is not enough that the technologies themselves exist it is the services they offer that create competitive advantage, and which is what matters not only in health services delivery, where the client is going to continue to be increasingly suave and demanding, but also in the applications of IPTV in other domains. This would even be more so in those Asian countries where the healthcare consumer pays part if not all of his/her healthcare bills. As mentioned earlier, service blending rather than bundling would create better client value, hence market share. In countries such as China, with a huge potential market, IPTV architecture needs to move from a client-server to peer-to-peer model, which would also facilitate worldwide circulation, with less regulation by the State Administration of Radio, Film and Television, SARFT. The security of distributed content would also be a major market driver in the health industry, with the high profile of issues relating to patient information privacy and confidentiality. Some argue that open standards, the essential basis of IPTV stifles creativity, which might make the interoperability issues that the industry continues to battle difficult to resolve. These examples illustrate the complexities of the factors that would be key to the nature and direction of the emergence of these important technologies regarding their applications in the health industry in Asia, and indeed, elsewhere. Nonetheless, healthcare delivery in the region would largely shape and would depend on the innovative value offerings that the technologies engender in the coming years. The region's immense market growth-potential coupled with its technological classiness on the one hand, and of the blend of fixed and mobile telephony create interesting convergences with budding significant integration and influence on global healthcare ICT markets that the region's position in global outsourcing and software development already secure. Furthermore, does the fact that China's Lenovo purchased IBM's PC business in 2004, not foreshadow an intended greater role of the country's ICT firms on the world ICT stage? Indeed, the World Information and Technology Services Alliance, estimated that investments on the region on software, hardware, IT solutions and other ICT to be US$650bn in 2004, and increase to US$800bn by 2007. With the region's noteworthy cost-expertise ratio, in the outsourcing market, especially regarding the provision of business process outsourcing (BPO) and IT development services, the region would likely maintain its competitive edge relative to other parts of the world. However, it faces stiff competition from Eastern European countries in the years ahead, not to mention the regional competition between countries such as India, the Philippines, Vietnam, and China. The effects these developments would have on healthcare delivery in the region would vary depending on the type of outsourcing model, and the intensity of competition with overseas clients particularly in Europe and the U.S who would likely pay more than local clients for these services. This would likely be the case for healthcare establishments requiring the customary IT-assisted BPO, where telecoms and Internet connections enable inexpensive remote providers to offer functions such as call center, client care, data input, or research services. On the other hand, those seeking total service solutions, that is want to outsource their entire IT Departments, and customer service for management by a remote, service partner, might not have to worry so much about overseas competition. Those that need software and ICT service outsourcing, another variant of outsourcing, involving perhaps even ongoing involvement with the details of software development such as coding and other manual tasks that developing IT resources demand would. The high level of and ubiquity of IT technical expertise in most parts of Asia, though might not make healthcare ICT outsourcing costs totally out of reach even for those services that well-off foreign clients might seek, after all. This is more so as the prices of telecoms bandwidth, an important cost driver for IT services companies would likely keep falling in the near future.

Furthermore, most of these more competitive services, if sought, would likely be by the larger health establishments with secure funding sources, more so as outsourcing companies themselves would increasingly need to offer service differentiation as prices alone would become less secure survival guarantors. In other words, even smaller establishments seeking to outsource would increasingly become discerning and expect more value for their money, which means that Asian outsourcing companies would need scale and service differentiation for more effective competition, at all levels, in particular as many of their clients would likely be purchasing outsourced skills back into the enterprise, becoming competitors themselves. This is more so due to the fluidity of price-sensitive services, hence the need for outsourcing firms to assist their customers to innovate, rather than merely provid e them services. The ability of ICT firms to work with their clients to generate innovative ideas is even more pertinent in healthcare delivery, where as we previously noted, improving healthcare delivery involves understanding the underlying processes of the issues that ultimately foster or hinder health services delivery, and devising the appropriate healthcare ICT solutions for modifying them. This modification, which achieved could move the health system towards realizing the dual healthcare delivery objectives also mentioned earlier. In this regard, and similar to currents mobility trends in general, mobility is increasingly becoming a key aspect of service provision, with wireless services, increasingly sophisticated in order to meet the demands for these mobile services, and Asia is one of the most advanced wireless services markets globally. The region has the largest market for organic growth prospects in essential mobile services, with currently almost 50% of global mobile subscribers, and has a buzzing next-generation mobile services industry, with as many as 75% of global 3G subscribers from just Japan and Korea, both most aggressive about 4G technologies. With increasing demand for first-rate mobile content in countries such as China, data including SMS content might provide the much-need carrier revenue that could ease concerns over the chances of market demand not catching up with what some would term the frenetic innovation rate in the mobile services domains in Asia. The increasing use of these technologies in both mobile voice and data services in healthcare delivery could also bring voice services back into contention as veritable revenue sources for carriers in Asia, the double revenue sources likely offsetting upfront investments in infrastructures and technologies by operators. This is plausible considering for example the data and information-intensive nature of the health industry, and the potential to transmit lab results for example from healthcare provider to patient or to other providers using this medium, and efficiently and cost-effectively too. There are other aspects of healthcare delivery for example health promotion and disease prevention campaigns that would benefit more from multimedia content delivery that non-voice applications for example, SMS, would be deficient in achieving, although most subscribers in Asia currently use the latter. The likely next mobile/wireless battlefront would be 3G carriers therefore not only providing multimedia content but also doing so inexpensively. This is because they would be competing for subscribers most of who also have access to speedy data and multimedia through broadband services and increasingly prevalent WiFi services, reducing their need to access the internet through a phone, especially if expensive to do so. As previously noted, products rather than services currently dominate the consumer markets in Asia, and there are indeed, "loaded" mobile phones on the market, with a variety of features that appeal to the average consumer. Terminal developers are however, starting to break loose from the hitherto tight grip of carriers some of who actually market both applications and terminals. This is an important development as handset manufacturers keen to market 3G services are doing the exact thing, marketing novel applications along with their sophisticated handsets, and capturing valuable market share in a subtle but effective way, for example with mobile TV applications. These changing dynamics have implications for healthcare delivery as individuals could watch their favorite health program on the go. With more than five million new cell phone subscribers in China monthly, the opportunities for the delivery of health services are potentially immense, particularly to persons living in the country's remote regions, prospects that in fact apply to other developing countries in Asia. It is important for these companies not only to develop innovative products capable for delivering equally novel services, they would need to be able to work with the health industry in understanding the processes involved in healthcare delivery and the services that handsets could help deliver in the particular markets in which they are interested. These services would clearly vary among countries, a further indication of the immense market potential that healthcare delivery offers in the region. Even the massive potential mobile gaming market in Asia, estimated to be over US$1 billion in another year, minus Japan, could involve the health industry, with carriers and even handset developers broadening their data service offerings to target the "health games" market, which would likely increase and indeed, significantly in Asia. In countries such as Japan, for example, offering an increasingly aging population, avenues for cognitive stimulation has undeniable market potential. China also has promises a major mobile health gaming market, as does South Korea, which currently has the largest gaming market. This is not necessarily due to population aging, but the fact that health games for every segment of the population, would in future become just as ubiquitous as the current games concepts in the broadband markets, with entrepreneurs coming up with creative and interactive service ideas that would appeal to a mass market in general. Mobile and wireless services would therefore be prominent in healthcare delivery in the near future in particular with the emergence of next-generation technologies capable of facilitating all facets of healthcare delivery including primary, secondary, and tertiary prevention service provision. Pricing might be a limiting factor, if it is too high for a mass market, a key issue that carriers would have to consider, and why some Telco's are exploring the concept of limited mobility services, for example Reliance Telecom in India, with minimal mobile technologies deployed to facilitate affordable access in countries with less pervasive connectivity. Access to broadband services is still mainly via the internet cafe, although pre-paid home services are also increasingly common, in the poorer Asian countries, but with services more affordable, and connectivity improved, broadband speed billed to reach 1.2 gb/sec by 2020, there is no doubt about the immense market opportunities that would open up. The market potential of both broadband and mobile technologies in healthcare delivery in Asia is indeed, enormous, but the firms operating in these domains need to formulate the appropriate service offerings as mentioned earlier. Fixed carriers also need to take a cue from mobile operators in providing for their subscribers and work with content providers to offer qualitative and sellable services. This would also ensure that they are able to make reasonable profits from these services. There is no doubt that Telco's and other firms need to pay more attention to the health industry as it offers them incredible latitude to develop, working with industry insiders, innovative products and services that the immense Asian market is literally awaiting, to achieve th e dual healthcare delivery goals mentioned earlier. The companies ought to start to appreciate the fact that the very peoples that use computers, telephones, cell phones, and that watch TV, and send/receive text messages and emails, and conduct transaction s on the Internet, and on their mobile phones, also become ill, and see their doctors, undergo surgeries, and need health information to prevent diseases. If these persons already have the products, and have subscribed to certain other non -health services, why should these companies not be interested in developing health services that they could market to these same persons via the products and services to which they have already subscribed, and exploit scale and scope economies? There is no doubt that most people care about their health and want to live and be healthy. It is furthermore, in the interests of these companies that these individuals are, were they, the companies themselves to survive. Why would the companies then not want to pay attention to health issues when in fact they derive double advantage from so doing, a guaranteed market to which they could sell additional, in this case, health-related services? In fact, Asian countries also should be keen to create the enabling environment for these interlocking factors to play out the best way they could. This means embracing policies that would open up new and profitable markets for Telcos and other healthcare ICT firms, which would enable them, recoup their often-massive investments in technical infrastructures; that would create service offerings that would help in keeping their citizens healthy; and those that offer opportunities for the achievement of the dual healthcare delivery objectives. In the end, the health of Asian countries has intimate links with their economies, and even those with poorer economies need to institute these measures, as the realization of the dual objectives is crucial for them because of the even more limited financial and other resources required to fund health services delivery. With such shortages, not only could they not afford escalating healthcare costs, they need to provide their citizens with qualitative health services, which would increase the chances of their peoples being healthy and more economically productive. The increasingly widespread use of a variety of information technologies in the region is a first step toward achieving these dual objectives, which would likely not materialize without taking the additional steps we have been discussing thus far, among others, applied contextually based on the expositions that they process cycle exercises reveal.

References

1. Available at: http://www.healthcareitnews.com/printStory.cms?id=5120
Accessed on June 26, 2006

2. Available at: http://www.witsa.org/
Accessed on June 29, 2006

An Analysis of East Asian Healthcare ICT Markets

We have discussed Asia as a single entity thus far, but as we mentioned earlier, it is possible to explore the region in a number of different ways, one of which we would utilize hereafter in looking at healthcare ICT in an important part of the region namely, East Asia. It comprises People's Republic of China (PRC); Hong Kong, China; Republic of Korea; Mongolia; and Taipei, China. The PRC has maintained its vigorous economic growth despite global economic foibles. Its gross domestic product (GDP) grew by 7.3% in 2001, projected 2002 growth, 7.4%. Economic growth slowed in the latter part of 2001, but recovered in early 2002, and its growth rate was actually 9.1% in 2003. In fact, the country's first production census realized at the end of 2005 that there has recently been a gross undervaluing of the country's GDP, the rapid growth of the services sector not accounted for, which made the economy's growth rates for 2003-2005, actually about 10% per year in real terms. The relentless growth of the economy over the years has prompted some to fear it would eventually overheat a potential bubble-burst that could spell disaster for not just the economy but could trigger spasms with global reverberations. With economic growth in developing Asia, East Asia included, in 2006 expected to fall to 7.2% and even further to about 7% in 2007 as cyclical support for growth draws back, even these collective projections, which would no doubt camouflage some diversity, apply to the PRC, whose back-to-back, double-digit growth in recent years fell below 10% in 2005, albeit fractionally. The People's Republic of China (PRC) in 2005 had an absolute increase in foreign exchange reserves, about the same as in 2004, a noticeable improvement in its current account surplus for the year, regardless, the country at $819 million, accounting for about 44% of developing Asia's stock of foreign exchange reserves at year-end, 2005. This was an increase from about 27% at end -2001, amassing roughly 56% of the region's rise in reserves during the same period 2. While developing Asia's share of the United States merchandise trade deficit has not changed significantly since 2000, $289.6 billion, or 37.8% of the total US trade deficit, 0.6 percentage points increase from 2004, the PRC gained shares, $201.6 billion, or 26.3% of the total deficit, a 1.4 percentage points increase. This is unlike Korea and Taipei, China, whose shares fell by an aggregate of 1.2 percentage points, which combined with the gains of the PRC resulted in a net 0.2 percentage point increase for the East Asian sub-region. This is an indication of the country's low -cost production advantages on the one hand, and of favorable intra-regional trade growth with exports of parts and supplies to its markets for inexpensive assembly into export goods, on the other. The increase in the world electronics cycle, which started in 2005, and expected to continue throughout 2006, would buoy growth in many regional economies, in particular in East and Southeast Asia, which would be especially rapid in the PRC and India, particularly if domestic demand also increased. What do these economic trends portend for healthcare delivery in East Asia, for example? With interest rates likely to increase, hence the chances for fiscal gerrymandering limited in many developing Asian countries, it would be necessary to bridle deficits in many of these countries. Again, what does this mean for healthcare delivery in these countries? What would it mean for example to reduce fuel subsidies and set more realistic pump prices for access to health services delivery in these countries, in particular for those living in remote and rural locations? Yet, could these countries afford to ignore the fiscal burden of fuel subsidies or indeed of subsidies to energy, such as electricity, among others? Indeed, growth rates would fall in the PRC in 2006, and projected combined economic growth in developing Asia would fall to 7.2%, and 7.0% in 2006, and 2007, respectively[2]. Although these are still healthy growth rates in developing Asia historically, there is no doubt that these countries need to make adjustments in order to meet their sustainable economic development goals. The PRC, for example, wants to speed up the reform and development of health care, as stated in the Report on the Work of the Government delivered by Premier Wen Jiabao at the Third Session of the 10th National People's Congress on March 5, 2005[1]. In the same report, it stated that it planned to complete the development of a disease prevention and control system and of a public health emergencies system in 2005. It also proposed to focus on medical and health care work on rural areas, to upgrade its healthcare infrastructure and increase the numbers of healthcare professionals in rural areas. It planned to pursue a pilot project for a new system of co-operative medical and health care services in these places and explore means to establish a medical assistance system, prevent, and control infectious, endemic, and occupational diseases, including the prevention, treatment, and control of the spread of HIV/AIDS. It also planned to reform the urban medical service system, including standardizing medical fees and medication costs to reduce health-services provision costs, to strengthen urban community health services, and vigorously foster customary Chinese medicine.

Furthermore, it planned to focus attention on the health of the elderly and the disabled, and to continue research on population development strategies, stick with its family planning low birthrate policies, including establishing a reward system for compliance with these policies. Is it not desirable for the achievement of these goals, which essentially constitute primary, secondary, and tertiary prevention health services delivery, which against the backdrop of the need for rational utilization of limited financial resources in order to meet sustainable development goals, seems indeed imperative? In other words, would it not be preferable for China, and indeed, other Asian countries to achieve the dual objectives of qualitative healthcare delivery to their peoples at all levels of care, efficiently, and cost-effectively, the achievements of which the implementation of the appropriate healthcare ICT could help facilitate? In China's 11th Five-Year Program (2006-2010), the Government aims at a lower economic growth route, and on stemming the rapid population -growth, in urban and coastal areas, projected at 9.5% in 2006, down to 8.8% in 2007. Even if the projected population-growth acceleration in Korea of 5.1% in 2006 materializes, neutralizing the deceleration in the PRC to give East Asia an average of 7.7%, same as in 2005, how fast could the PRC hope to slow growth and for how long? Should the PRC therefore not be seeking ways to achieve the dual healthcare delivery objectives in order to be able to deliver successfully, its healthcare goals mentioned earlier? What role could healthcare ICT play in this regard? Securing the link between the economy and health is crucial for the achievement of either of these goals. Should China, where increasingly high investment levels have led to overcapacity in many industries, and where deficient Financial systems, labor market, and state companies' reforms, and increasing income gap, trade frictions abroad, and worsening natural milieu, threaten sustainable economic development, not ensure the realization of the dual healthcare delivery objectives? Would this not in turn ensure the healthy citizenry that make sustainable economic prosperity possible? With gross domestic product (GDP) growth of 9.9% in 2005, projected to be over 9% up until 2010, the country's rapid economic expansion has created the structural weaknesses mentioned earlier, that threaten the investment (5.9 percentage points to the total GDP growth or 60% of overall growth)-and export (7.1% or 71% of overall growth)-based economy. China, indeed, plans to reform its health system in the near future, in particular to reduce healthcare costs and protect its peoples' health3. According to a recent statement by Li Jian'ge in the People's Daily, vice-director of the Office for Restructuring the Economy of the State Council, the Central official departments and local authorities the State Council plans to institute medical insurance procedure for urban employees. He also noted that th e state's health administrations, including the Ministry of Health, would oversee countrywide hospitals rather than run them. The administrative authorities will also inspire competition among hospitals and other healthcare organizations throughout the country. Li also advised hospitals to restructure and improve the quality of service provision to patients. Furthermore, China has begun to split hospitals and pharmacies, the latter becoming stand -alone drug retailers. The State Drug Administration (SDA) will also employ Good Manufacture Practice (GMP) and Good Sales Practice (GSP) in the market, assuring the drugs quality. Indeed, China's drug producers must now print the recommended retail prices on their packaging, one of the country's efforts to stop the ever-increasing prices of drugs and medical services4. The new policy, issued June 28, 2006, in a circular by the National Development and Reform Commission, the Ministry of Health and six other government departments indicated that the government would readjust the fixed drug prices and tauten its oversight on market prices. Government even plans, on an experimental basis, to fix the prices of some drugs at the factory gate, and seek to review the prices of and standardize medical services in hospitals. It plans to prohibit major public hospitals from selling drugs at prices 15% more than their purchase prices. With soaring drug and medical service prices being key social problems in the country in recent years, and government previous efforts to improve the situation meeting with minimal success, should it not be exploring the potential benefits of healthcare ICT in achieving its goals.

The proposed changes to the country's health system mentioned above no doubt would have a positive influence on the peoples' health, provided of course their implementation is successful. They are also essentially efforts to achieve the dual healthcare delivery objectives of qualitative healthcare delivery while simultaneously reducing healthcare spending, which the deployment of the appropriate healthcare ICT could help achieve. Would we then likely see increased investments in these technologies in China over the years considering its resolve to achieve the dual healthcare delivery goals? No doubt, the country already deploys sophisticated ICT in healthcare delivery, for example, the International logistics firm TNT recently opened its latest medical logistics facility for Asia in Shanghai, the first specialized life-science products logistics and transshipment center in China, capable of transporting within a day, medical products from Shanghai to any specified ER in China. Built at a cost of 1-million-euro, the TNT-funded life-science products transshipment center is within Shanghai Waigaoqiao Bonded Zone, tailors logistic services to high-value medical products' manufacturers and distributors, and supplements TNT's regional life-science transshipment center in Singapore to provide Asia-wide service coverages. There is no doubt about the increasing opportunities for enterprise-wide healthcare ICT solutions not just in the supply chain, but also in customer services, human resources management, and in other non-health administrative and financial management domains. Another example is its tracking system aimed at containing the possible spread of the bird flu, ready for demonstration in June 2006, for related authorities and poultry industry in China[6]. By mid -March 2006, everything was already in place to launch definitive testing, according to Perry Law, President of the Canad a-based Smart-tek Communications, Inc at a conference held in Beijing to highlight the prospect of the system, who expressed the hope that the system would help China form effective collaborative networks against bird flu throughout its enormous territories. The system, "RTAC-PM," short for "RFID Tracking Alert Containment and Poultry Monitoring," designed to monitor livestock and

targeted specifically at the poultry industry, would in tandem with the efforts of the health Ministry help contain the possible spread of the H5N1 Avian Influenza. Says Law, "At its core, the system utilizes the Internet to report detailed, real-time information about events in the poultry supply-chain to a central monitoring station." It uses radio frequency identification technologies, allowing a central agency that the food -supply authorities control, to monitor the flow of products over a specified zone that could be a town, or a district, and even the entire country. It has built-in alert monitoring protocols, and provides instant alert warning of events that signal anomalies that, subject to inquiry protocols, could point to threats of disease outbreak to the central agency. The system thus offers information crucial to the central agency's rapid response to such threats. Examples of alert events are disproportionate mortality rates during growth, and unusual movement patterns by poultry farmers suggestive of attempts to cover-up disease outbreaks, and they would enable the central agency dispatch inspectors to investigate, thu s facilitating optimal resource utilization in high-risk areas, with the potential to saves costs significantly not to mention human lives. The system gathers information about the production cycle of each specific flock at the chick producer, growing farm , and processing plant, the entire life cycle from chick to maturity being only about eight weeks, minimizing the logistics of the exercise. The system uses customized tags and tagging equipment, the RFID bird tag designed to accommodate bird growth and durability, and the tag is reusable. The central agency could therefore collect data for examples date of birth, birth location, breed, and farmer information, which authorized users could access online. Besides recording bird movements, the system could also track those of containers, cages, and trucks used for poultry transportation, and could track the finished product used both at home and exported, even to the consumer. The system thus offers total egg-to-stall traceability. China would therefore not unlikely have market openings for such tracking systems for use in the health industry as well in order to synchronize tracking data and make surveillance more effective. In fact, there would likely be more market openings in the near future for modifying/facilitating all the processes involved in healthcare delivery. However, it would be necessary to first decompose the issues in the health system that need tackling, some of which we mentioned earlier, then decompose these issues, which would expose additional issues and their processes. It would also reveal the need for further decomposition, and exposition, the processes so revealed modified, including expunging as necessary, or facilitated, the quality of service provision improving along the way, this process cycle continuing ad infinitum. Thus, there would be need for healthcare ICT diffusion at all levels of health services provision in the country for it to achieve the dual healthcare delivery goals. The healthcare issues of its citizens far-removed from the cities and who are less financially endowed averagely than those living in urban settings for example, would likely be different from those of their city-dwelling counterparts as would the processes that would need facilitating, hence the technologies that would serve to improve service provision best in these areas. Software and healthcare ICT vendors seeking to do businesses in China also therefore need to understand the issues in the different parts and segments of the country s health system, in order to appreciate the workings of the health system and its processes that healthcare ICT solutions could help facilitate. Such firms also need to track Government policies in order to stay abreast of developments that could trigger or hinder healthcare ICT investments. On March 18, 2006, for example, Ge Yanfeng, an official with the China Development Research Center (CDRC) under the State Council, noted that the inappropriate utilization of market mechanisms has led to a gross injustice in health resources distribution, signaling probable changes to the country s radical and much criticized market-oriented health reforms7. His comments made at the preparatory meeting of the China Development Forum in Beijing that under the reforms, lower-end health institutions, for examples rural hospitals and community hospitals in urban areas, are barely surviving suggests possible future focus areas. He also mentioned the outcome of a study the CDRC and the World Health Organization (WHO) collaborated on, and lamented the ill effects of commercializing China s health reforms and the need to correct them. Henk Bekedam, WHO representative in China, blamed too little input and government interference from for the inefficient use of China s limited health resources, and observed that there are at present 11 government departments playing different roles in health services, with no overall coordination. Do such issues not call for the decomposition/exposition exercise earlier mentioned with a view to highlighting faulty processes and rectifying them with the deployment of the appropriate healthcare ICT? Indeed, the WHO representative suggested that the State Council establish a special organization to coordinate these departments and that government should institute a long-term plan for the health sector and clearly define its roles. Also at this meeting a Health Ministry official, Gao Weizhong, stressed the need to halt profit-seeking tendencies in health institutions and for government to play a key role in future health reforms, if China were to provide qualitative health services to its 1.3 billion peoples. Ge noted that it would cost China an estimated US$19 billion to US$25 billion U.S. dollars, or roughly, 15% of China's gross domestic product in 2005, to build a new health system that would make health services available and affordable to all, a plan he noted the country could afford. In a similar vein, on January 7, 2006, Health Minister Gao Qiang noted at the 2006 national health work conference that China will strictly limit the size of large hospitals in order to lower the cost of medical treatment for the people, and enable them to access health services easier and cheaper. He stressed the need for Chinese hospitals not to purchase luxury medical equipment and use top techniques in the treatment, as those in developed countries do. He also told the conference about government plans in 2006 to stiffen control over the expansion of large hospitals and purchase by these hospitals of large medical equipments with bank loans and public funds. He advised local health authorities to offer hospital and medicine service at a realistic price to farmers, urban laid -offs, jobless, migrant workers, the elderly and children. He also said that luxury rooms in hospitals should not exceed 10% of the total sickbeds, and that hospitals should utilize income from special beds and medical services requests in establishing funds for service provision to the needy, noting, "The patients with financial difficulties or in critical condition must be treated first, instead of being charged first." Again, these developments indicate the direction the country's health services is heading in the next few years, and suggest the government's determination to achieve the dual healthcare delivery objectives and the likelihood of increased healthcare ICT, which no doubt facilitates the achievement of the objectives. On the other hand, premiums are growing and so are losses due to a dearth of specialized firms, in the country's health insurance sector. Premium s paid rose by an average of 46% annually from 2002 to a total of US$3.2 billion in 2004. Premiums from health insurance in the first ten months of 2005 reached US$3.3 billion, up 15.5% over a similar period in 2004. The demand for health insurance in China is increasing, illness, one of the three greatest concerns of about 65% of Chinese residents, some surveys revealed, and unofficial estimates show, the market could grow to US$36billion by 2008. This growth potential notwithstanding, commercial health insurance plays a minor role in the domestic market now, constituting just 10% of the residents' overall medical costs. With the country having only two specialized health insurance companies: PICC Health Insurance Co Ltd and Ping An Health Insurance Co Ltd, "Compared to the strong market demand, the supply of specialized health insurance services is rather weak," says Chen Wenhui, director of the life insurance regulatory department of the China Insurance Regulatory Commission (CIRC)s. He was speaking at an International Symposium on the Development of Health Insurance and Third Party Administration in November 2005, adding, "This is partly because of the high technical requirements and potential risks of health insurance." Noted Wang Xujin, an insurance professor at the Beijing Technology and Business University, also at that event, "A lack of specialization is the major reason for the risks Health insurance, which is hugely different from life insurance in terms of actuarial analysis, risk control and other factors must be offered by specialized providers". Yet, there are problems in the way of this ideal with many health insurance providers concerned about the high risks in the business, loss ratios for example, as high as 200% for some insurers lately, others having to suspend the sale of health insurance products. That every Chinese life insurance firms able to underwrite health insurance policies, and since 2004,

208

property insurers, to sell short-term health insurance, only further complicates the picture. There is no doubt about the chances of commercial health insurance growing in China, however, the insurance industry needs to find answers to issues such as adverse selection. It is also uncertain if information asymmetry therefore is not a key reason for the massive loss ratios, a problem that would escalate with insurers not traditionally in the healthcare industry foraying into this domain. Does this not support the need for the sort of process cycle analysis mentioned earlier by these insurers in order to understand fully, the health and behavior patterns of their potential clients? Could healthcare ICT not help in this regard, and indeed, with health information dissemination among the clients, which could help prevent ex-ante moral hazard for example, which would prevent unnecessary spiking of insurance premiums for even low -risk persons that could result in pricing them out of the market, making health insurance unprofitable in the end? These issues also apply to health service provision by government, although the provision of health services for all, both high and low risk persons, would in theory, prevent adverse selection. What would the likely plans of government to reduce the prices of health services be on service utilization for example? Could the health system avoid ex-post moral hazard with individuals over-utilizing services and incurring unnecessary costs in tax and premium inflations for examples? Would such overuse of the health system not deplete the financial resources allocated to health? Could the deployment of the appropriate healthcare ICT not help in, for example, actualizing the disease prevention and health promotion programs that could reduce the need for health services utilization? In short, the need for healthcare ICT diffusion would not just benefit the health, but also the health insurance industry. Would elimination the issue of information asymmetry for example not help keep people healthy, and would this not drive down the prices of premiums, as insurers would need to pay less out while making more money from increased clientele population? Would this not serve the purpose of government in ensuring wider coverage? Would health information dissemination by making people healthier for example promoting physical exercise, smoking avoidance, eating right, and other healthy lifestyles, also not reduce health spending by government-run health services, while offering qualitative health services, in other words, government achieving its dual healthcare delivery goals? Does it not make sense therefore to embrace and implement the technologies capable of making all of these happen? This is in fact what we are likely to see in the years ahead happen in the country's health system, as all healthcare stakeholders increasingly appreciate the immense promise of healthcare ICT in the realization of their respective healthcare objectives. A joint report from the State Council and the World Health Organization indicated in late 2005 that China's eight-year health reform program has run into more than a few problems, chief among which the unequal distribution of benefits across the country and how to resolve it[9].

China has the largest population in the world, spread across the country in both urban and rural settings. Part of understanding health service provision in the country is appreciating the diversity of health issues and delivery practices including the country's traditional medical practice, exported to 164 countries and regions around the world in 2005, with export earnings about US$830 million, according to the China Association of Traditional Chinese Medicine[10], a 14.55% increase from 2004. The earnings accounted for just 6% of China's total export of medicine products and in the main from the export of low value-added extracted herbal substances and raw materials. In 2005, China made US$69.57 million from the export of extracted herbal substances alone, exports projected to increase. The country also imported herbal medicines though, US$240 million worth in 2005, increasing by 6.4% year on year and constituting 2% of the total medicine products imports. There is no doubt about the significance of Chinese traditional medicine in the overall healthcare delivery scheme, and indeed as an industrial chain covering the agriculture, industry, and commerce, with for example, 448 plantation bases for standardized traditional Chinese medicine and 18 provincial level plantations[11]. It is not only economically justifiable, but also smart for software and healthcare ICT vendors to explore the prospects of developing ICT solutions to address the issues affecting this industry and in relation to others in the value chain, and to facilitate/modify the processes involved in the interplay between these industries. Indeed, such process cycle analyses are also critical for all stakeholders in the traditional medicine industry to embark upon, exercises with the potential to stimulate investments, which would boost employment in this and associated industries, and by extension, exports, earning valuable forex for the players, including the country. This is besides the benefits accruable to the individuals that utilize traditional medical services, which in the end constitute major elements of the health services delivery chain, and who by receiving qualitative and affordable services, indicate government's success in achieving the dual healthcare delivery objectives in this regard. There is also little doubt about the importance of such exercises regarding Western medical practice. Research for example shows that heart disease, cancer and stroke are now the main killers of middle-aged individuals in China, high blood pressure and smoking, the main risk factors increasingly prevalent with the country's economy forging ahead [12]. The research, which examined the chief causes of death in adults, found that over the past almost half a century, the same chronic diseases prevalent in the West has replaced infectious diseases as the major killers. The study of almost 170,000 Chinese men and women over 40 years old showed that the cause of deaths of about 75% of the 20,033 individuals during the research period was heart disease, cancer, or stroke, findings based on medical data collected in 1991 with follow -up assessments in 1999 and 2000. The study, published in the September 15, 2005 issue of the New England Journal of Medicine, also showed that of the deaths of individuals between the 40s to mid -60s, Chinese mortality rates from each of the three diseases were higher than for individuals of similar ages in the U.S. According to lead co-author Jiang He of Tulane University's Department of Epidemiology in New Orleans " We are very surprised by this finding ' This study indicates that chronic disease is not only (the) leading cause of death in wealthy countries, but also (in) developing countries, such as China. " The findings also echoed the observations Robert Beaglehole, the WHO's director of chronic diseases, on China's health scene, that " I think it's probably exactly what it was like in the United States a couple decades ago. " He added, " ...When it was apparent that young people in the prime of their lives were dropping down dead from heart attacks (in the U.S.), it drew attention to the problem which had sort of a human impact as well as an economic impact ". Experts concur that China's health transition, measured, is in harmony with its growing economic prosperity, with more peoples moving from the farms into cities, physical activity lessening, eating habits, worsening, and smoking rising. Do these facts not call for urgent action to disseminate health information, in the most efficient and cost-effective way to reverse the trends associated with these risk factors for the prevalent diseases mentioned above? Indeed, the study also showed that more deaths occurred from the top three chronic diseases in China's rural areas than in cities, which suggest that these issues are not restricted to the cities, which in turn suggests the need for developing health promotion and disease prevention programs, for these different populations. This underscores the need for the country to embrace the concept of healthcare ICT-enabled, targeted, and contextualized health information dissemination, which would cater for the specific health information needs of the populations to which we target the materials. The project would also utilize and build on the existing healthcare ICT infrastructures that each targeted population has. As Beaglehole also noted, China should in fact also focus on strategies aimed at tackling both these chronic diseases and the high-profile infectious diseases like AIDS and bird flu that also pose major health hazards to its peoples, which again would benefit from the deployment of the appropriate healthcare ICT. These technologies could actually assist the countries in achieving the right balance between the two, which is crucial to resource optimization, hence costs savings. The study also found that Chinese men are a little more at risk than women are, with 68.7% of male participants dying from the top three diseases versus 62.6% of females. There is no doubt that these diseases are preventable, and in order of their contributions to deaths, high blood pressure is the most preventable, followed by cigarette smoking, and physical inactivity and being underweight. Lung cancer caused the highest number of deaths, with 63% of the men interviewed being smokers. Along with the prevention, programs though must be efforts made to diagnose these conditions promptly, and to treat them effectively, including limiting their chances of long-term sequelae or managing these effectively. In other words, it is increasingly imperative in China to embrace technologies that heuristically would enable seamless transition from one to the next in a series of measures characteristic of the disease prevention paradigm. In short, we need healthcare ICT that would integrate seamlessly our primary, secondary, and tertiary prevention efforts, making it at once possible to deliver qualitative health services in these different domains, and to do so cost-effectively and efficiently. It is clear form the foregoing that the process cycle analyses mentioned above would help in revealing aspects of health services delivery in the country that need attention, and the most appropriate healthcare ICT solution to rectify the problems identified. The concept of "hospitals on wheels", for example, is an attempt by China to address the health issues in rural and remote areas. The central government in 2004 equipped counties in central and western China with 1,004 coaches to provide door-to-door health care for farmers, the amount that the National Development and Reform Commission and the Ministry of Health have invested in the program, 230 million yuan (US$27.7 million)13. The coaches are for common disease diagnosis, small operations, health check-ups, and health education for the farmers, who live in rural locations and hitherto had limited access to health services. County-level hospitals will use the vehicles to conduct medical check-ups related to AIDS and other contagious diseases, supervised by provincial governments. Many consider this development a shift in emphasis toward more focus on healthcare delivery to persons living in rural and remote areas. Does it also signal interest in investing in tele-health technologies, which would serve the same purposes as efficiently if not even more, and more cost-effectively? Local officials and residents cautiously welcome the "hospitals on wheels" concept, Xiong Guanglin, the mayor of the city of Bazhong in Southwest China's Sichuan Province, for example, lamented the previously low investments in the health sectors in western rural areas. In his city, over 90% of women in urban areas give birth in hospital, an equal percentage of babies delivered at home in rural areas. According to Xiong, 70% of the country's residents living in rural areas receive only 30% of its resources in the health and Medicare domains. In fact, farmers pay their medical bills in some poor parts of China, which because they could hardly afford, most ignore, which further worsens their health, and because they are unable to farm, makes them even poorer. Government plans to stop this vicious cycle via the new scheme, the central government reportedly allotting 10 yuan (US$1.2) yearly to every rural resident in central and western China since 2003, to help them enroll in a new medical insurance scheme. Reportedly, the plan would also collect 10 yuan (US$1.2) for each rural resident from local governments and the same amount from each rural resident. It is likely that we would continue to see new government programs aimed at improving access to health services in the rural and remote areas where a significant proportion of the Chinese population reside. This would likely create substantial market openings for healthcare technologies including tele-health technologies. There would also likely be increased investments in synchronizing health services delivery at the three prevention levels mentioned earlier. With the magnitude of its population, more emphasis ought to be on primary disease prevention efforts rather than wait for diseases to develop before doing something about them, which latter, even despite the country's increasing prosperity is far more expensive to achieve than the former. Furthermore, as noted with the vicious cycle of disease and poverty mentioned earlier regarding rural dwellers, the link between economic prosperity and health is universal, and without the right attention paid to the health, and in particular to the achievement of the dual healthcare delivery objectives mentioned earlier, the prospects of the country's economy being compromised is anything but bleak. China does not lack the technical expertise to initiate a massive healthcare ICT diffusion effort. Its computer giant Lenovo Group, which has a third of market share, recently announced its plans to further expand its position in China by creating new market demand and building brands[14]. With the capacity to respond to customers' service demands in two hours and solve problems within 24 to 48 hours in over 1,250 cities in China, 365 days a year, it is the first computer firm to offer this service level of service and coverage in China, and well placed to be actively involved in the country's "healthcare ICT revolution". In an interview on June 27, 2006, Chen Shaopeng, senior vice-president of Lenovo and president of Lenovo China, noted that the firm would also visit 100,000 customers to assess demands and help solve problems with their Lenovo computers. Perhaps he was right in also observing the influence the ongoing computer price wars would have on the company, as it might simply not be enough for the firm to add services to its value proposition, if its sales started to drop because other firms are pricing it out of the market. In other words, with the increasing prosperity of China would be more discerning clientele who would be just as perceptive with pricing as they would with service offerings. Furthermore, the markets that Lenovo appears to be targeting, consumers in smaller towns, rural areas, and elderly customers, since for example, about 80% of families in Beijing had a computer at the end of 2004, but in nearby Inner Mongolia Autonomous Region, less than 20% did, according to the National Bureau of Statistics are not likely exactly rich. The prospects of Lenovo spreading its reach successfully, to the smaller cities and rural regions, which no doubt have massive markets, would therefore likely play out on the pricing plate. With experts predicting growth in computer ship ments in China to 30 million units in 2008, from 20 million units in 2005, and the demand for consumer and enterprise computer technology products in the fourth- and fifth-layer markets, primarily counties, soaring, market opportunities even for foreign firms, particularly those with the right product/service mix, are simply immense. Lenovo is no doubt strong in the service arena, with over 2,000 stores, 600 service centers, and 57,000 engineers in 1,250 cities, which significantly raise entry level in this domain, in particular for foreign competitors. Dell is a strong competitor in China, and it plans to offer consumers wider product options. For example, it is establishing a partnership with its partner, Intel's competitor AMD, from which it would also source microprocessors, with a view to offering cheaper computers, but Lenovo has been collaborating with AMD since 2004, debuting computers at 2,999 yuan (US$375), a successful alliance resulting in 80% of Lenovo's consumer computers using AMD's processors in 2005. Even then, Dell's partnership with AMD is enabling the former to offer lower-priced products to consumers in smaller cities or rural regions. It is also attracting enterprise clients as demand increases for relatively inexpensive AMD's processors that support 64-bit processing technology and dual-core processors. There is no doubt that the price war is on, a scenario that when the dust settles, literally, would likely foster healthcare ICT diffusion in China's countryside, a key requirement for its full entry into the coveted e-health age. With more of its peoples not just owning computers but also knowing how to use them, it would be far easier for the country to initiate healthcare ICT-enabled programs at the different disease prevention levels nationwide. It would also be much easier for example, to have countrywide electronic health records systems, which would offer real-time access to valuable patient information at the point of care (POC). With the potential of such real-time access to reduce morbidities and mortalities, hence save costs, China would finally be able to realize its dual healthcare delivery goals, comprehensively. The achievement of these goals, as our discussion so far indicates, is the accrual of a variety of health and non-health processes derived from pertinent issues relating to healthcare delivery in particular locales, facilitated/modified by healthcare ICT-enabled targeted and contextualized initiatives. Thus, even though the exercise, that is the process cycle analysis, which encompasses these efforts, might be long and complicated, there is no doubt that its results are worthwhile. The projected annual growth rate of China's software industry, 30% between 2006 and 2010, and worth, 1.3 trillion yuan (US$162.5 billion) by 2010, which Ding Wenwu, deputy director of the electronics and information technology products department at the Ministry of

Information Industry (MII), made at the 10th China International Software Exposition on June 01, 2006, are impressive. He also noted that software exports would be up to US$12.5 billion by 2010, thrice those of 2005, US$3.59 billion 15. Considered "the core of the information technology (IT) industry," and "of strategic importance to the enhancement of our national strength and innovative capability," according to Ding, it is little surprise that the industry is making remarkable progress in China, worth 390 billion yuan (US$48.75 billion) in 2005, versus 44.05 billion yuan (US$5.5 billion) in 2000. Ding admitted though that the industry lags behind its counterparts in developed countries, and in meeting the country s demands of social and economic development, crucial aspects of its role in the healthcare industry, which underscores the need for not just healthcare ICT, but ICT diffusion in general as a priority in China in the next few years. As we noted earlier, it is not in the country s best interests for its economic progress to outpace its health status, as the deficiencies in the latter would in time, likely be detrimental to progress in the former. The MII s Vice-Minister, Lou Qinjian, indicated on May 31, 2006 the imminent release to the public of a special policy to boost the development of the software and integrated circuit industry, drafted by the MII, and submitted to the State Council. He added that the MII would take tangible steps to buttress the country s software industry via measures such as establishing venture capital groups or government procurement. Progress in the software would no doubt spill over into the healthcare industry. As previously noted, the markets for healthcare ICT including software is huge in China, and growing, its workers numbering 900,000 in 2005, projected to be about 2.5 million by 2010. Intellectual property rights (IPR) protection would improve the overall software industry milieu and further increase market demand. Measures such as announced in April 2006, by the MII and the National Copyright Administration mandating all PCs produced and sold in China to have authentic operating software systems installed, would no doubt stimulate demand, and improve the revenues of software firms. Indeed, four Chinese software firms namely, Huawei, Haier, ZTE and UTStarcom reporting sales revenues of more than 5 billion yuan (US$625 million), twenty-six, above 1 billion yuan (US$125 million), the latest rankings showed. There is of course enough room in the healthcare ICT industry for foreign firms to compete. Cisco Systems, Inc., which made US$ 24.8 billion, and US$ 5.74 billion in total sales and profits, respectively, in FY2005, for example was recently in China looking for partners with risk investment of US$200 million[16]. The firm had earlier given investment of US$300 million to over 30 firms with innovated capacity in China, interested in the role of supp lying platform in the country, its business growth highest in Western China, although its presence noticeable in the other three regions, namely, Eastern, Southern, and Central China, its profile growing in fact in all four regions. Foreign software and healthcare ICT firms must, however, expect stiff competition in China, which plans to increase the number of software export bases to 15 by 2010, up from its current six software export bases, in Beijing, Shanghai, Tianjin, Dalian in Liaoning Province, Shenzhen in Guangdong Province, and Xi'an, of Shaanxi Province. This move aims to enhance the software export and outsourcing industry, as Yi Xiaozhun, vice-minister of commerce recently noted [17]. According to Yi, "Exports of software and information services will play a leading role in the service sector in China, "whose service trade in 2005 was worth US$158.2 billion, 10.9% of total trade, which was much less than the world average, 19%. This underscores the reason for this move by the Chinese government, which wants to increase service trade turnover to US$400 billion by 2010, and with the increasing focus on exports would likely be an increase in domestic market openings. As noted earlier the MII's projection for software exports would triple in five years from 2005, software outsourcing, according to Li, "a shortcut that will allow the Chinese software industry to catch up with developed countries." China's software outsourcing industry would, however, be competing with those in other Asian countries such as India, the Philippines, and Vietnam, and in East European countries. Developments within and outside China would increase the influence on its ICT industry in general. In May 2006, AsiaInfo Holdings, Inc., a key telecom software solutions and security prod ucts and services provider in China, announced it signed contracts with China Mobile to construct network support management systems for the latter's headquarters and six of its provincial subsidiaries including Guangdong, Sichuan, Guizhou, Jiangxi, Shanghai and Shandong18. This new application in AsiaInfo's AIOpenXpert network-management product suite, featuring a data collection and management platform, comprehensive business monitoring, report management, and flawless integration with the BOSS disaster tolerance system, would enable China Mobile to monitor system operations in real time and enhance operating efficiency. The system would also help in forecasting business development trends and potential problems to facilitate extension and fine-tuning of the network and business support system beforehand. The Asia-Pacific Development Information Program is also giving China technical assistance in the preparation of a comprehensive and integrated national e-strategy, especially to foster intersectoral involvement in the development and application of ICT. There is no doubt that healthcare ICT would gain increasing prominence in the ICT sector in China in the coming years, with market expansion also likely to continue apace.

References

1. Report on the Work of the Government delivered by Premier Wen Jiabao at the Third Session of the 10th National People's Congress on March 5, 2005.: Available at:

http://www.chinability.com/2005%20government%20work%20report.htm

Accessed on July 01, 2006

2. Asian Development Outlook, 2006 Available at:

http://www.adb.org/Documents/Books/ADO/2006/documents/ado2006.pdf

Accessed on July 01, 2006

3. Available at:

http://english.people.com.cn/english/200010/16/eng20001016_52747.html

Accessed on July 2, 2006

4. Available at: http://www1.cei.gov.cn/ce/doc/ceng/200606012378.htm

Accessed on July 2, 2006

5. Available at: http://www1.cei.gov.cn/ce/doc/ceng/200603275352.htm
Accessed on July 2, 2006

6. Available at: http://www1.cei.gov.cn/ce/doc/ceng/200603202878.htm
Accessed on July 2, 2006

7. Available at: http://www1.cei.gov.cn/ce/doc/ceng/200603202877.htm
Accessed on July 2, 2006

8. Available at: http://www1.cei.gov.cn/ce/doc/ceng/200511230887.htm
Accessed on July 2, 2006

9. Available at: http://www1.cei.gov.cn/ce/doc/ceng/200509141469.htm
Accessed on July 2, 2006

10. Available at: http://www1.cei.gov.cn/ce/doc/ceng/200605081011.htm
Accessed on July 2, 2006

11. available at: http://www1.cei.gov.cn/ce/doc/ceng/200510273580.htm
Accessed on July 2, 2006

12. Available at: http://www1.cei.gov.cn/ce/doc/ceng/200509161215.htm
Accessed on July 2, 2006

13. Available at: http://www1.cei.gov.cn/ce/doc/ceng/200408028555.htm
Accessed on July 2, 2006

14. Available at: http://www1.cei.gov.cn/ce/doc/cenl/200606283052.htm
Accessed on July 2, 2006

15. Available at: http://www1.cei.gov.cn/ce/doc/cenl/200606021668.htm
Accessed on July 2, 2006

16. Available at: http://www1.cei.gov.cn/ce/doc/cenl/200606231467.htm
Accessed on July 2, 2006

17. Available at: http://www1.cei.gov.cn/ce/doc/cenl/200606222596.htm
Accessed on July 2, 2006

18. Available at: http://www1.cei.gov.cn/ce/doc/cenl/200605111472.htm
Accessed on July 2, 2006

Healthcare ICT Markets in East Asian Countries

Internet penetration in the Republic of Korea also called South Korea, is 51%,

the highest in Asia, the country's broadband Internet access penetration the highest worldwide, despite not being one of the world's most developed nations, on a GDP per capita basis, although its economy is the 4th largest in Asia in currency terms. The Korean government has deliberate policies aimed at promoting ICT diffusion, for examples providing all elementary and secondary schools with free Internet access, encouraging computer literacy among all its citizens, even those in rural areas, about a fifth of the population, and offering low-interest loans to firms providing broadband access, among others. This pervasive ICT penetration creates the enabling milieu for the use of these technologies in the delivery of qualitative and cost-effective health services. It also promises significant market opportunities for ICT firms both local and foreign in a vigorously market-oriented economy. Indeed, many contend that among the factors that stimulated the rapid broadband growth in the country was such competition among operators that peaked six years ago with the introduction of DSL access to compete with the then prevalent cable TV broadband access, the result; low broadband access prices, some of the least globally. Furthermore, by allowing its Ministry of Information to keep all income made from regulatory activities such as license fees, which it utilizes to fund ICT diffusion and related government p rojects, the country ensures that these technologies continue to be more widely available. In 1994, Korea had less than a million Internet users, the penetration rate, just 1.6%. However, its high subscription levels to non-Internet online services even then, due to the dearth of Korean content on the Internet, formed the nucleus of the later-explosive shift to Internet services as content in Korean became ubiquitous. Furthermore, with the launching of broadband access in July 1998 came Internet access, the number of subscribers soaring to ten million by the end of 2002. The increase continued over the years as virtually all services requiring broadband access such as games, which was and continues to be very popular in Korea, audio and video streaming, and e-commerce were only obtainable via the Internet. The country s dense urban geography also makes broadband access uncomplicated. Since the launch of Thrunet s cable modem services in July 1998, and of Hanaro Telecom with the advent of local loop competition in April 1999, the broadband market explosion has continued essentially unabated. Even Korean Telecom, the erstwhile dominant market force, which was reluctant initially to invest in and enter the ADSL market, preferring to stick with ISDN, did finally in June 1999, as did many other operators. The increased competition has created not just options, but lowered pricing for Koreans, which has resulted in the country s enviable Internet penetration rates, with the potential for the use of these technologies not just facilitating health service provision, but also shaping it. The former, a key traditional benefit of these technologies, the latter their constitutive effects are both critical that the country embraces increasingly, in order to maximize their equally and if not more important, additional transformational potential. Considering that, Koreans have a number of broadband -access options, for examples, ADSL, cable TV, local area networks (LAN,) broadband wireless local loop (WLL), and of course, satellite, the opportunities for health services provision via these technologies seem vast, particularly with some of the lowest broadband prices, often flat rate and uniform and most generous bandwidths, globally. It makes no sense to hook up to the internet via dial-up connectivity in Korea any more due to the telephone charges that come with it, which becomes uneconomical to pay overall with broadband connectivity. There is no doubt that the evolution of broadband technology has created immense opportunities for improving the country's society in many ways including its health, and by opening up opportunities for qualitative and cost-effective health services provision, among its other benefits for example, in e-commerce, its economy overall. However, not only broadband technologies that are changing in profound ways, Korean society, and that would , in the near future, its health services. Other ICT, for example, mobile communications technologies, are playing decisive roles in the country too. In fact, the technologies that would enable seamless mobile and scalable real-time and anywhere networking, are going to feature more prominently in health services delivery in Korea, and indeed, in many countries in East Asia. Korea did not adopt digital service fast enough, relative to some other Asian countries, it went the way of the CDMA standard, and not the more widely used GSM.8, when it eventually did, yet its mobile penetration still ranks quite high, with more mobile phone users than fixed-line users as far back as 1999, beating many Asian countries to it. With a population of 48,846,823, according to the United States Census International Programs Center 2006 estimates, one of the most homogeneous countries linguistically, and densest in population in the world, Korea has a relatively large market suited to scale economies and a liberal economic atmosphere, albeit with more reform efforts required, conducive to investments. Because it also has a high literacy rate, including computer literacy, the country offers remarkable market opportunities in the ICT industry, including healthcare ICT. Its economy, the 12th-largest worldwide, continues to grow, its Per capita GNP, just $100 in 1963, over $12,000 in 2003, its Gross Domestic Product (GDP) growth rate, 3.1% in 2003, and 60% services-based (2003,) economic performance in 2004 billed to improve to almost 5.0%, even if based mostly on energetic exports. The country's large ICT equipment industry with notable names such as Samsung and LG reflect this export orientation, which besides its reputation for producing ICT at rational costs, has buoyed local manufacturers, and improved the quality of their products, a major competitive factor for foreign firms planning on exploiting the healthcare ICT market in Korea. The market, however remains, on the other hand, wide open considering the country's continued emphasis on exports. Its large ICT equipment-manufacturing base regardless, foreign firms could aim to collaborate with local firms, and the country still promotes open and competitive ICT-projects tenders. There have been concerns lately about the country's economic growth potential slowing because of increasingly noticeable structural problems and rapid population aging. Inflexible labor laws, immature financial markets, accountability issues, stalled economic reforms, and the shift of corporate investments, to countries such as China, with cheaper labor, are also some of the reasons for this concern. These issues are bound to influence healthcare ICT investments in the country also. The country's health insurance system, with universal health insurance coverage since the late 1980s, funded with money the insured, employers, and government contributed , also utilizes healthcare ICT to a remarkable extent, for example in payment processing. Two strategic policies, Health Vision 2010 and Welfare Vision 2010, guide the country's health systems development, and the Ministry of Health and Welfare's Health Care Development Plan for the C21st, focuses on four major areas, namely, setting up lifetime health maintenance and an efficient healthcare delivery system. Others are promoting the growth of the health care industry and health legislation/administrative reforms in order to improve the social welfare system 1. There is no doubt therefore, about the country's intention to improve its health services, and equally none that it has not just the technological base to exploit the immense benefits of healthcare ICT in facilitating the achievement of these objectives, but in doing so efficiently and cost effectively. Nonetheless, there is substantial room for foreign healthcare ICT vendors and operators in Korea. The fact is that despite its technology base, Korea is yet to maximize the opportunities that healthcare ICT offers in achieving its healthcare delivery goals. As with other countries in East Asia, and indeed in other countries of the world, increasing healthcare cost is a major challenge, and one that along with improving the quality of healthcare delivery, the appropriate deployment of healthcare ICT could in fact help overcome. Healthcare ICT diffusion and utilization in Korea do not reflect the pervasive and increasingly sophisticated penetration of information technologies, mentioned earlier, the cause: legal constraints, for example laws that forbid non-face-to-face consultations. Defective management also plagued some earlier healthcare ICT projects, rendering them effectively flawed, not to mention a lack of national healthcare ICT policy orientation. The country implemented its first telemedicine project as far back as 1994, in collaboration with the Korea Information Infrastructure (KII) initiative, with a number of pilot projects involving intersectoral public/private sector partnerships since then. The goal, to deliver qualitative health services via healthcare ICT to the country's peoples living in remote, inaccessible, and rural locales, and to offer ambulatory/domiciliary services to dementia patients. The projects have faulted for a variety of reasons including non-cooperation by doctors and some users' inability to afford the services, not covered in the national health insurance scheme2. There is however, progress in the country's efforts to improve healthcare delivery using information technologies both in the medical and non-medical domains. Developments in the health field, for example, changing disease patterns and progress in their prevention and treatment are key determinants of not just the country's emerging health reform policies, but also the nature and extent of future healthcare ICT investments. Chronic diseases for example are increasingly prevalent in the country, with resultant increasing focus on not just their treatment but also their prevention, which healthcare ICT, appropriately implemented could facilitate. The Korean government also plans to institute a comprehensive community health care system, the implementation of the programs under which no doubt would require significant healthcare input. Indeed, the status of the country's health industry has direct association with progress in public health and improved quality of life, albeit with, by extension, economic growth and sustainable development and its information-intensive, knowledge-based, and value-added nature, implies it would benefit from health information technologies, which are indeed, capable of enabling, facilitating, and shaping its future. It is little wonder then that the Korean government plans to establish a "Bio Health Technopolis" at Osong in Chungcheongbuk-do Province, in its southwest by 2006.

With improvements in the country's socioeconomic structures and lifestyles, and in health and medical care, have been changes in its mortality patterns, chronic non-communicable diseases now more prevalent than acute and communicable diseases, the prevalence of the former increasing as the population ages, more persons having chronic degenerative diseases. These developments have profound influence on the country's health policies, and resource allocation and utilization, with more emphasis on supplementing treatment-focused health care policies with those focused on disease prevention and health promotion. This shift clearly points in the direction of the future of healthcare ICT investments in Korea, considering the significant roles that these technologies play in the cost-effective and efficient delivery of the health programs aimed at achieving these preventative health services goals. With the level of broadband and Internet penetration in the country, delivering qualitative multimedia healthcare content for example, aimed at primary prevention is likely to speed up in the years ahead. As noted earlier, it is not sufficient for the country, or any other for that matter to have extensive internet penetration, at least in regard health services delivery. It is just as important, if not more so, for example, for the end user, say healthcare providers to embrace and use these technologies. In other words, besides the potentially large scope for content provision in realizing primary prevention projects, an aspect of healthcare ICT utilization in secondary p revention that would create business opportunities for both local and foreign, for example, European firms is change management, and in relation to human resources, business process outsourcing (HR BPO). In fact, business opportunities in the healthcare ICT industry in Korea would be eclectic, ranging from technical to service provision, as the country intensifies its utilization of healthcare ICT in achieving the dual healthcare delivery objectives of delivering qualitative health services to its peoples w hile simultaneously and in fact reducing health spending. To buttress the point about the country's drive to improve health service provision, and paradoxically, its need to achieve the dual health delivery objectives mentioned above, its health and social welfare expenditures have increased annually. The budget of the Ministry of Health and Welfare for 2004 was roughly, US$ 9.7 billion, 7.7% of the government entire budget, or an increase of 8.6% versus the year before. The country had 60,000 doctors for example in 2002, and in 2004, 95 881, along with 20 446 dentists, 54 381 pharmacists and 192 480 nurses, the country also now has more healthcare facilities. These increases are in keeping with the increasing sophistication of the healthcare delivery expectations of its peoples, which the increased living standards, widespread education and increased awareness of health issues, and longevity, and in fact universal health insurance, have engendered. The increasing suave results in increased demand not just of the country's health, but also its social security system, to cope with which, its current fundamental framework must necessarily adapt, in both content, and quality. Such adaptation would no doubt benefit from appropriate ICT input, for example implementing the necessary changes to the system's current supplier-focused approach. The Ministry of Health and Welfare principally administers social security schemes, for examples, the National Pensions Scheme (NPS), the National Health Insurance Scheme (NHIS), Public Assistance (livelihood protection, medical aid, veterans relief, disaster relief), and Social Welfare Services (for the disabled, seniors, children, women and the mentally handicapped). It is clear from the above that the country would no doubt continue to require significant ICT deployment in order to execute in the most cost-effective and efficient manner, many of the programs of each of these service areas, and indeed, of those of the 13 World Health Organization (WHO) collaborating centers in the country. Healthcare ICT plays a major role in health insurance claims in the country for example as noted earlier, in other words, also, ICT implementation in Korea would increasingly embrace both the medical and non-medical processes

231

involved in healthcare delivery, and indeed, all the activities carried out by the various functional service areas subsumed under the Health Ministry. It is important, therefore for European and other foreign firms interested in the Korean healthcare ICT markets to understand these processes and those that are of high priority in the country's efforts to improve healthcare delivery to its peoples. As also previously noted , emphasis is shifting from communicable to chronic, non-communicable diseases in the country, the recent establishment of the WHO Collaborating Centre for Cancer Registration, Prevention, and Early Detection at the Korea National Cancer Centre, testimony to the interest in fact, of international organizations in assisting Korea in addressing issues relating to this shift in orientation. Health promotion for example, is a key aspect of preventing these chronic noncommunicable diseases, strategic directions for which should include core functional areas such as capacity building involving health promotion leadership, infrastructure and financing, strategic partnerships for education, and governance, health communication and health promotion effectiveness. In April 2002, the Ministry of Health and Welfare publicized the Comprehensive Health Promotion Policy, with health goals, part of its Health Plan 2010. Consider the issue of nutrition in the country. While there is undernutrition in a small proportion of the deprived socioeconomic classes in the country, overnutrition is rife among persons with higher energy in takes and less physical activity, hence the need for a dichotomous approach to addressing this issue. The country has major plans to improve the nutritional status of the population including programs such as the revision and dissemination of dietary guidelines, putting in force mandatory nutrition labeling, offering nutrition services to vulnerable groups such as the elderly and children, and diffusion of science-based nutrition information, all of which would require significant healthcare ICT input in their implementation3. As technological progress now makes it possible for health information technologies to move beyond enabling action, to even shaping it, businesses with value propositions that include these capabilities, that is, for offering constitutive healthcare ICT and services would no doubt have a distinct competitive edge, in an already technologically advanced market. The recent invitation to South Korean companies to take advantage of Malaysia s Multimedia Super Corridor (MSC) as a regional centre for the location of their information and communications technology (ICT) operations, including research and development, contact centers, technical support centers and data centers, attests to the international recognition of their expertise4. Malaysia s Minister of International Trade and Industry Datuk Seri Rafidah Aziz, said on July 07, 2006, said at a seminar on "Business Opportunities in Malaysia" in Seoul, on the first leg of her nine-day trade and investment mission to South Korea and Japan , th at MSC since formed in 1996, has been the nucleus of an emerging knowledge-based economy. According to the Minster, "Currently, there are more than 1,500 companies with MSC status. This will ensure they get fiscal and non-fiscal incentives under the Bill of Guarantees. Exports of ICT-related products and services increased to US$730 million (RM2.7 billion) in 2005, with more than 40,000 high value-added jobs created . Incidentally, developments in the services sector, which the Minister said under the Ninth Malaysia Plan (9MP), will become a new source of growth, and which she said "(excluding government services) in Malaysia currently contributes about 50.3 per cent to Malaysia's gross domestic product" reflects the growing importance of the service sector in the country. However, this trend is not peculiar to Malaysia, as the service sector is also gaining prominence in Korea, where it contributes over two-thirds of the GDP. Another important aspect of the Korean market is that foreign firms would have to compete with the chaebols (conglomerates) in the domestic market, although the largest chaebols are still small by global standards, in sales terms for examples Hyundai Motors, less than 10% of General Motorss. Also important to the market is the fact that many non-health factors influence the country s health status, for example, its temperate climate with four characteristic seasons, with Typhoons usually between June and October, two to three of which, typically, directly or indirectly, affect the Korean peninsula annually. When typhoon Maemi for example hit the country s south-east on September 12, 2003, the death toll was 130 persons, with 4089 households and 10 975 persons affected, and property damage, KRW 4.7810 trillion (about US$ 4.1 billion). There is therefore likely to be an increase in the markets for a variety of health information technologies critical to disaster preparedness and response, for examples, surveillance technologies, and electronic health records systems for the provision of ready, real-time access to patient health information, among others. The country being an integral part of the global community would also need to tackle the problems with HIV/AIDS and bird flu that the rest of the world either confronts or potentially does, among some infectious diseases it still has to deal with. These health problems also underscore the likely increase in the market for surveillance and tracking technologies in the country, among others. South Korea will also continue to strengthen health promotion programs utilizing the National Health Promotion Fund, including as defined in the 1995 National Health Promotion Act, health education, disease prevention, improvements to nutrition, and encouragement of healthy lifestyles6. In keeping with this policy, it pursuant to this policy, In keeping with the goals of its health policy to improve the quality of life (QOL), and foster healthy life span the country would likely to continue to invest in healthcare ICT that would promote healthy lifestyles, and improve accessibility to preventive services. It would also likely continue to invest in efforts to improve its social environment including those that support healthy lifestyles, in which efforts, healthcare information technologies would no doubt play increasingly important roles. To be sure, nongovernmental entities would also be actively involved in these efforts, for examples, companies promoting health via healthcare ICT enabled, multimedia-content, targeted, health information dissemination, and periodic workplace health examinations. These firms therefore, also would create immense market opportunities for healthcare ICT vendors and operators to market value-added products and services. On the aggregate, the interactions real and potential, between European and Korean markets in the healthcare ICT sector are likely to be increasingly strong and mutually economically rewarding. The latter s focus on exports has and would continue to find markets in Europe, in the health sector for example, with electronics devices made by Samsung and other Korean companies garnering increasing market share worldwide. However, they face stiff competition from other and larger global firms, even from Asia, for example, Matsushita, the Japanese electronics firms that Samsu ng Electronics is only about 14% of its size. This export focus, some would argue also opens up its domestic markets to forays by foreign firms. Korea is an OECD country, and indeed, its economic growth has been so swift it advanced its per capita income to two-thirds of the OECD average[7]. Yet, the country needs to focus its fiscal policy on controlling expenditure considering in particular the increasing pressure of its budget due to population aging, and with its National Pension Scheme, which is not sustainable as it were, hence requiring urgent reform. These fiscal pressures are going to increase the country's interests in exploring options for reducing health spending, for example, while not compromising the quality of its health services provision, dual healthcare delivery goals that the implementation of the appropriate healthcare ICT could help achieve. There is likely to be an increasing focus on ambulatory/community/domiciliary health services provision to the elderly, and indeed, all chronically ill persons with the availability of increasingly sophisticated technologies for patient monitoring, market for which technologies would therefore likely increase, particularly with the population being in the main highly computer literate. There would also likely be an increase in the market for assistive technologies, a variety of adaptive and rehabilitative devices becoming more commonly used to help persons with disabilities and the elderly live independent, high quality lives, for examples telecare alarm systems such as fall detectors, text-telephone or TTY(Teletypewriter,) and speech recognition software. Korea needs to encourage competition even in its high-powered ICT industry as some secotrs such as health are lagging in the diffusion of these technologies, and rectifying this anomaly by strenthening competition in the service sector is crucial to the country's economic growth and sustainable development. The country also need to adopt an inclusion policy for the elderly and women, in the labor market, not least because of its rapidly aging population, which could significantly compromise its workforce by 2050. It needs to encourage seniors to stay on the job longer, but they need to be healthy in order to do that. This again, underscores not just the critical connection between health and economic performance, but in this particular instance, the need for Korea to implement more healthcare ICT in the provision of healthcare to its seniors, for efficiency and cost-effectivenss reasons among others. The Korean government has in fact increased subsidies to promote the employment of senior workers, and other groups, but it has to reduce employment subsidies too, and give more employees, currently only about 50%, coverage under the Employment Insurance System , the law in fact mandates coverage for 85%. It needs to expand the percentage of the unemployed receiving unemployment benefits, presently only 25%, and coverage of employment-based social insurance program s, including health and pensions, to non-regular workers. In other words, Korea needs to address the increasing dualism in its labor market, with non-regular workers, now almost a third of the country's workforce, which raises equitability issues and could compromise efficiency. By offering non-regular w orkers better social safety net and increasing employment flexibility for regular workers, the government would render employing non-regular workers cost-ineffective for firms, and foster labor market flexibility. These labor reforms are crucial to the country's future economic progress, the transition to which would be much easier were the government to couple its vision of labor laws revision with that of health reforms. In other words, for the government to appreciate for example, the important link betw een the two. For example, what would be the consequences on the country's overall health status for only a quarter of its unemployed to receive unemployment benefits, vis-à-vis the potential escalation in health spending that the minimal if at all even existent adverse selection in its health system notwithstanding, and in short, could this benefits-lack result in significant moral hazard, ex-ante, or post? On the contrary, how could providing this population unemployment benefits in tandem with healthcare ICT-enabled, targeted and contextualized health services influence these considerations? Finally, could the possibly significant healthcare costs savings that deploying healthcare ICT appropriately in addressing issues in health services not offset the costs of implementing the labor reforms mentioned earlier? These issues underscore the need for potential foreign healthcare ICT to understand the medical and non-medical issues at play in the future of the healthcare ICT market in the country, on the one hand, on the other, to decompose these issues in order to tease their underlying processes. Engaging in such a process cycle analysis would facilitate the determination of package of value propositions to secure the required competitive edge in the market.

Hong Kong, China is one of the two special administrative regions (SARs) of

the People's Republic of China (PRC). The other is Macau. A British colony from 1842 until handed over to the PRC in 1997, it retains a significant degree of autonomy, including its capitalist systema and way of life, guaranteed under Hong Kong Basic Law for fifty years after the transfer of sovereignty. Hong Kong has had a series of political and economic problems since 1997, including the precipitous fall in land prices shortly after the handover, events linked with the Asian finacial crisis, and the massive July 01, 1997 protest rally over proposed laws by its government threatening press and religoius freedom, among others, and over the appalling state of its economy. However, it also had major health problems, most notably the 2003 Severe Acute Respiratory Syndrome (SARS) outbreak, which adversely affected travel, and further worsened its economy and indeed, that of the entire region. Most of Hong Kong's 425 square miles is undeveloped, actually about 75%, and of its 7 million residents also live and work in high-rise buildings in the city and neighbouring locales. The country is monsoon-prone, with heavy winds and rain, and experiences typhoons occasionally. The economy is trade-and tourism -based, the combination of its geography, including its climate, and its population, which increasing life expectancy and immigration continue to increase despite its low -birth rate, and economy, an important factor in the nonmedical/medical intermix of variables that determine the direction of healthcare delivery in the country, including the nature and extent of its healthcare ICT markets. The service sector contributed 86.5% to its GDP in 2001, and it has advanced ICT systems[8]. Life expectancy at birth has been increasing in Hong Kong for more than thirty years, 78.54 years and 84.31 years among males and females, respectively in 2003[9]. As noted above, its population has been increasing, and indeed, aging steadily, in 2003, 11.69% aged 65 and above, versus 7.0% in 1983, and 9.3% in 1993, the elderly dependency ratio, 161 per 1000 population aged 15 to 64, compared to 102 in 1983, and 132 in 1993. Considered one of the four East Asian Tigers, the others being Singapore, Korea, and Taiwan, countries with hitherto relatively poor economies but that achieved phenomenal economic growth between the 1960s and 1990s via a combination of export-oriented economic development, minimized domestic consumption, a focus of widespread education, and egalitarianism. Although much less in the public eye with the remarkable performances of other Asian economies, they continue to do well in relative terms. For example, Hong Kong s Gross domestic product (GDP) grew in real terms during the decade to 2003, averagely at 3.23% yearly, Per capita GDP by 1.49% in money terms during the same period, up to US$ 23 000 (HK$ 179 300) in 2003, with impressive performance in 2004. Public health spending reached US$ 4.4 billion, or 12.35% of total public expenditure in FY 2003-2004₉. Hong Kong s health indices are indeed enviable globally infant and under-five rates, and maternal mortality rations constantly low. Major causes of death are chronic noncommunicable diseases, many of which as we discussed in the case of Korea, have increased as Hong Kong also became more affluent, and which are in fact, in the main preventable. In 2003, WHO figures indicate that the four chief killer diseases were malignant neoplasms (11 510 deaths), heart diseases (5309), pneumonia (3867) and cerebrovascular diseases (3462), accounting for about 66.3% of all deaths that year alone₉. While the incidence of preventable infectious diseases is low among children, due to widespread and effective immunizations, communicable diseases still pose major health hazards in Hong Kong. There were 5624 tuberculosis (TB) notifications in 2003, a 9.9% fall versus the previous year, notification rate 79 per 100 000 population, mainly because of population

239

aging and overcrowding, the cumulative total of cases of HIV infection, and AIDS, 2244 and 669, respectively in 2003. These figures indicate the importance of preventive health services in the territory, both for noncommunicable and communicable diseases. Indeed, the Government set up the Centre for Health Protection under the Department of Health on 1 June 2004. The goal was to attain effective prevention and control of diseases, working with local and international stakeholders. Again, as discussed earlier, the achievement of this goal requires a thorough appreciation of the various issues, both medical and nonmedical, involved. To appreciate these issues, it would be necessary to decompose them and expose the underlying issues and their processes. Some of these processes would need expunging, others modifying, and yet others facilitating, being wary of course, of any psychological fallacy, throughout the process cycle analyses. The idea is to change the processes in order to achieve the necessary stages that all eventually result in the attainment of the set goal. The processes that would emerge, in the medical domain, primarily for example, primarily because even these processes would themselves interplay with others that are not necessarily medical, say in, primary, secondary, and tertiary prevention, would no doubt be amenable to the necessary changes that the implementation of the appropriate healthcare ICT would help effect, successfully. The measure of such success would not merely be the achievement of the set goal, but also efficiently and cost-effectively, dimensions that themselves should be measurable benchmarks for the deployment of these technologies in the first place. It would therefore not be sufficient for Hong Kong s Department of health for example to want to institute disease surveillance, but it has to be able to do so expediently and nimbly. The utilization of the appropriate health information and communications technologies is capable of making these happen, the technologies in fact becoming " embedded " in the health system, deployed most fittingly, help ing to shape it in a quality improvement continuum. This is testimony to the heuristic value of the sort of process cycle exercise mentioned above, which itself assumes the perpetual imperfection of the territory's health system, or that of any other entity for that matter. Thus the territory in seeking ways to achieve one objective would likely end up achieving two, that is the dual healthcare delivery objectives mentioned earlier, possibly more. With the resources for healthcare provision limited, even in prosperous territories such as Hong Kong, it is only intuitive to adapt this process cycle approach to conceptualizing health service provision, the complexities involved in certain situations only going to make the outcome the desired. In the same vein, healthcare ICT vendors both local and foreign need to understand the markets they are interested in also using this or a different conceptual framework. The framework should nonetheless lead to the sort of decomposition/exposition cycle that only could exert the rigor imperative for the sort of continuous quality improvement exercises that would surmount the ongoing challenges any health system would inevitably face. In a milieu where besides the Hospital Authority, a statutory body that manages all public hospitals provides medical treatment and rehabilitation services to patients through outreach services, specialist clinics and public hospitals, 38 in 2003, and the goal of Government is the provision of reasonably-priced, and qualitative health services, the need for process analysis becomes even more acute. Not only is the onus on Government under these circumstances to ensure qualitative service provision, it must also do so in such a way that it would be able to continue so to do. Furthermore, in compliance with its pledge to ensure that none of its citizens lack healthcare due to lack of means, it must provide health services comparable to, and perhaps surpass those provided in the private sector that an individual could be missing otherwise, if he or she could not afford private healthcare. These considerations, coupled with its stated commitment to providing qualitative client-oriented health services make it imperative for government to explore ways to achieve the dual healthcare delivery objectives. In other words, were the authorities in Hong Kong to embrace the ideas we have been discussing, we could expect to see significant increases in its investments in healthcare ICT in the years ahead. With the remarkable improvement in health services, and possibly increased varieties of service-offerings that such investments would bring would also be increased healthcare ICT investments in the private health sector, at least among those practitioners that intend to avert the moribund fate their practices wou ld face, otherwise, and this is only the first stage. They would then have to compete with one another on at least initially an even keel, literally, with those that survived the first stage amply imbued with sophisticated healthcare information and communications technologies. The next stage would not only offer the residents of Hong Kong eclectic value added services, but also increasingly inexpensively. Regardless of the combination of public/private healthcare service provision that emerges from this unfolding dynamics, the aggregate effect would be positive on the territory's overall health status, and economic growth and sustainable development in the long term. Hong Kong has a well-developed ICT infrastructure, and with being connected to the Internet early, since 1991, low internet access prices, liberal economic policies, and the prominence of the banking and financial among other information intensive industries in the territory, it is hardly surprising that it has high internet penetration in both households and business sector. It became one of the earliest economies to launch broadband services in 1998, since when dial-up has given way to high-speed technologies for Internet connectivity, the territory just behind Korea globally in broadband Internet, and number three globally for second -generation mobile penetration[10]. In fact, Hong Kong has one of the most competitive mobile sector markets in the world. There were 4,878,713 Internet users in Hong Kong in 2005, 3,763,300 main telephone lines in use, and 8.214 million cell phones in Hong Kong in 2004[11]. Fifty percent of Hong Kong homes had personal computers (PC) in 2000, 71% in 2004, over 91% connected to the Internet in 2004, the increasing broadband connectivity a chief reason. There is relatively high Internet connectivity in the health sector in Hong Kong, although no official survey has measured its nature, extent, and usage, an exercise profusely conducted in other economic sectors[12]. The Department of Health (DoH) has conducted a number of H ealth Manpower Surveys (HMS) amongst healthcare professionals that practice in Hong Kong since 1980[13]. However, the survey, which aims to obtain current information on the characteristics and employment status of all healthcare personnel working in Hong Kong, for use in health labor planning, does not include questions on the availability of ICT in the health sector, nor the use of these technologies by healthcare professionals. However, the Hospital Authority (HA), which manages the territory s 43 hospitals and institutions, 45 specialist outpatient clinics and 74 general outpatient clinics, keeps some data on ICT[14], which reveals that all HA hospitals and institutions have Internet connectivity via a secured Demilitarized Zone (DMZ) network infrastructure in 2005. This dearth of information on ICT use in the health sector, even in a territory such as Hong Kong with advanced ICT infrastructure and extensive penetration is not surprising. Rather it typifies the well-known lag in the health industry, a very information-intensive industry, in the adoption of healthcare ICT, which by some estimates is as much as a decade compared to other similar industries, for example, the banking industry, which exists many countries, even the developed ones. There is no doubt that the territory could achieve much more in delivering qualitative and cost-effective health services to its peoples exploiting the potential to the fullest of its ICT infrastructure and the

243

extension diffusion of these technologies among its peoples. This underscores the point we made earlier about these technologies not merely being enablers but constitutive. However, it is important to apply them in the most productive manner in order to realize maximum benefits from these technologies. An approach for both local and foreign firms interested in doing business in the healthcare ICT that would create business opportunities would therefore be a thorough exploration of the various issues underlying, and that have the potential to foster or hinder governm ent's healthcare strategic objectives. Subsequent to this would they be able to be able to channel their innovative potentials toward appropriate value propositions in both the public and in the private health sectors. For examples, the overall health targets of the territory include, restructuring and enhancing health education and preventive programs, ensuring adequate provision of medical services to cater for a growing and ageing population, moving forward proposals for reforming the health care system, and developing and promoting the use of Chinese medicine[6]. It would be important to appreciate fully the issues involved in achieving these goals in order to be able to offer the most appropriate value-added technologies and services that would facilitate their realization. In other words, there is likely to be immense business opportunities in the years ahead in the healthcare sector in Honk Kong as it is in the best interests of the territory to harness the potential of the technologies that it already has in abundance the infrastructures for their operations, in delivering qualitative and cost-effective healthcare to its peoples. In fact, by not investing more in healthcare ICT in addressing the various issues in its health services both nonmedical and m edical, the territory would be attracting investments in another aspect of its economy, thus broadening its economic base, and accruing side-benefits including job creation, technology, and knowledge transfer, among others. In any case, with its increasing dependence on tourism, and considering the devastating effects of SARS in 2003 on its economy, it is only prudent that the territory takes the issue of healthcare ICT adoption, and not just providing every doctor with PC and Internet access, seriously. Considering the enormous numbers of visitors from mainland China, for example, would it not make sense for Hong Kong, to implement an advanced National Health Information Network and be able to communicate and share patients' health information not just among its healthcare professionals but also among those in China? Would this not enhance the prospects of qualitative healthcare delivery to Chinese tourists that fall ill while on a trip to Hong Kong? Furthermore, with the SARS outbreak exposing weaknesses in epidemiological surveillance and in the health care services preparedness to respond to SARS and other extremely contagious diseases, not just in Hong Kong, but in many countries, and with a potential avian flu pandemic, looming, is the need for even more effective epidemiological surveillance and health care services preparedness not imperative? With the relative minimal health impact of SARS creating a massive economic impact, 8,000 persons infected worldwide, some 800 dead, but according to Asian Development Bank (ADB) estimates the economic impact, around $18 billion in East Asia, roughly 0.6% of GDP, the answer would unarguably be affirmative[15].

Taipei, China, also known as the Republic of China (ROC), Chinese Taipei, or

Taiwan with a population of roughly six million individuals, has a buoyant economy that is expanding at the rate of 5% per annum, with practically full employment and low inflation. Its economy is export-oriented, almost fully industrial, the electronic sector, the most intensive, the country, a key global PC manufacturer and the world's largest PC monitors supplier. The U.S and Japan provide more than 40% of the country's imports, and along with Hong Kong, and China, the former the trade conduit between Taipei, China and mainland China, recipients of about 55% of its exports. Despite its buoyancy, confronted with the chances of continued relocation of labor-intensive industries to those countries where labor is less expensive, it has to improve the technology and service bases of its economy. In addition, the country is diversifying its trade markets, its exports to the U.S down as those to Southeast Asia and mainland China increase, and it continues to develop its European markets, which would likely grow over they years as the country further liberalizes trade and eases trade barriers that cosseted local industries from foreign competition. These factors would likely open up new markets for European healthcare ICT firms over the years, the extent, and nature of these markets determined by a varieties of factors, some manmade, others not. For example, on September 21, 1999, Chi-chi, Taiwan, China experienced an earthquake, which measured 7.6 on the Richter scale killing 2405, injuring 8664, its total economic impact, an estimated US\$ 9.2 billion, followed by a major aftershock, which measured 6.2 on September 26, and another earthquake, a 6.4, in the Chiayi area on October, 22[16]. There is no doubt about the health implications of such natural disasters, and the need to take measures to deal with them, both prior and subsequent to their occurrence, and of the crucial role that ICT could play in this regard. In other words, the country would need to continue to invest in the appropriate health information and communications technologies for d isaster preparedness and response in the coming years, hence a potential major market opening for both local and foreign firms, including those in Europe, where the country is vigorously seeking trade openings and trading partners, as noted above. There is no doubt that Taipei, China would continue to improve its preparation for natural disasters, and that this would create business opportunities in the healthcare ICT sector. Indeed, after the September 1999 earthquakes, part of updating the country's health emergency plans included the establishment of a Health Information Network covering public health workers. However, the country needs a nationwide health information system that would enable the seamless communication and sharing of patient information by healthcare professionals in the public and private health sectors, even routinely, in the absence of natural disasters. In fact, according to the WHO, in spite of the many natural disasters, which occur in East Asia, and elsewhere in Asia, the majority of disaster-prone countries have not revised their national health emergency contingency plans[16]. Countries, such as Taipei, China, need to move away from mere emergency response to emergency preparedness were they to limit the adversities that these disasters bring. This would no doubt require the country to invest more in healthcare ICT, which are crucial facilitators at every stage of the preparedness, and even response efforts to these natural disasters. Would having patients' health data and information in virtual storage accessible anywhere anytime for example not help in the continuity of treatment of for example, evacuees that might have sustained injuries or had ongoing health problems after a natural disaster, their health information held in irretrievable file cabinets due to loss to floods, fire, or other such catastrophic events? Does the continuing rural to urban population shift and the advent of mega-cities in such disaster - prone countries such as Taipei, China, not warrant proactive city-precise emergency preparedness, including the implementation of meteorological advance warning systems, surveillance systems, tracking systems, and electronic health records systems in a coordinated, intersectoral effort to minimize the consequences of the disaster? East Asian countries, including Taipei, China, would also need to confront the health issues that such rapid increase in urban population brings for examples, those relating to overcrowding and traffic congestion and environmental pollution, for examples respiratory diseases, which might affect negatively, its efforts to reduce the prevalence of and control communicable diseases. Taipei, China, continues to have major outbreaks of communicable diseases, for example, hand -foot-mouth disease (enterovirus 71) in 1998, with high case fatality amongst young children, and Dengue is still of major regional health concern. The surveillance of these and other communicable diseases is critical were responses to such outbreaks to be efficient, timely and cost-effective. This means Taipei, China would need to have implemented, appropriate healthcare ICT for data collection, analysis, and feedback. It would also need to avoid such problems as defective coordination among different surveillance programs in the country, which underscores the need for seamless data and information sharing via the availability and usage of the appropriate healthcare information and communications technologies, of course integrated nationwide with lab information systems. These latter would not just ensure accurate diagnosis but also for the information sharing at local and national levels crucial for effective surveillance. There would be need for technologies to track vaccinations, and logistics support, and a variety of other issues involved in preventing and managing communicable diseases. The above points to a few of the health issues that Taipei, China faces for which it would likely invest on healthcare ICT in the near future. It is important for not just the country, but also any European healthcare ICT organization or any such vendor elsewhere, including those within Taipei, China, to approach the efforts at ensuring the delivery of qualitative health services to the country's peoples by exploring the medical and indeed, the nonmed ical issues that it confronts as we have done thus far. It would make it possible to expose systemically, the underlying issues in healthcare delivery contextual to the country, and those interrelated with regional and global health issues and the processes that determine them, hence the technologies best suited to modify them. Antibiotic resistance for example, is not peculiar to Taipei, China, it is in fact a regional, issue, and it exists outside the region. In the first instance, the country would need to address the issue internally but would also need to collaborate with regional partners to deal with it at that level. It would therefore need tracking networks in the country to address the problem. However, it would also need to collaborate with for example, the Regional Network for Antimicrobial Resistance Monitoring established in 1991, which involves 14 focal laboratories in 13 countries and areas, namely Australia, Brunei Darussalam, China (2 laboratories), Fiji, Hong Kong (China), Japan, Malaysia, New Zealand, the Philippines, the Republic of Korea, Singapore, Tonga, and Viet Nam [17]. There is no doubt that the country would benefit from international technical expertise in dealing with some of these issues, including in capacity, in particular for the surveillance of communicable diseases and the investigation of disease outbreaks, and of course in the appropriate deployment of the right healthcare ICT in tackling the health and associated problems communicable diseases cause. Surveillance is the hub of all communicable disease control efforts, and the health information department in many countries typically handles this critical function, gathering information, chiefly in order to develop national policies, and to ensure that legacy systems, at local and national levels have the capacity for the intensive data management required for the exercise, and share information effectively. Taipei, China would therefore need to build capacities at both levels and ensure their effective communication. The country also needs to encourage the increased implementation and use of healthcare ICT in dealing with the issues that chronic, noncommunicable diseases pose. With many of such problems preventable, it would increasingly need to invest in technologies geared toward primary, secondary, and tertiary prevention efforts, in the years ahead.

The increasing liberalization of the Mongolian economy, another of the East

Asian countries, is attributable to its political reorientation towards democracy in recent times, although the overthrow in January 2006, of the democratically elected government would no doubt undermine progress in the direction the country s economy heads, which would doubtless influence healthcare delivery, and investments in healthcare ICT. This wou ld at be so regarding the political will and the financial wherewithal to implement the necessary health reforms that the country needs. A large country, with little arable land, and a significant nomadic population, roughly a third of its peoples clustered in and around the capital city, Ulaanbaatar, there are clearly logistics problems involved in healthcare deliver, among others. Mongolia s economy is mainly agriculture-based, including livestock, which constituted 20% of GDP in 2003. Others in 2003 were trade and services (28.8%), transport and communication (15.1%), manufacturing (6.0%) and mining (9.5%), accounting for roughly 75% of the country s exports. The country is landlocked, its population in 2003, 2 504 023, the adult literacy rate, 97.2%. Birth rate is falling, and life expectancy is averagely 66.63 years[18]. Unemployment in Mongolia rose to 6.7% during 2004, females,

55.2% of the total registered unemployed. Educational enrolment rates at all levels for school age girls are increasing, more than for school-age boys. Over 36% of its peoples are poor, that is, earn roughly less than S$ 20 per month per person, about 30% and 43% of urban and rural dwellers poor by this yardstick, respectively, and with its very ruthless winters, the country has significant, including health issues to address regarding poverty and homelessness. Each household averagely spends 5% of its consumption on healthcare according to the WHO Household Income and Expenditure Survey (HIES) 2002-2003, with richer spending thrice as much as the poor, spending on self-prescribed medicines, about 50% of total personal health spending, about 75% of the total health spending of the poor[18]. The non-poor have more health complaints than the poor do (7.4%/4.6%), more of who utilize health services than the poor (74%/63%). The inequality in income distribution in the country is thus spilling over into health services utilization, and indeed the health status of its peoples. Indeed, the other statistics mentioned above all have implications for health service provision in the country, including on the nature and extent of investments in healthcare ICT both in the public and private health sectors. What for example, would be the implications for service provision in a country with a significant nomadic/semi-nomadic population? Would there likely be need for extensive telehealth services under such circumstances? Would the relatively high and increasing literacy rate in the country facilitate the diffusion and use of healthcare ICT, in for example, primary prevention programs? How could such programs for example help reduce health spending on medicines particularly by the poor who could least afford to spend such a high percentage of their meager resources on healthcare? What are the likely market opportunities that the answers to these questions would engender? Several other factors, nonmedical, and medical, are important drivers of health services delivery of Mongolia, for example, the Mongolian Parliament's promulgation in 2002, of the Public Sector Management and Finance Act, with its implications for managing and financing all public sector services and institutions, including the Ministry of Health (MOH). The MOH for example now has direct say in the decision-making process for financial resources allocation to health care institutions and programs, which theoretically should facilitate policy formulation on and acquisition of the required healthcare ICT for the execution of its programs. The prevalence and patterns of diseases in the country also have major implications for service development and resource allocation. Communicable diseases pose major health hazards in the country, for example, Brucellosis, controlled in the 1980s, because of a successful vaccination program in animals is a re-emerging in the country, with a major economic impact on its agricultural sector. Would the country not need to explore the technologies that could help with reducing the prevalence of this and other communicable diseases, for example, healthcare ICT that it could deploy for surveillance and tracking purposes among others? The country also has to deal with chronic, noncommunicable diseases at the primary, secondary, and tertiary prevention levels, all of which healthcare information and communications technologies could in achieving, efficiently and cost-effectively. As earlier noted, the magnitude and nature of the healthcare ICT markets would be much clearer with a fuller understanding of these and other medical and nonmedical issues that the country faces, and the underlying processes that interlace to result in the desired outcome, the delivery of qualitative healthcare, efficiently and cost-effectively, to the peoples of Mongolia. The country is undergoing such momentous changes nowadays that make such analyses necessary. On the one hand, with many of the country's erstwhile nomads literally camped outside the capital city under less than ideal conditions, long, harsh winters having decimated their livelihoods, the migration city-ward unrelenting, and the living conditions in these city-edge shanties worsening, the health system needs to deal with the health problems typical of such milieus, foe example, communicable diseases. This, again, underscores the need for healthcare ICT-enabled programs aimed at addressing these diseases. On the other hand, the rich customs and nomadic traditions of Mongolia are proving to be strong incentives for tourists who are flocking to the country for these reasons in increasing numbers lately, in particular with festivities ongoing to mark 800 years of Mongolian statehood, garnering precious foreign exchange for the country. It is only fair that Government ploughs some of these funds back into improving the health and welfare of these nomads. Furthermore, the country needs to invest more in healthcare ICT in order to make health services delivery more efficient and cost-effective, with the additional expectations of its tourists regarding the accessibility and quality of health services in the country. The country's telecommunication network has 4,000 km of analog microwire and 30,000 km of openwire lines[19]. The country has 325 exchanges with network capacity for 100,000 telephone lines, an increase by 8.1% to 93,801 in the number of telephones. With an economy sensitive to world market prices and exports values, which if they fell for its major export products, cashmere, and copper, could result in government tax revenues falling, and budget deficits worsening, these could have adverse implications for resource availability to fund health programs. The country therefore, needs to initiate efforts toward achieving the dual healthcare delivery goals of qualitative health services provision, while simultaneously reducing health spending, a key approach being the implementation and use of the appropriate healthcare information and communications technologies in healthcare delivery. However, it has to develop further its telecommunications and other infrastructures in order for this to happen, embracing which idea would therefore create immense business opportunities in not just the ICT sector, but also in the applications of these technologies in the health sector. The country is keen to attract foreign investments, and has preferential tariffs with the U.S, European Union and Japanese markets for products of Mongolian origin in some industrial sectors, and with labor abundant, relatively well educated, and inexpensive, its economy increasingly liberalized, the investment climate, even for healthcare ICT products and services is favorable. In fact, investments in telecommunications networks, among other industrial sectors, are entitled to 10 years of complete tax exemption and a 50% tax exemption in the subsequent 5 years by law, the Foreign Investment Law and the Taxation Law [19]. The country has also removed 99% of imported goods tariff, hence has a zero-sum import tariff structure. These measures no doubt would influence investments in healthcare ICT by both local and foreign firms, and the government singly or in collaboration with these ICT operators and vendors, the future of these technologies in health services provision in the country. As noted earlier, the country's changing demographics would certainly influence its health status, and the future development of its health services, including its healthcare ICT industry. Consider for example the following findings of a report released on July 10, 2006 in Dublin by the Institute of Public Health in Ireland. The report noted the impact of the built environment on a number of health problems such as obesity, cardiovascular diseases, asthma, and psychological stress[20]. The report analyzed several international research publications that studied the health impact of building design and maintenance, and the association between health and open spaces, and the networks within the built environment. According to the report, children, the elderly, and persons living in disadvantaged socioeconomic circumstances are more vulnerable to the effects of the built environment. The report also observed that a variety of health problems could result form living poor quality housing facilities, where traffic density is high, and where there is or no access to quality green spaces, but also that a sustainable urban planning approach with active collaboration between planning and health professionals could avert these problems. This could also reduce the prevalence of cardiovascular disease, stress, and asthma. The report noted the abundant evidence to indicate that urban sprawl contributes to increased prevalence of obesity, with many people dependent on cars for transportation, commuting times increase, and there are fewer opportunities for physical exercises, and to increased social isolation. Owen Metcalfe, Associate Director of the Institute, said at the report s launching, "This report establishes the inextricable links between place and health, and shows that there is a need for dialogue and cooperation between public health professionals, planning professionals and policy makers when it comes to urban planning and design. Planning for public health involves much more than curative services ¯ it is about healthy human habitat and supportive social structures. We hope that this document will serve as a useful reference and create opportunities for dialogue that will lead to the creation of more sustainable communities, and a healthier society across the island of Ireland."

Indeed, it is a useful reference for all countries, including Mongolia, which, with the increasing migration of erstwhile nomad s to the cities, in particular the capital city, Ulaanbaatar, mentioned earlier, could end up with the health problems mentioned in the above report, in addition to those relating to communicable diseases that we mentioned earlier. The report also underscores the need for the sort of process cycle analysis mentioned above in order to understand fully the various factors at play in the success delivery of qualitative health services, factors that may be medical or nonmedical. Could such analyses and in-depth appreciation of these issues by healthcare ICT operators and vendors not help guide investments strategies for example, in Mongolia, by both local and foreign firms? Could they not also help government in policy formulation, not just in health, but also in rural/urban planning, and in allocating resources, including on healthcare ICT, in executing determined programs? Would this not likely yield the desired results of qualitative healthcare delivery efficiently and cost-effectively? Richard R. Jackson, Professor of Environmental

Health at the University of California, Berkeley School of Public Health, who delivered the keynote address at the launching of the Institute of Public Health report, mentioned the integrated approach to urban planning in the US that assisted in combating the spread of TB and Typhoid in the early C20th, in his address. According to Professor Jackson, "Business leaders, physicians, planners and architects worked together to overcome the poor living conditions that contributed to the spread of disease, improving sanitation, and by considering issues such as available sunlight and air quality. This could not have been achieved if they remained isolated in their specialities." This is precisely true. There is no gainsaying the necessity for intersectoral collaboration in tackling contemporary health issues. In fact, as we have repeatedly mentioned, the issues impinging on healthcare delivery are legion, and complex and arduous as it may sound, they need subjecting to process cycle analysis, which would reveal the further intricacies, some that have stealthily been or are potentially capable of compromising thus revealed, along with their processes. It would then be possible to modify these processes, jettison some, and speed up others, exercises that might be achievable using the appropriate healthcare ICT, which we would also be able to determine in the course of the analysis. Global economic competitiveness is going to define our world from now on. Prudence is going to be a maxim of the competitive ethos. With accountability also going to be, increasingly sine qua non for new and additional capital availability, at all levels, hospitals, local governments, health regions, health authorities, even national governments are going to have to justify their investments, including on healthcare ICT, a purpose such process analyses amply serves. Again, as Professor Jackson observed regarding this integrated intersectoral approach, urban design modifications, for example, could help identify and tackle the new generation of health problems, "American life spans have doubled since that time, from 40 to 80 years, yet only seven of those added years have come from medical care. The other 33 years have come from a Public Health approach that has seen imp rovements in housing and workplace environment. Similarly, we now face epidemics of chronic illnesses such as diabetes, obesity, depression, osteoporosis and cancer, which are devastating to the quality of life. Fundamental changes to our built environment are necessary to help combat these new epidemics." Mongolia would certainly also need to incorporate housing and environment improvement in its health reforms efforts, which as should be the case elsewhere, need to be ongoing. There is no doubt that these efforts would also influence its planning for investments in ICT infrastructure and the use of these technologies in healthcare delivery. Computer ownership per 100 residents in Mongolia is 1.64, telephone lines per 100 residents, Internet users per 100 residents, 1.23, telephone lines and subscribers per 100, 5.18, and 8.84, respectively[21]. It has 5.4% teledensity, digitalized networks, and a remarkable cellular growth, from 1800 users (1996) to 235,000 users (2002)[21]. Internet subscription has increased by 8% from 2002 figures. The ICT sector contributed 1.99% to the GDP 1.99% in 1995, 5.66% in 2000 and increasing, 6.3% in 2003, for example. Major Cable TV providers include "Hiimori", "Sansar", "SuperVision", "Manai Delgets", "Minii Mongol" based in Ulaanbaatar and several others in four other cities, over eighty thousand households with CATV in 2002. The country had two wireless TV operators in the same year. There were 2.4PCs per school in the country in 2002, its telecommunication basic network, 3100km analogue, and roughly 900km of digital microwave lines that same year, when there were also 7 ISPs, now six, offering dial-up access, email, web hosting, satellite, xDSL, and e-commerce applications and services, among others. Its total international Internet bandwidth was then about 10Mpbs. The country has an ICT Department within the Ministry of Infrastructure, and an Information and

Communications Technology Agency (ICT Agency). Its bandwidth is increasing, due to increased fiber optic access in China that ensued with collaborations between RailCom, TransTelecom, and China Unicom . These statistics point to improvements in the country s ICT infrastructure that augur well for the increasing deployment of these technologies in healthcare delivery in the country. Mergers and acquisitions are reshaping the Mongolian ICT landscape, for examples, those of NGOs, the Mongolian Information Development Association (MIDAS) and the Mongolian Information Technology Association (MONITA) and ISPs, Magicnet, and Bodicomputer. The proposed privatization of the Mongolian Telecommunications Company (MTC), and the membership of Mongolian ICT-based NGOs into the World Information Technology and Service Alliance and the Asian-Oceanian Computing Industry Organization, developments ushering a new era of the more active involvement of the country s ICT sector in the global stage, would also encourage foreign investments in its healthcare ICT sector[22]. Indeed, new mobile operators are in the country, which would increase further ICT cellular penetration facilitating, the development, and implementation of additional and novel, healthcare delivery programs in the country. Indeed, the country initiated a telehealth project connecting six locations in the country to a major Hospital, where experts review cases seen in these locations, including lab investigations and offer diagnosis and suggestions for treatment to doctors at the locations. This is just one example of the variety of ICT-enabled healthcare delivery programs that we would likely increasingly see in Mongolia. With its literacy levels relatively high, the prospects of the success of these programs are encouraging, as are those of the potential increase in business opportunities that the increase in such programs would engender for both local and foreign healthcare ICT vendors and operators in the country in the years ahead.

References

1. Available at: http://www.wpro.who.int/countries/05kor/health_situation.htm
Accessed on July 0, 2006

2. Briggs, J. Telemedicine and related technologies in South Korea, 2001

3. Available at: http://www.wpro.who.int/NR/rdonlyres/992473A8-DC95-441D-859B-07707E4A0C52/0/kor.pdf
Accessed on July 8, 2006

4. Available at:

http://www.btimes.com.my/Current_News/BT/Saturday/Corporate/
BT576209.txt /Article/
Accessed on July 8, 2006

5. Available at:

http://www.economist.com/countries/SouthKorea/profile.cfm?folder=Profile-
Economic%20Structure
Accessed on July 8, 2006

6. Available at:

http://www.wpro.who.int/countries/04kor/national_health_priorities.htm
Accessed on July 8, 2006

7. Available at:

http://www.oecd.org/document/18/0,2340,en_2649_34569_35428626_1_1_1_1,00.h
tml Accessed on July 8, 2006

8. Available at: Hong Kong Country Commercial Guide inc Macau 2004:
Economic Trends, Strategis, 24 July 2003. Accessed on July 08, 2006

9. Available at: http://www.wpro.who.int/countries/05hkg/
Accessed on July 08, 2006

10. Available at: http://www.itu.int/ITU-D/ict/cs/hongkong/
Accessed on July 9, 2006

11. Available at:

http://www.cia.gov/cia/publications/factbook/geos/hk.html#Comm
Accessed on July 10, 2006

12. Available at: http://www.itu.int/ITU-
D/ict/cs/hongkong2/material/HKG_CS.pdf
Accessed on July 9, 2006

13. Available at: See www.info.gov.hk/dh/health_new/background/index.htm
Accessed on July 9, 2006

14. Available at: www.ha.org.hk/

Accessed on July 9, 2006

15. Available at: http://www.wpro.who.int/NR/rdonlyres/E975F458-1CF4-4D5B-81AC-8612E03CC44D/0/DP4_ADB.pdf

Accessed on July 9, 2006

16. Available at: http://www.wpro.who.int/NR/rdonlyres/92D9464A-6BBC-426A-9963-AAFE442E009F/0/14_EHA.pdf

Accessed on July 9, 2006

17. Available at: http://www.wpro.who.int/NR/rdonlyres/572C5084-4ADB-4634-8E85-EE8993DA3E3D/0/05_CSR.pdf

Accessed on July 9, 2006

18. Available at: http://www.wpro.who.int/countries/05mog/

Accessed on July 9, 2006

19. Available at: http://www.un.int/mongolia/economy.htm

Accessed on July 10, 2006

20. Available at: http://www.publichealth.ie/index.asp?locID=160&docID=648

Accessed on July 11, 2006

21. Available at: http://www.apdip.net/projects/dig-rev/info/mn/ Accessed on

July 11, 2006

22. Available at: http://www.digital-review.org/05_Mongolia.htm Accessed on
July 12, 2006

The Euro-East Asia Healthcare ICT Markets Dyadic

Severe weather is one of the many natural disasters comm on to both Europe

and East Asia. Typhoon, Monsoons, and earthquakes hit many East Asian countries with noteworthy frequency. Harsh winters, overheated summers, excessive rains and floods, and in some parts, even earthquakes, are frequent occurrences in Europe. These events interruptions in water and power supplies, disruptions in communications, and in many cases large-scale evacuations of individuals to safer areas, including refugee camps, with families truncated, health services disrupted, yet a variety of health problems emerge due to unsanitary living conditions, among others. Disaster preparedness and response are therefore, major issues common to both Europe and East Asia. There disasters are not all natural, though, nor are they all due to severe weather if even so. We have seen in recent times the emergence of new microbes, viruses, causing epidemics, and potentially, even pandemics. We have seen novel bacteria, and the resistance of even known ones to treatment. There is also the threat of terrorism , local and imported, also common to both Europe and East Asia, with potentially devastating immediate, short-and long-term implications for health and health service provision. Both regions thus on the one hand, have many health and related issues in comm on yet have those that are contextual. They could therefore no doubt benefit from each other in many ways regarding addressing their healthcare delivery issues, including those concerning disaster preparedness and response. Many of these issues are uncomplicated and require measures that individual countries in each region could handle without outside help, but there are also many that require the involvement of international technical and other assistance. In general, the principles of disaster preparedness apply to all countries starting with a consideration of the needs of the family unit[1, 2], in particular those of children[3], who are even more vulnerable at these times. In the U.S, the Joint Commission Joint Commission on the Accreditation of Healthcare Organizations have stricter standards for hospitals' backup communications[4], hence many communities now have hospital-to-hospital radio communications using amateur or Ham radio operators via a local Metropolitan Medical Response System (MMRS)[5,6,7]. It is clear even from the above that healthcare ICT plays a major role in communication between relief personnel prior to and during disasters, and in several other aspects of disaster management such as surveillance and tracking activities, and indeed, in public health education. It is also important to recognize the overlap in many areas between preparedness and response, hence the need for efforts in both directions to be in tandem. Each country also needs to have a National Disaster Response Plan, all involved in its implementation trained well in advance in all its aspects, and there are valuable courses and manuals to help with such trainings[8, 9]. In short, countries in both regions need to invest in healthcare ICT to prepare for and respond to these disasters efficiently and effectively, both of which could

264

save many lives. Countries in the more advanced countries already have sophisticated communications infrastructure, yet many have had to depend on Amateur Radio Disaster Services (ARDS), when disasters essentially wiped out existing telecommunications avenues. This underscores the need for investments in these technologies, even in developed countries, in electronic health records and data management technologies that ensure data and information safety and accessibility, which would not only guarantee communications between emergency relief personnel, but also enable the sharing, in real time, of crucial patient information between healthcare professionals. The UK's National Health Service (NHS) has programs such as Connecting for Health in England . It also has the Informing Healthcare in Wales, and the National eHealth / IM&T Strategy in Scotland. Other European countries would also need to have such programs but in fact also a National Healthcare ICT Policy. Indeed, these technologies could help countries in both regions and elsewhere in the world achieve the dual healthcare delivery objectives of providing their peoples with qualitative health services while simultaneously reducing health spending. The decision on July 12, 2006 by German Chancellor Angela Merkel's cabinet to approve controversial reform plans aimed at shore up the country's beleaguered health system and reduce corporate tax rates, underscores some of the themes of our discussion on the importance of healthcare ICT in healthcare delivery[10]. Thus, it not only underscores the finiteness of resources allocable to health services in any country, and the need to reduce health spending while simultaneously delivering qualitative healthcare, but also the connection of health to the economy. The German health service costs an annual 144 billion euros (US$183 billion,) and health spending is increasing, population aging, and recent high unemployment, expected to rack up a shortfall in 2007 or roughly 7 billion euros. It is little wonder that Merkel's government plans to increase

265

healthcare charges by 0.5% from 2007 to help finance the pecuniary-challenged health service, a move unpopular among voters and that threaten the grand coalition government. The Government also plans to reduce, in its company tax reforms, corporate tax rates from a nominal 38.65% to 29.16% with effect from January 2008, both the health and tax reforms going to parliament later in 2006. The country's Finance Minister Peer Steinbrueck noted detailing the tax plan, that it would make Germany more attractive to invest in, and bolster its comparative advantage. Although the tax changes will cost the government more than 5 billion euros annually in the medium term, it seems overall that the benefits accruable from the plans, which include the introduction of a flat capital gains tax from January 2008, capital gains currently subject to personal income tax rates, particularly in preventing capital flight outweigh the costs. Indeed, Government plans to go ahead with the plans, despite protestations by Germany's eight industry associations, which cautiously welcomed the plan but released a joint statement recently indicating that tax burden would escalate with the plans in the investment phase. Government plans to use the extra tax revenues to help buoy service's financing, including healthcare delivery, in particular children's health. Government had earlier introduced a 3-percentage-point rise in the country's consumption tax to 19%, to which parliament concurred in June 2006, many of course piqued by this VAT increase, which they claimed would slow if not stagnate the country's economic recovery. The financial crunch facing Germany's health services is not peculiar to the country and neither are the prospects of healthcare ICT diffusion and the implementation and use of the appropriate health information technologies to address its issues resulting in the achievement of the dual healthcare delivery objectives mentioned earlier. The Bush administration in the U.S., for example, on July 11, 2006 projected that the elderly will confront another double-digit increase in their

Medicare premiums in 2007, leading to monthly payments of almost $100₁₁. The monthly premiums for supplementary medical insurance will increase from $88.50 to up to $98.40, or more, an 11.2% increase, projections, which if the presupposition underlying it that Congress would cut Medicare payment rates for doctors by about 4.7% in 2007, did not materialize could mean even higher insurance costs for seniors. According to Mark McClellan, administrator for the Centers for Medicare and Medicaid Services, the increased volume of care provided Medicare patients necessitate the higher premiums, as doctors are utilizing services more in providing these services, for examples, imaging, physiotherapy, lab tests, and prescription medications use, on the rise. What is more, a CMS fact-sheet released the same day noted, "Use of these services varies substantially across practices and geograp hic areas, with no clear impacts on health", and according to McClellan, "We can t keep pumping more money into a payment system that is not sustainable". How true, but what then is the answer? Does this not underline the need to seek ways to achieve the d ual healthcare delivery objectives? The premiums help support physician services and outpatient care (Medicare Part B,), which taxpayers also finance. Government programs fund the premiums of roughly 7 million of the poorest beneficiaries, ex-employers help some retirees, but most of the country s 43 million beneficiaries pay for themselves, and would also the increase in premiums. What are the chances of these increases compromising and perhaps eliminating the access to health services or at least some of them, by these senior citizens? Could we avert such situations by exploring credible ways to achieve the dual healthcare delivery objectives, specifically promoting healthcare ICT diffusion and utilization of these technologies, appropriately, in the execu tion of healthcare programs at the primary, secondary, and tertiary prevention levels? Do such measures not also apply to other countries including in Europe and East

Asia, and indeed, in the rest of the world? As Kirsten Sloan, national coordinator for health issues of the American Association of Retired persons (AARP) noted, we could reduce costs for seniors by reducing costs in the entire health care system via increased utilization of technology. She also noted that legislation aimed at making medical care paperless cut health spending, and indeed, medical errors, improving the quality of healthcare delivery and saving lives all at once. According to Sloan, "We're going on several years of repeated double-digit increases, and it's also roughly three times the rate of the Social Security (cost-of-living) increase" It puts a real squeeze, particularly on moderate-income seniors." The observation by McClellan that premiums for the new drug benefit have been lower than projected, the average premium projected a year ago to be roughly $37 a month, which fell to $24 a month as seniors and the disabled sought plans offering lower monthly premiums, attests to this squeeze.

Increasing healthcare costs no doubt put significant strain on the budgets of many countries, and influence their public finances. New Organization for Economic Co-operation and Development (OECD) data in fact confirms this for its member countries, many of which are in both regions under consideration. *OECD Health Data 2006,* an all-inclusive database of comparable health statistics in major developed countries, showed that health spending continues to increase in OECD countries and, if current trends persist, governments would have to increase taxes, slash spending in other sectors or make people pay more out of their own pockets in order to sustain their current healthcare systems[12]. The data indicated that health spending has grown more rapidly than GDP in all OECD countries apart from Finland between 1990 and 2004, accounting for 7% of GDP on average, in 1990, and 8.9% in 2004, an 8.8% increase from 2003. With many of these countries obtaining most of their health services funding via taxes, these developments are ominous for their peoples, particular the poor, this is more as projections indicate probable increases in health spending as a percentage of GDP even further because of expensive new medical technologies and population ageing. Again, we see the potential of healthcare ICT to cut costs without compromising care as they could obviate the need for many of these pricey technologies by strengthening aspects of health services delivery that do not require the use of costly technologies. In other words, by facilitating the prevention of diseases in the first place, or their treatment in ambulatory/domiciliary/community settings, rather than in hospitals, thus eliminating the often-substantial costs involved with the latter, yet not compromising care, healthcare ICT could help achieve the dual healthcare delivery objectives mentioned earlier. The public share of health spending is increasing in many countries in these regions, for examples in Korea, from 38% in 1990 to over 50% in 2004, the percentage of direct, out-of-pocket spending 37% in the same year, versus in Greece, 45%. On the average, p rivate insurance contributes only 6% of total health spending in OECD countries. Nonetheless, it is an important health-funding source for some individuals in some European countries such as Germany, the Netherlands, and in France, in which latter, it covers between 10% and 15% of total health spending, and is more prominent in payments for prescription medications rather than for hospital or ambulatory care, in many countries with publicly funded health systems. Money for more than 75% of drugs spending in several European countries in 2004, for examples, France, Germany, Austria, Sweden, and Spain came from public funds[12]. Regardless of where the funds come from, however, an ever-increasing health spending is unsustainable in any country be it in Europe or in East Asia, or indeed, in any country in the world. Furthermore, the higher a country's health budget, the more it compromises its ability to provide other important services to its peoples. What is more, that the country spends an increasing proportion of its economic resources on health does not necessarily translate into the provision of better health services. In fact, the reverse is sometimes the case[13]. Studies have also shown that investments in new medical technologies have led to increased and often unnecessary service utilization, which drives up costs[14]. The reasons for increased service utilization under these circumstances vary with health system, ranging from the absence at least in theory of adverse selection in publicly funded health systems, to that of Tort law reform in others, where healthcare professionals practice "Defensive Medicine" in order to avoid litigation, among others. Yet, in either instance, healthcare ICT could reverse the trend, in publicly funded systems for example, obviating the need to invest significant amounts of money on medical technologies that would be redundant in some circumstances, or would at least not duplicated in others, in particular, the infrastructure-intensive, diagnostic imaging technologies, or those for treating cardiac and cancer patients. At the most basic levels, we could, via intensive, healthcare ICT-based, primary prevention programs, start to see the need to coalesce secondary prevention services, with reduction in the prevalence of diseases requiring the use of costly technologies such as magnetic resonance imaging (MRI), computed tomography (CT) scanners, cardiac catheterization, and coronary artery bypass graft (CABG), among others. Healthcare-ICT related services such as business process outsourcing and client resource management would make the need to duplicate certain health services unnecessary, thus saving costs, possibly significantly. There thus needs to be system changes in many countries were they to reap the immense benefits of healthcare ICT in achieving the dual healthcare delivery goals mentioned earlier. This would require policy changes in regard healthcare ICT in these countries, many, both in

Europe and East Asia, which currently lack a National Healthcare ICT Policy, the essential starting point for such systems reforms. Many countries in Europe have actually embarked on the path of widespread healthcare ICT adoption. In January 2003, the U.K government struck a £168m "broadband" deal with BT, which aimed to enable the NHS improve its infrastructure to connect hospitals and GP surgeries across the country to a fast internet connection. The high-speed network would underline the NHS modernization program. It would enable for example, online appointment scheduling, easier access by healthcare practitioners to patient information at the point of care (POC), and the electronic transfer of prescriptions. The deal gave credence to Prime Minister Tony Blair's declaration in November 2002 to bring broadband to all GP surgeries and schools in the U.K by 2006. It would take much less time for patients to see a specialist as doctors exploit the capabilities of the network to carry out online diagnoses using imaging or video-conferencing, for examples, and patients receive treatments form doctors in their local hospitals with remote expert guidance saving transportation costs, even lives due to prompt and effective treatment. Government also envisaged experts in one region being able to share knowledge with a variety of hospitals and care centers, and the streamlining of health service provision. However, things have hardly turned out the way Government hoped in many ways. Many would insist that the gridlock in the system persists, and that the fundamental problems of the NHS remain unsolved, for example, the management issues arising from the increasing market orientation of health service provision in the country, one of which in fact include the vagaries inherent in the development of pervasive healthcare information and communication technologies. Many have called for example, for an independent investigation into the £6.2bn upgrade of the NHS IT system, querying if the robustness of the plans to meet NHS demands. Nonetheless, Government is adamant that the 10-year IT (NPfIT) program aimed at connecting over 30,000 GPs in England to nearly 300 hospitals by 2012, and has an online booking system, a centralized health records system for 50m patients, e-prescriptions and fast computer network connections between NHS organizations, undergoes periodic evaluation, and is resilient[16]. There is no doubt that the development process of such massive projects is fraught with hitches, some of which could escalate costs. There is also no doubt that investing in these technologies involves much more than implementing them successfully. For example, what if afterward, the end-use refused to have anything to do with them, or did not utilize fully their potential? What about issues of the safety and confidentiality of patient information, or its security, and what in fact would happen were these technologies, which necessarily have different origins, could not communicate with one another, or did defectively, causing communication delays? Such concerns have led some to propose that the Health Select Committee helps resolve uncertainty about NPfIT by requesting the government to commission an autonomous technical assessment as soon as practicable. Government on the other hand remains sure that the technical architecture of the national program is apposite, would deliver benefits to patients, and ensure value for taxpayers' money. These issues, policy, technical, management, end-user, and many others are not peculiar to healthcare ICT efforts in the U.K. In fact, they are issues every country would likely confront, as they are inherent in technology implementation, including healthcare ICT. They also illustrate possible market openings and which, for every country of interest to ICT vendors, they need to identify and elucidate. In other words, that any health system attempting to implement new healthcare ICT would likely confront end-user resistance is doubtless, particularly were the implementers oblivious to the importance of end-user buy-in, from the outset of the ICT project. Even if they were not, there would likely be ongoing need for training and for building on the support garnered by prior change management efforts. There would also be need for example, for any country serious about disaster preparedness to examine on an ongoing basis, the biosurveillance challenges it faces. In the U.S for example, a federal advisory group is working on recommendations regarding the data elements required to help healthcare providers and public health agencies communicate and share crucial healthcare data during an array of scenarios including pandemic outbreaks, natural disaster, and biological attacks[17]. On July 07, 2006, this biosurveillance workgroup from the American Health Information Community met to advance toward its goal of making recommendations that would enable physician offices, hospitals, ER departments, and labs to send within 24 hours, information in a standardized and de-identified format to public health agencies. This workgroup exemplifies the need for the sort of identifying, understanding, and elucidating issues germane to healthcare delivery and the role of healthcare ICT in addressing these issues mentioned above that not only healthcare ICT vendors keen on doing business in any country, but on which the country itself needs to embark, on an ongoing basis.

Eighteen million people in the EU and about 58,000 EU citizens commit suicide annually, tens more attempting it. Do these statistics not point to the urgent need to formulate and implement an action plan for mental health promotion and the prevention of m ental illnesses in all EU member states? What role could healthcare ICT play in such programs? Would an appreciation of the ramifications of such statistics not help a healthcare ICT in devising strategic market options? Would it not help an EU country in policymaking, program development, and in healthcare ICT investments decisions? Would addressing these issues vigorously not help reduce the significant health and economic burden of these disorders, and facilitate the achievement of the dual healthcare delivery goals mentioned earlier? There is no doubt that early intervention and preventive initiatives could help save the lives of many persons that have depression, yet on average, EU member states allocate only 3% of their healthcare budgets to disease prevention in general, that of mental illnesses, a small part of this amount, annually. Would this not have to change in light of such grim statistics as mentioned above? A recent EU report noted that 25% of Europeans would likely experience mental health problems in their lifetime, and that more than 27% of European adults have mental ill health annually[18]. The EU report also noted that depression and anxiety disorders, and stress-related disorders, are the most prevalent mental health problems, and that by 2020, neuropsychiatric disorders, with depression most prevalent, would constitute the commonest cause of illness in the developed world. A key objective of the Program of Community Action in the Field of Public Health (2003-2008), termed " The Program Decision ", which the European Parliament and the Council adopted on September 23, 2002 a key instrument behind the development of its health strategy is harnessing health for economic growth and sustainable development[15]. Article 152, § 1, of the EU Treaty guarantees a high degree of human health protection, which broadly expressed the intent of the " The Program Decision " to support an integrated and intersectoral health strategy embodies. One of the chief aspects of this intent, which is in keeping with a new European health strategy, launched on 15 July 2004, is to develop connections with relevant Community programs and actions and with national and regional initiatives, to promote synergy and shun overlaps[19]. The EU also plans to improve the analysis and knowledge of the effect of health policy formulation, and of other EU policies and initiatives, for examples, that of the internal market on health systems, and how these could enhance its goals of health promotion and disease prevention. It also plans to develop criteria and approaches for evaluating policies for their effect on health as well as other links between public health and other policies. Again, these plans underscore the need for understanding and elucidating health issues, both peculiar to countries, both in Europe, East Asia, and indeed, elsewhere in the world in order to determine the best approaches to addressing them. This exercise, or process cycle analysis, essentially involves identifying health issues and those influencing health, decomposing them, to expose more underlying issues and their processes, eschewing historical fallacies. Process cycle analysis would reveal the processes that need addressing and in what manner, that is, whether to expunge, facilitate, or modify them in some way or another, and which health information and communication technologies would best do the job. It is, therefore not surprising that the EU's plan stressed the need for cooperation between Member States regarding information about health systems. Other priority issues include the effects of patient and healthcare professional mobility on health systems, healthcare quality assurance, and health technology evaluation, cross-border collaboration in health services, and economics and health. The pivotal role in the EU actualizing these priorities is self-evident, an indication of the domains of likely future healthcare ICT investments, the EU's interests in better understanding if, why and how cross-sector health, has economic benefits, also indicative of the crucial link between healthcare delivery and the economy. It is also indicative, though, of the importance of aiming to achieve the dual healthcare delivery objectives mentioned earlier, which creates the prospects of buoying both health and the economy simultaneously. To underscore the key role that healthcare ICT would play in the healthcare delivery scheme in future, including in financial and economic issues, the EU also wants to develop a

Hospital Activity, and Resources Information System to fortify the cross-analyses of health accounts information of hospitals and their impact on health services provision, and on patients' access to it. The EU would support its members' efforts to implement the System of Health Accounts it set up under the Community Statistical Program, again, the foregoing an indication of the non-health information systems whose role nonetheless influences healthcare delivery. These accounting and other non-health information and communications technologies would continue to feature prom inently in healthcare ICT investments budgets throughout the EU, and elsewhere in Europe in the coming years, creating for example, intense competition between vendors of enterprise software-based and the increasingly popular, web-hosted, customer relations management technologies, for example. This is more so with the increasing emphasis on customer-focused healthcare, and efforts to reduce waiting times, and enhance client satisfaction. With the mobility of patients and healthcare professionals likely to be a major issue in a milieu that is actively promoting labor mobility, these technologies and those that would facilitate cross-border access to patient information, hence improve the quality of healthcare delivery, would gain market ascendancy in Europe. There is no doubt, that East-Asian firms, keen to enter the European healthcare ICT markets would benefit from understanding the tide of health services provision on the continent. The key goal of the first two years of the "The Program Decision", for example involved establishing the basis for an all-inclusive and coherent approach, via a focus on three key priorities: health information, health threats, and health determinants, initiatives designed to fashion self-sustainable means for member states to synchronize their health -related activities, 130 projects chosen by 2004 for funding[20]. Collaboration with international organizations for examples the World Health Organization (WHO), the Council of Europe, and the Organization for Economic Co-operation and Development (OECD) are ongoing. For example, the EU would offer financial assistance for WHO-activities, unless otherwise agreed in exceptional circumstances, in keeping with the Financial and Administrative Framework Agreement between the European Commu nity and the United Nations, which became effective on April 29, 2003, areas of cooperation including data and information gathering, health monitoring and disease surveillance. Considering the previously mentioned, these areas would continue to attract significant healthcare ICT funding in the years ahead. The EU also has direct grant agreements with the OECD, which would address public health programs for examples, performance assessment of health care facilities for quality strategies, health economics and cost-effectiveness issues in the different levels of prevention, labor mobility issues, including of healthcare professionals, System of Health Accounts support outside the EU s Statistical program. In other words, there is also a wide scope for healthcare ICT investments in actualizing programs relating to this agreement. The global budget for the program in 2005 was €61,460,411, administrative and operational budgets, the indicative global amount for grants, €48,316,546, the EU co-funding up to 60%, typically, and with projects with strong European benefit, and in new member states or candidate states, sometimes up to 80%. There are compelling reasons that not just EU countries but also indeed, all countries have a stake in health, the most fundamental being the maintenance of the health of their peoples, but there are also economic reasons, which attest to the intimate connections between health and the economy mentioned above. In other words, countries in Europe would increasingly invest in healthcare ICT that would help them achieve the dual healthcare delivery objectives. The contribution of the Commission on Macroeconomics and Health (CMH), whose final report appeared in 2001, to this link between health and economy is undoubted, in developing countries[21], as is its value in guiding investments in health, even if its bearing to EU countries, with different health issues seem unclear. The CMH report not only confirms that investing in people's health in developing countries, a noble objective in its own right, has noteworthy economic paybacks, for the peoples and their countries. Despite its focus on developing countries, which incidentally some of the countries in East Asia, are, some of the empirical evidence gathered referred to industrialized countries, not to m ention the intuitiveness of the applications of the concept of the economy/health connection to all countries, whether developed or developing. The report noted a variety of cost-effective investments that could result in the achievement of the dual healthcare delivery goals, which essentially is saving lives and money simultaneously. In short, that healthcare investment in the less financially endowed would not only help lift the poor from the poverty abyss, but the country's economy overall from it. This further highlights the need for the implementation and use of healthcare ICT in healthcare delivery in these countries in particular, and indeed, in all countries, including those in Europe. With 87,000 recorded protests incidents in 2005 in China, over the effect of the country's economic policies on the poor, for examples, farmers displaced to make way for industrial growth, and with the country's population aging, and birth rates falling, due to deliberate government policy, could China for example, afford to ignore this need? Would China for example, not have to invest in technologies that could save it money while it could deliver qualitative health services to its aging population? Should it not continue to seek ways to sustain its economic development in the likely event of a dwindling labor force? What could a healthy seniors' population offer the country in the years ahead when it might need them to keep its industrial engine rolling? Do these queries not suggest the likely healthcare ICT investment scenario in the country in the near

278

future, for example, the increasing use of ambulatory/community/domiciliary technologies? The characteristic quantitative effect of life expectancy on economic growth is that a 10% increase of life expectancy at birth boosts economic growth at least by 0.3 to 0.4% points of GDP per year[21]. The CMH report on developing countries and its focus on investing in communicable diseases in the main are instructive, and with the main types prevalent in each country identified, the most appropriate healthcare ICT for addressing them would be more readily determinable. Does this not underscore the point we made earlier about the need for process cycle analysis in every instance by interested parties be they healthcare ICT vendors, non-governmental, or governmental organizations? While East Asian developing countries might be focusing more on communicable diseases, hence healthcare ICT vendors seeking to business there more on the technologies most appropriate for addressing the issues the decomposition/exposition exercises revealed and their processes, the reverse would be true of vendors in East Asian seeking to do business in Europe. That said, that does not mean that Europe does not have communicable diseases, or that East Asia lacks noncommunicable diseases. In fact, the latter at least in the more affluent countries, are starting to see increased prevalence of chronic noncommunicable diseases, and the former, communicable diseases such as HIV/AIDS, Syphilis, and Tuberculosis, in some areas not to mention the avian flu, which is in fact causing global health concerns these days. There is no doubt that we need to determine the priority interventions that would, and perhaps, significantly reduce the burden of disease in the country in question. In Europe for example, the burden of disease in the main due to chronic noncommunicable diseases, the approaches to addressing the issues would likely involve more complexity in terms of the need for multidisciplinary, intersectoral collaboration in devising sophisticated healthcare ICT-enabled programs that would help in achieving the dual healthcare delivery goals. The programs would involve primary prevention, which lends itself to the use of these technologies particularly in a region where the telecommunications infrastructures are available. They would also involve secondary and tertiary levels disease management strategies, for examples for mental health, and cardiovascular disease, and intricate infectious diseases, for examples, nosocomial, and medication-resistant infections. Prevention at these levels would benefit from healthcare ICT, for example, sophisticated mobile technologies that the likes of LG and Samsung Electronics of Korea, could compete with European companies for, successfully in the European healthcare ICT markets. Sales of LG, until recently better known for household air conditioners, and plasma TV, although now ranks high in mobile phone manufacturing, increased an estimated 21%, to $23.6 billion (24,659 billion won) in 2004, although it dipped slightly to 23,774 billion won in 2005. Its sales of handsets increased from 6.9 million in 2000 to 44 million in 2004, 20 million in the U.S alone. The company has supplied American carrier Verizon Wireless, to which it sold 11 million handsets in 2004, 6 million to Cingular/ AT&T the same year. LG Electronics was the first firm to launch a CDMA (Code division multiple access) platform -based digital mobile phone, with avant-garde multimedia and data transmission capabilities, features that are invaluable in delivering a variety of primary, even secondary and tertiary prevention health programs. The company is a major manufacturer of CDMA/GSM handsets, UMTS 3G handsets, Mobile TV Phone (SDMB/ TDMB/ MediaFLO/ DVB-H), its 2005 global sales of 55 Million Units amounting to US$ 9.9 Billion, impressive[22]. Samsung is the quintessential Korean electronic firm, the 44 million handsets LG sold in 2004 just roughly half of Samsung's output, and LG s 3G technologies head start, threatened in both Korea and China. Incidentally, Samsung has reported an 11% fall in quarterly profits, battered by decreasing margins for cellular phones and flat screen TVs. The company reported that it made 1.51 trillion won ($1.59bn; £864m) in the three months prior to June 31, 2006, versus 1.69 trillion won in 2005, although it expects recovery across its businesses in the remaining half of the year. The company also revealed its $1.9bn deal to manufacture LCD display screens for Sony of Japan, under whose terms it will manufacture LCD panels for 50" flat screen TVs subsequent to a "significant" demand rise. With firm having to contend with a global market awash with LCD TVs, and stiff competition from Nokia and Motorola in the "cut-throat" mobile phone market, seeing its second quarter mobile phone profit margin drop to 9.5%, from 12% during the same period in 2005, the major world chipmaker, seems to be struggling. Nonetheless, these issues, and LG and Samsung, exemplify those, including the potential competition foreign firms venturing into the healthcare ICT markets in East Asia would likely face, and possibly in European markets too. On the other hand, European firms need to be looking at healthcare ICT more suited to the management of communicable diseases in developing countries, as these constitute although not exclusively as noted earlier, the major burden of disease in these countries.

The dyadic interactions between Europe and East Asia in terms of business opportunities and market openings in the healthcare ICT sector would, therefore, reflect the dynamics of health and non-health factors, in particular what is happening elsewhere in the economic sectors of the countries in these two regions. However, and as noted above, it would not just be a matter of developed versus developing, as health and economy are extremely complex issues, whose intricacies require in-depth analyses to unravel. The fundamental issues confronting health systems in developing countries differ from that Europe face, which makes extrapolating such findings as of the CMH mentioned above somewhat tricky. Some might also argue that because the health status of the EU countries is already relatively high, achieving additional health system improvement would be harder and more expensive, hence u nlikely to accrue significant economic payoffs. Furthermore, there are differences in demographic variables, for example, population aging, and health indicators that could significantly influence the economic burden of disease in these regions. To be sure, the dichotomy of developing and developed countries is not absolute in terms of the individual as there is affluence in the former and poverty in the latter, and there are prospects of transitioning from one group to the other. In fact not only was Portu gal and Ireland until recently deemed developing countries, there is poverty in some parts of Europe, and according to the most recent Eurostat figures the working poor, are becoming poorer, the purchasing power of workers on the minimum wage varying between 1 to 7.5 among the EU-28, seven member states not having a minimum wage[23]. This report also indicated that Luxembourg, with the highest per capita income in the EU, and the highest minimum wage, also has the largest number of workers stuck on that minimum wage, versus others in the same year, 2004, the U.K (1.4%, the same incidentally for the U.S), 15.6% in France, and 3.1% and 4.5% in Ireland, and Poland, respectively. The migration issue further complicates the picture in Europe, with potential significant effects on its health and economy, even if the migrants are more prone to impoverishment in the short term. There are about 20 million migrants in the EU, and the numbers are increasing daily. Defined as third-country nationals with temporary or permanent legal residence, migrants, include immigrants, refugees, and asylum seekers, among others, and exclude automatically, EU citizens. Caritas Europa's recent, third report on poverty in Europe, noted that asylum seekers are among the most susceptible groups of the EU population, lacking not just pecuniary wherewithal, but also social empowerment, the combination of education, housing, employment, and health problems these migrants confront a potential wellspring of future socio-economic problems in their host countries. They face health risks for example, due to deprived living conditions, lack health insurance, and do not have the funds to pay for healthcare. Would these countries not need to major policy reorientation to avert the long term health and economic, not to mention social consequences of these issues, and what role could healthcare ICT play in their efforts in this direction, for example in social inclusion, health promotion, and disease prevention? Do these issues not support the need for the sort of country-specific process analysis mentioned earlier, rather than depending on broad, dichotomy-based assumptions, were efforts to address them to succeed? There is no doubt that there are costs linked to illnesses. Even basic COI (Cost-of-illness) studies, which reckon resource quantity (funds), used in disease treatment vis-à-vis the extent of its negative economic costs (lost productivity) to society, indicate this much, the limitations of such studies, for example, causality direction of the health/economy dyadic, regardless. COI studies attempt to recognize and measure all the costs linked to a specific disease or risk factor, direct, indirect, and intangibles costs. The point here is that in exploring the healthcare ICT markets, there is need for process cycle analysis, which could be at different levels, country, regional health authority, hospital, which, among others would reveal funds guzzling issues and processes that need modifying. Depending on a variety of factors that govern their overall strategic interests, a healthcare ICT firm might want to, as the governments or local authorities ought to do, make this an ongoing exercise in perpetuity, because no health system could ever be perfect, and as long as it confronts constraints, must evolve for the better or risk oblivion. Thus, it is necessary for example to know the drivers of direct costs, that is, those on the health sector concerning disease prevention, diagnosis, and treatment, and might include costs of ambulances, in/outpatient, medications, rehabilitation, and community health/healthcare, among others. It is also important to know those of indirect costs, that is, costs due to lost productivity potential of ill patients, or those that died precipitately. Some have included in this estimation the loss of future earnings (discounted), the so-called human capital approach, and others have adopted the scenario-based, willingness to-pay technique, estimates of indirect costs, often a matter for contention. Intangible costs, which aim to account for the psychological aspects of illnesses to the ill person and to his/her family, are even more difficult to measure, hence more contentious. Nonetheless, an exploration of these different drivers, and their costs, for examples via the disease prevalence, or the more data-intensive incidence costing methods, would reveal perhaps even cryptic issues and processes that underlie them, and which the application of the appropriate healthcare information and communication technologies could help modify and improve, hence reducing the costs, while not compromising healthcare delivery. Cardiovascular diseases for example are some of the commonest noncommunicable diseases among Europeans. The economic burden of coronary heart disease (CHD) in the UK (direct and indirect costs,) was GBP 1.73 billion (EUR 2.5 billion) in 1999, GBP 2.42 billion (EUR 3.5 billion) and GBP 2.91 billion (EUR 4.2 billion) in informal care, and lost productivity (24.1 % due to mortality and 75.9 % to morbidity), respectively[24]. The overall yearly cost of all CHD-related burdens, GBP 7.06 billion (EUR 10.2 billion), was about 1 % of 1999 GDP and 11 % of total national health spending for 1999[21]. Such estimations could also reveal the costs and their drivers for other diseases, and even enable comparison of costs for diseases and costs within and between countries, facilitating policy formulation and program development. By understanding these issues, healthcare ICT firms would be better able to develop the appropriate product and service mix, and develop the right strategies for the markets either in Europe or in East Asia that interest them. It is not always that these firms have either the resources or willingness to embark on such analyses, in which case, they need to hire someone to do the job. With regard countries, should the U.K for example, knowing that in 1999, CHD had the highest burden their direct, indirect, and total costs respectively, GBP1730, GBP 5325, and GBP 7055, not do something to reduce these costs21? What role cou ld investing in the appropriate healthcare ICT for example play in this regard, considering that many of the risk factors for these conditions are preventable for example? The same questions apply to other " high-burden " diseases such as obesity/diabetes, m ental illnesses, and substance use/dependence not just the U.K, but in most of Europe, where they constitute significant disease-burdens. These disorders need prioritizing and measures taken to reduce their prevalence and their burden in both human and material terms, and governments in countries where they are prevalent cannot afford to do otherwise. Considering that these diseases are preventable in the main, this says something for the sorts of health information, and communication technologies that these countries would need to invest on in the years ahead in order to tackle these problems. Let us illustrate this point further with some figures. In 2001, the US Surgeon General s report estimates of the direct and indirect costs of obesity were US$117 billion (US$61 billion direct costs; US$ 56 billion indirect costs), albeit underestimates, the condition s effects on social well-being, and among those outside the labor force excluded25. In 2001, the direct and indirect economic costs of physical inactivity and obesity in Canada were US$5.3 billion (EUR 3.5 billion), US$1.6 billion (EUR 1.1 billion), and US$ 2.7 billion

(EUR 1.8 billion) in direct and indirect costs, respectively. In the same year for obesity, the costs were US$4.3 billion (EUR 2.8 billion), US$ 1.6 billion (EUR 1.1 billion) and US$2.7 billion (EUR 1.8 billion), in direct and indirect costs, respectively, both physical inactivity and obesity, in total, 2.6 % and 2.2 %, respectively, of the country's total healthcare costs[26]. In 2001, estimates also revealed that treating obesity in the U.K, cost the NHS roughly GBP 500 million (EUR 715 million) annually, and with costs to the entire economy of reduced productivity and lost output added, another GBP 2 billion (EUR 2.8 billion) annually. The devastation that Typhoon Bilis, which hit the Philippines and Taiwan on July 14, 2006, and China, caused is another example of the need to appreciate the health issues of each country fully in order to better determine the most appropriate healthcare ICT required in the delivery of cost-effective and qualitative health services to the country's peoples. The floods and storms of the Typhoon killed at least 115 persons, in China's southeast Fujian, Hunan, and Guangdong provinces[27], more than 100 people in Hunan province alone, thousands of homes and hectares of farmland, swept off, train services, disrupted, and power lines cut, torrential rain predicted to continue across southern China for the next many days. Such rain only in June 2006 killed at least 349 people also in China. In fact, seasonal heavy rains and typhoons cause hundreds of deaths in China yearly. Should the country not invest in and deploy the appropriate healthcare technologies to address the varieties of health issues that these natural disasters cause? Do these examples not underline the contextual approach that healthcare ICT vendors should adopt regarding their strategies in their markets of interest? The healthcare ICT sector is no doubt evolving in many countries, including those in the regions under consideration. However, this evolution would likely have a pattern, based on the issues and approaches we have discussed thus far among others. These issues would be different for each country, and indeed, for each region, but what would be the same for all is the need to achieve the dual healthcare delivery objectives mentioned earlier. Besides considerations for individual's health, investing in healthcare information and communication technologies would also be a means to an end, that of sustainable economic development. These are two potent reasons that governments cannot afford to shun the important role that these technologies could play in their achieving these health and economic objectives. We have not identified the markets for specific healthcare information and communications to any precise level for the same reasons we have advanced in this discussion regarding the need for process cycle analysis to a more or less extent in the particular setting in which we are interested. To do otherwise would either mean having particular information on the specific healthcare ICT projects that that setting, a country, health region, or hospital, for example, has lined up, or merely speculating on them. It is possible to obtain the former information from the appropriate sources since it would probably be on open tender, but it is important to be able configure a strategic view on the direction the health system of interest is headed as this might be crucial for the distinctions value proposition that confer competitive advantage.

Part of the process analysis involves also determining the technical issues involved in healthcare ICT diffusion, implementation, and utilization in these settings, which would also likely reveal the nature and extent of their markets. Interoperability for example, is a major technical issue in healthcare ICT implementation in many countries, although it has other dimensions for examples, research and development, regulations, and standards, among others. In this connection, some developers are addressing the interoperability issue from a Service Oriented Architecture (SOA) software design perspective, for example, hoping by overcoming the challenge to launch a new age of efficient network services, cross-organizational business collaboration and novel services with valuable applications in the health industry. SOA is essentially a novel, software development methodology that rather than of individual programs that perform, a variety of functions enables the design of individual functions that could blend to offer a variety of diverse services, the programs compiled when required and extensively reused, SOA thus lithe and cost-effective. It is also likely to be invaluable in connecting organizational, services, platforms, and networks, facilitating the seamless information communication and sharing that the typically disparate systems in the health sector needs, yet the need to scale the interoperability hurdles, literally, is crucial for this to happen. That this requires addressing at levels other than the technical is not in doubt considering the need for business to drive IT rather than the reverse, which again underscores the need for process analysis, which reveals underlying issues and processes and the best health information and communication technologies to modify/improve them. The IST-funded, ATHENA project, for example, involves research, research, technological and industrial partners, and aims to develop solutions to the different interoperability issues that firms confront at various levels, such as data, services, processing and business levels[28]. Researchers are utilizing semantics, mostly semantic data transformation to help translate information stored in different formats and systems among dissimilar enterprises, focusing in the service area, on model-driven SOA to address the issue of running different applications on diverse architectures, for examples, Web services, Grids or P2P[28], and a 'process abstraction concept' at the process level for automated cross-organizational processing. The researchers' success with the latter for example would mean no longer the need for wagering between efficiency and security in connecting corporate applications for information sharing to protect some crucial data from general view, a scenario that applies in particular to health systems, besides companies' supply chains, for example. With ATHENA, the abstraction concept translates to every business partner or authorized user-department in a health system is able to define public processes positioned above its internal, private processes keeping private and confidential processes, and data cloaked, simultaneously. In other words, the researchers hope to develop an integrated yet secure milieu. According to Rainer Ruggaber at SAP Research in Germany, one of the principal developers of SOA solutions, "Though this concept is not new, the value of our solutions revolve around the creation of an integrated but secure environment. It means that my internal processes are linked to my public processes which in turn are connected to your public processes and to your internal ones but where outside access to the private processes of both sides is restricted." There is no doubt interoperability solutions in SOA will have important applications in any sector including the health sector where efficient, seamless information communications and sharing are key processes in its operations. For example, the SOA-based, SODIUM project has developed two prototype systems addressing risk management and healthcare utilizing a standards-based approach to determine, comp ose, and execute mixed web, peer-to-peer and grid services, trials underway in Romania and Norway. Its scientific coordinator, Aphrodite Tsalgatidou recently noted, "SODIUM is providing solutions on top of existing standards to create a unified way to discover and compose heterogeneous services" The main challenge for us is to achieve syntactic and semantic interoperability." He added, "In crisis management, for example, emergency services have to use a variety of services some of which will be P2P, others will be Web based and others will be Grid based. All of them have to work

289

together." As noted earlier, there are varieties of natural and manmade disasters that countries in both Europe and East Asia regularly confront. With risk and crisis management, being no doubt domains where interoperability is crucial, would countries in these regions not therefore need to explore the potential of ATHENA, and similar technologies, for example? Have the researchers not for example, and as we have advocated thus far, critically examined the issues involved in interoperability, decomposed them, and determined their underlying processes and those that need modifying and improving for more efficient and cost-effective, systems interoperability, in fact able to offer novel and intuitive value propositions in the process? In fact, another SOA-based project, ORCHESTRA, aims to address procedural, technological and communications challenges that compromise efficient risk management. According to project coordinator José Esteban, "Our architecture will allow interoperable risk management services to be created to overcome the barriers between different actors who use different procedures, databases, systems, and languages The standards-based approach aims to ensure compatibility between systems, databases and services including those that are already in use by different public administrations across Europe." These technologies would certainly be useful in healthcare d elivery, and would play a key role in improving interoperability standards. In fact, the ATHENA project has fashioned the Enterprise Interoperability Centre (EIC) to use ATHENA results for forging accord, and as Ruggaber noted, "The EIC is currently working on business profiles for interoperability focusing on public business processes and building on existing messaging standards. Initially starting in the construction sector it will continue with scenarios in the automotive industry, healthcare, and logistics", the EIC aiming to facilitate the collaboration of stakeholders in securing the wider applications of research findings. ATHENA is also involved in the Enterprise

Interoperability Research Roadmap that the European Commission would publish in July/August 2006, and intends to contribute to EU policies aimed at improving systems interoperability among European firms. These examples buttress many of the points we have made about the importance of process cycle analysis. The direction of the dyadic between Europe and East Asia with regard the healthcare ICT markets would in future hinge on this sort of analysis. New and sophisticated information technologies emerge routinely, many with features applicable to healthcare delivery although not necessarily set out to deliver such services. The question is whether ICT software and other vendors are aware of developments in the health industry or are at all interested in them. The examples of ATHENA and others mentioned above indicate that at least some are collaborating with research and other organizations to design and develop ICT focused on issues that bear direct relevance to healthcare delivery. However, the markets for healthcare ICT is unimaginably wide open considering the innumerable processes that currently hamper healthcare delivery efforts, hence yearning for technologies to improve them. The issue of hospital wait lists for example, plagues many European and East Asian countries, and these issues no doubt could benefit from appropriate healthcare ICT applied to addressing some of the underlying issues and processes involved. Would a healthcare ICT vendor that conducts process cycle analysis in its preferred market in order to understand fully these underlying processes, and then designs and develops the appropriate technologies to tackle the issues successfully not likely to find sufficient market opportunities to recoup its costs, for example, or be gratified additionally by the social grace of perhaps saving lives? These are clearly questions that these companies would need to ask in time seeking market opportunities in the health sector, not just in Europe and East Asia, but also worldwide.

References

1. Federal Emergency Management Agency (FEMA). Are you ready? An in-depth guide to citizen preparedness. Washington, DC: FEMA. August 2004.
Available at: www.fema.gov/areyouready/
Accessed July 12, 2006

2. US Centers for Disease Control and Prevention and the American Red Cross. Preparedness today: what you need to know. US Centers for Disease Control and Prevention and the American Red Cross. February 23, 2006.
Available at: http://www.redcross.org/preparedness/cdc_english/CDC.asp
Accessed on July 12, 2006

3. Johnston C, Redlener I. Critical concepts for children in disasters identified by hands-on professionals: summary of issues demanding solutions before the next one. *Pediatrics*. 2006; 117:458-460

4. Joint Commission on the Accreditation of Healthcare Organizations.
Comprehensive Accreditation Manual for Hospitals. Standard EC.1.4. Washington, DC: Joint Commission on the Accreditation of Healthcare Organizations; 2006.

5. Available at: http://www.hamquick.com/articles/art_what_ham.php
Accessed on July 12, 2006

6. Amateur Radio Disaster Services (ARDS). American Radio Relay League.
Available at: www.ares.org Accessed June 20, 2006

7. US Department of Homeland Security. Metropolitan Medical Response System
(MMRS), Federal Emergency Management Agency (FEMA).
Available at: www.mmrs.fema.gov/default.aspx
Accessed July 12, 2006

8. Available at: http://www.training.fema.gov/EMIWEB/IS/is800.asp
Accessed July 12, 2006

9. U.S Department of Homeland Security. National Disaster Medical System. US
Washington, DC: Department of Homeland Security.
Available at: www.ndms.dhhs.gov
Accessed July 12, 2006

10. Available at:
http://www.expatica.com/source/site_article.asp?subchannel_id=52&story_id=31
520&name=Merkel+cabinet+agrees+to+health+charge+hike Accessed on July 13,
2006

11. Available at:
http://news.yahoo.com/s/ap/20060712/ap_on_go_ca_st_pe/medicare_premiums&
printer=1;_ylt=AthTr2bFOtN2OFjcW85_NKCWwvIE;_ylu=X3oDMTA3MXN1bH
E0BHNlYwN0bWE- Accessed on July 13, 2006

12. Available at:

http://www.oecd.org/document/37/0,2340,en_2649_201185_36986213_1_1_1,00.html Accessed on July 14, 2006

13. Jencks SF. Cuerdon T. Burwen DR. Fleming B. Houck PM. Kussmaul AE. Nilasena DS. Ordin DL. Arday DR. Quality of medical care delivered to Medicare beneficiaries: A profile at state and national levels.[see comment]. [Journal Article] *JAMA*. 284(13):1670-6, 2000 Oct 4.

14. Laurence Baker, Howard Birnbaum, Jeffrey Geppert, David Mishol, and Erick Moyneur The Relationship Between Technology Availability And Health Care Spending *Health Affairs* Web Exclusive, November 5, 2003

15. Available at: http://news.bbc.co.uk/2/hi/health/5177860.stm Accessed on July 14, 2006

16. Available at: http://news.bbc.co.uk/2/hi/health/4896198.stm Accessed on July 14, 2006

17. Available at: http://www.healthcareitnews.com/printStory.cms?id=5205 Accessed on July 15, 2006

18. Available at: http://www.irishhealth.com/?level=4&id=9895 Accessed on July 15, 2006

19. Available at:

http://ec.europa.eu/health/ph_programme/howtoapply/proposal_docs/workplan 2005_en.pdf Accessed on July 15, 2006

20. Available at: http://ec.europa.eu/health/ph_information/information_en.htm Accessed on July 15, 2006

21. Available at:

http://ec.europa.eu/health/ph_overview/Documents/health_economy_en.pdf Accessed on July 15, 2006

22. Available at: http://www.lge.com/about/corporate/business_telecom.jsp Accessed on July 16, 2006

23. Available at: http://www.euractiv.com/en/socialeurope/places-working-poor-poorer/article-156738 Accessed on July 16, 2006

24. Liu, J. L. Y., Maniadakis, N., Gray, A. and Rayner, M. (2002), 'The economic burden of coronary heart disease in the UK', *Heart*, 88: 597 603.

25. Kuchler, F. and Ballenger, N. (2002), 'Societal costs of obesity: How can we assess when federal interventions will pay? *Food Review*, 25(3): 33 37.

26. Katzmarzyk, P. T. and Janssen, I. (2004), 'The economic costs associated with physical inactivity and obesity in Canada: an update', *Canadian Journal of Applied Physiology*, 29(1): 90 115.

27. Available at:

http://newsvote.bbc.co.uk/mpapps/pagetools/print/news.bbc.co.uk/2/hi/asia-pacific/5185314.stm Accessed on July 16, 2006

28. Available at: http://istresults.cordis.lu/ Accessed on July 16, 2006

The Future of Healthcare ICT Markets in Japan

Comprising over 3000 islands, many mountainous and volcanic, the
population of Japan, the world's second largest economy, almost 129 million
people, that of Tokyo, its capital and the world's largest cosmopolitan area, over
30 m illion, the country faces unique healthcare delivery challenges. Federal and
local governments provide health services in Japan, which has a universal health
care insurance system that aims to offer equitable access to care, with coverage
for all seniors. There is also private health insurance in Japan, including
employer-sponsored health insurance, persons without which could use a local
government-administered national health insurance program. The country,
whose total health expenditure per capita, the p er capita amount of the sum of
Public Health Expenditure (PHE) and Private Expenditure on Health (PvtHE), in
2003 was Intl $, 2,244, and total health expenditure as % of GDP in the same year
was 7.9%, is increasingly a consumer-focused health system, with persons able to

choose healthcare providers and services. Despite being Western-based in the main, the health system in Japan has a significant traditional component, which itself creates its own challenges, for example, regarding practice regulation, and communication and information sharing between the two health systems. The country's aging population is another key challenge to Japan's health system. Life expectancy at birth m/f (years) is 79 and 86 years respectively. Seniors constituted just 5% of the population in 1950, but 11.6% in 1989, a proportion projected to reach 25.2% by 2020, the rate of increase in seniors' population in Japan much faster than in other industrialized countries. This means an equally rapid increase in the country's expenditures on its health and welfare systems for this population segment, an increase that would bear significantly on the future of not just its health systems, but also on the nature and extent of healthcare ICT investments in the country. Increasing national health spending, long hospital wait times, the administrative and financial burden of a substantially paper-based health system, ex-ante moral hazard due to negligible healthcare costs to patients, are some of the other challenges the health system in Japan increasingly confronts. There are several others including high prescription medications' costs, the misdistribution of healthcare professionals, and problems with the coordination of healthcare provision by the array of practice traditions. Could the implementation of the appropriate healthcare ICT not help overcome these challenges?

There is no doubt that Japan's economic growth is back on track, the country

having mostly overcome its post-bubble woes, its current impressive output growth billed to continue through 2007, at between 2% and 3%, the buoyant domestic demand, propped by increasing corporate bottom -line and increasing

297

employment and indeed, wages₁, the former projected to fall to 3½% by 2007. With deflation curbed, and inflation high enough to counterbalance and keep it confined, experts argue that Japan s medium -term fiscal goal should be a primary budget surplus sufficiently large to steady the public debt-to-GDP ratio by the early 2010s, rooted in more inclusive spending and tax initiatives. Thus, confronted with a rapidly aging population and an increasingly suave public with expectations of higher living standards, the country needs to institute the necessary measures to promote the efficiency of market operations, including the required regulatory market reforms that would bolster creativity and competitive forces. These issues no doubt have significant implications for the future of healthcare delivery in the country. Japan has to take necessary cost-containment measures for example regarding its health spending, yet, has an aging population whose healthcare needs constitute the bulk of health spending in the country, not to m ention on its welfare system, both likely to put increasing pressure of its finances in future. Most of its healthcare professionals and its healthcare resources are in the urban centers and many of its peoples in far-flung mountainous and other remote areas with limited access to healthcare resources compared to those living in the cities. Even among the city-dwellers, long hospital wait lists, and short physician consultation times, essentially constitute healthcare access restrictions, which could have m ajor health implications in certain cases, including the risk of death. The Japanese health system thus has major access and other issues that need scrutiny. In short, there could hardly be any effective solution to these issues otherwise. Thus, it would be necessary to decompose these issues in order to expose the underlying component issues and their respective processes, which would be the starting point in understanding the causes and solutions to the problems and challenges that confront the country s health systems. For example, without such an exercise, it would be difficult if not impossible to know the processes hampering the efficiency and effectiveness of the health systems and their interrelations. Whereas, understanding these processes and their roles in the overall system, and its ability to achieve its set objectives, could instruct which of facilitation, expulsion, or modification in some way that would be the right choice in fixing these processes, hence improving the system's performance in general.

The implications of this progress could be far-reaching for the system, and for

the country's sustainable economic growth at large. In other words, it could mean for Japan, the delivery of qualitative health services to its peoples while simultaneously reducing its health spending, for example, the dual health delivery objectives, which are clearly most appropriate for the country to realize the economic objectives, mentioned earlier, in addition to the intrinsic desirability of those of healthcare delivery. This is besides the fact that realizing either would influence the other anyway, economic prosperity making more resources available for even higher quality healthcare delivery, which latter would be an enabler of even further economic growth. Should the country therefore, not be keen to invest in the means by which it could achieve these dual objectives, for example, in healthcare information and communication technologies that research has shown could help these dual goals? A 2005 Rand Corp. study for example found that nationwide adoption of EHR in the U.S, could result in over $81 billion in annual savings via improvements in healthcare efficiency and safety, saving which Healthcare ICT-enabled prevention and management of chronic disease cou ld ultimately double at the same time increasing health and other social benefits[2]. The study, published in *Health Affairs* on September 14, 2005, noted the need for related systems changes though to realize these savings, which few would argue, is not a su bstantial chunk of the over $1.7 trillion annually that the U.S spends on healthcare, and realizing similar savings few would contend either that Japan should not aspire to. Furthermore, in fulfilling, its commitment to provide access to health services to its citizens Japan s health system has to improve access to care at all levels, primary, secondary, and tertiary. Should it therefore not know whether or not to commit the enormous human and material resources required for the provision of tertiary care for example in every part of the country considering the likely variability in service utilization, on the one hand, and its equally likely abuse in locations for example with hitherto low utilization of such service? Could the health system not in fact rather outsource say the MRI service it proposed to introduce to that location to another nearby with higher service need , hence likelier prospects of return on investment? Furthermore, could the health system not develop more-relevant needs-based services for each location instead? Would this not make more economic sense than wholesale construction of health facilities, or implementation of costly medical technologies, risking underutilization, or abuse? These questions highlight the issues that health administrators in Japan or elsewhere for that matter would need to address in order to make rational decisions regarding investments in health services, including in healthcare ICT.

The country's health system is more and more patient-focused, but this shift implies added responsibility on the health system s part. For example, would it not need to make the necessary information available to the public on the price of services and their quality, and on the expertise of healthcare professionals, and service availability, among others to enable prospective clients m ake rational choices regarding healthcare providers and services? Would healthcare providers not have to differentiate competitively via value propositions for examples offering dedicated websites for health information provision, accepting email consultation, providing personal health records services, and online repeat prescriptions? Could the health system not enhance the operations of its insurance system incorporating predictive modeling technology, for example, thus making existing claims paying data veritable information sources on clients that could help with future policy formulation and program development and implementation? Could it not for example have benefits information system that would track information on medication purchases at point of sale (POS)? Could such information not make it possible for pharmacists and payers to determine a client's health insurance eligibility, coverage, and out-of-pocket costs? In addition, by integrating the system nationwide facilitate could it not facilitate the compilation of individual s claims history, hence help with the planning and implementation of resource allocation? Could combining this information for example with those other health information systems provide such as electronic prescribing information, electronic medical records, quality reports and system performance appraisal records, not help provide more comprehensive information on medications types and use, and their efficacy, safety, and costs? How much could Japan safe in administrative costs replacing the burdensome paperwork in its health system, which could be substantial, according to some estimates, up to 25 cents of every *healthcare* dollar spent in the U.S for example, where it also takes up a half-hour of a doctor's time for each hour spent with a patient ₃? As these questions show, do information and communication technologies not have key roles to play in the future of the Japanese health system, and does this not suggest the likely hike in investments in these technologies in the years ahead? Would this not in particular likely to be so were the country to achieve the dual healthcare delivery objectives mentioned earlier, and what indeed, are the chances that it would rather not? In other words, on a general note, there is likely to be significant increases in investments on healthcare ICT in Japan in the near future. The challenge to technology firms seeking to do business in the country's healthcare ICT industry would therefore be to determine in what technology areas these investments would be and their nature and extent.

To put the symbiotic link between the economy and health in Japan into

perspective, it is important first to note that the country has only recently come out of its long economic stagnation in the wake of early 1990s' asset price bubble with domestic demand driving essentially driving the economy after the earlier push by exports. Experts predict the economic expansion would continue with output projected to rise to between 2% and 3% in 2006 and 2007, respectively[4]. However, for Japan to sustain its impressive economic growth in the medium term, not to mention in the long term, the country has to confront some key challenges headlong, of which of direct relevance to healthcare delivery is ensuring fiscal sustainability with its population aging very fast. Coupled with its gross public debt already over 170% of GDP, its need for initiatives to cut down the large government budget deficit is undeniable, as is the question of these initiatives compromising the resources available for healthcare funding. Also crucial is the need to rectify increasing income inequality and relative poverty simultaneously curtailing government spending. Incidentally, income inequality and poverty, and an aging population that depletes the labor force, means that Japan needs to promote creativity to assist in improving productivity growth, which in turn means utilizing overseas goods, services, capital, technology, and labor to the fullest. These issues have significant implications not just for healthcare delivery, but also for the evolution of the country's healthcare ICT markets. They also underscore the need for technology firms both local and foreign that plan to venture into the country's healthcare ICT industry to understand fully these and related issues, their underlying processes and the appropriate technologies and services required to modify them, and move Japan closer to achieving its health and economic reforms objectives, including the dual healthcare delivery objectives. What would it mean for example for Japan to open its doors to foreign labor in terms of healthcare services provision? For examples, what adjustments would the health system need to make particularly regarding changing patterns of disease prevalence, such as the possible increase in the prevalence of certain genetic disorders due to consanguineous marriages, changing demographics also resulting in changes disease patterns, and increase in diseases due to poverty and poor living conditions? What role could healthcare ICT-enabled programs play at the primary, secondary, and tertiary disease prevention levels in this regard? Would employers be embracing healthcare consumerism and if so, what role would healthcare ICT play in implementing the necessary health education and promotion campaigns characteristic of such moves? Would the efforts to promote innovation and the increasing sophistication of healthcare tastes that the consumer-driven health service model engenders, coupled with the ongoing economic and market reforms not trigger competition among healthcare providers? Would such competition not result in more comprehensive service offerings delivered with cutting-edge healthcare ICT, in the quest for competitive edge? In other words, and are we not likely to see an increase in healthcare ICT investments in both Japan's public and private health sector in the coming years, and would this development not open up immense market opportunities for these technologies at various healthcare delivery levels? Should healthcare ICT firms both local and foreign not be conducting the process cycle analyses, trying to understand fully the critical health and non-health issues facing Japan that would determine the direction of its future healthcare-delivery policies, and resource allocation, particularly to healthcare ICT? In other words, not only the country's health administrators ought to be examining these issues, decomposing them, and teasing out the underlying issues and processes, the essential elements of the process cycle.

In the U.K for example, Lord Warner, the Health Minister on July 22, 2006,

confirmed the arrangements for the NHS Summary Care Record Taskforce, whose goal is to assist the start of the first phase of the NHS Care Records Service by tackling important issues and concerns. Chaired by H arry Cayton, the Department of Health's National Director for Patients and the Public, its membership includes the chairs of the BMA, and the Royal College of GPs. Others include President of the College of Emergency Medicine, the General Secretary of the Royal College of Nurses, and patients' representatives. The Taskforce will identify and examine the concerns of healthcare providers and patients alike, with a view to better understanding the various issues involved in implementing these technologies and the relevant services in practical ways beneficial to both p atients and the NHS, in collaboration with NHS Connecting for Health, developing a national implementation plan, starting in early 2007. Other phases of the project would continue for another couple of years. The Taskforce will likely also collaborate with the U.S Veterans' Administration, which stores health records for 23 million US ex-servicemen and women, to gain from their experiences in running electronic health record system s. In addition, NHS Connecting for Health is working on facilitating seamless relocation of GP patient records between practices when patients switch GPs, making patients' records available at the point of care (POC) even at the first visit to the new GP, and patients not having to wait 6 weeks to 3 months for their record to be available. Government plans to make it possible for hundreds of GP practices to transfer patient records by the end of 2006. Would Japanese healthcare ICT firms interested in exploring the British healthcare ICT markets not benefit for example, from having such information, in fact well in advance, which the sort of process cycle analysis we mentioned earlier could enable, not assist in strategic planning for products and services by such a firm? This exercise is indeed, also indispensable to employing more strategic approaches to doing business in Japan's healthcare industry, and that of any country for that matter. Furthermore, health services are increasingly going to have to justify every dollar spent hence would likely be looking for health information technologies that would not merely be enablers of functions and processes but would become there essential organic constituents as the following exemplifies. Some of the chief cost drivers in health systems including in Japan are hospital and prescription medication costs. The quest by health systems to reduce these costs is evident in the increasing markets for wireless based e-health diagnostic, monitoring, and treatment services, which enable and facilitate ambulatory/community and domiciliary health service provision. These services are, incidentally also likely to increase in Japan considering its rapidly aging population with many seniors having chronic non-communicable diseases suited for these management approaches, and they would increasingly involve the participation of foreign companies considering the country's likely movement towards economic alignment with the rest of the world, increasing its chances of exploiting the opportunities globalization presents.

It is important to solve its fiscal problems and to achieve a primary budget

surplus for both central and local governments in the early 2010s, for Jap an to restrict the growth in government spending, and in fact as set by the F Y 2001 Structural Reform and Medium -Term Economic and Fiscal Perspectives, at 38% of its GDP through FY 2006. , and this target is likely to be achieved. Nonetheless, slashing public investments might compromise healthcare delivery eventually, although structural factors and economic expansion in the main accounted for much the reduction in its primary budget deficit from 6.7% of GDP in 2002 to a projected 4% in 2006. On the other hand, such fiscal cutbacks do not necessarily have to compromise health service provision with the implementation and utilization of the appropriate healthcare ICT as mentioned earlier, which could result not just in substantial savings, but also in the achievement of the dual healthcare delivery objectives. The need for Japan to keep its efforts to achieve a primary budget surplus going, while at the same time provide qualitative health services to its peoples means that it would have to embrace these technologies on a large scale, sooner than later. With population aging likely to slow output growth perhaps even lead to an increase interest rate, Japan would need to take the necessary fiscal measures to stabilize its public debt to GDP ratio at minimal levels, for which it would likely need a sustained primary budget surplus of between ½% and 1½% of GDP4. It is therefore clear that the country cannot afford to let its health spending escalate, just as it cannot let the quality of its health services depreciate. Even if it had to reduce its public investment, which it did from 8.4% of GDP in 1996 to 5% in 2004, although still higher than the average in many developed countries, these reductions would likely be in conjunction with investment resource allocation to bolster productivity. This is a requirement that investments in healthcare ICT would no doubt meet, including increasing the efficiency of legacy systems, which would reduce the current rising costs of retaining present healthcare infrastructure, for example, many of which might become moribund consequent to the sort of process analysis of the country's health systems and related nonhealth and health issues mentioned earlier. This analysis would reveal processes in the health system that need facilitating, expunging, or leaving alone, among other options, overall improving the ability of the country's health systems to deliver qualitative health services to the public, cost-effectively. It would also reveal for example, those processes that the public health sector should continue to perform and those that the private health system, including the traditional healthcare practitioners would best perform. Such rational resource utilization would no doubt improve the efficiency and cost-effectiveness of the country's public, and other health systems overall. Such analyses would also reveal for example, the need for new processes to meet emerging healthcare needs, both consequent upon health and nonhealth issues.

N atural disasters, for example, occur in Japan from time to time. In fact, the country has been reeling under the strain of heavy rains and the flooding and landslides in its wake in the past week, with many of its citizens internally displaced, and many dead. By July 23, 2006, at least twenty-one across the country had dies in a week, southern Japan, particularly the island of Kyushu, worst hit by the torrential rainss. Kagoshima prefecture on the island's southern tip was the severely battered by heavy rainfall, with more rain expected in Kyushu for another day or so, thousands advised to vacate their homes for their own safety. With such developments as these relatively common in Japan, would the country not need to strengthen its emergency preparedness and response capabilities, and would this not entail continuing investments in the necessary information technologies crucial to realizing these capabilities? Many internally displaced persons need ongoing medical care and others would develop illnesses that require urgent treatment in their new locations. What would it mean if the healthcare professionals treating these individuals in their new locations had no access to their medical and treatment histories, or to any health information that could help in the initiation of the appropriate treatment and the avoidance of medical errors, due for example to avoidable drug interactions, and allergies? What would happen even if these displaced persons did not fall ill in their new locations or if those of current treatment knew their prescriptions and dosing, after they went back home but their hospitals and GPs' practices had been flooded and their paper-based health records swept away? Do these questions not raise issues regarding digitalizing the country's entire health system, with not just a national healthcare ICT policy in place guiding resource allocation for example on a fully-integrated national health information network? Would the country, as noted earlier based on findings of the Rand Corp. study not be saving substantially in the long term, hence recouping its initial investments, besides, and even more importantly providing its citizens with the necessary and qualitative health services in their hour of most need, literally, and indeed, always?

These considerations are crucial determinants of the likely direction of

healthcare ICT investments in Japan. The alternative is indeed too intrepid to contemplate, in other words, not making provisions for prevention of and response to emergency situations for tens of thousands of peoples affected/displaced by disasters both natural, such as earthquakes, floods, landslides, even a viral epidemic, and manmade, which could range from chemical to nuclear spillage, or bioterrorism, among others. What would happen if the garbage collectors, firefighters, ER nurses, and doctors, telephone services operators and water-work personnel started to become ill because of the spread of contagious diseases due to these disasters? Could the entire society be at risk of imminent collapse? What would be the consequences of such scenarios for the country's economy, and indeed, those of other countries in Asia, and the rest of the world? In other words, should Japan not prepare for these possibilities and not indeed participate fully in the global health society collaborating with others to provide the necessary healthcare ICT infrastructures crucial for disease surveillance and data and information sharing both internally and with others in the global health community? Would this not be in keeping with the necessary concerted efforts to prevent, for example the emergence of an avian flu pandemic? The question really for healthcare ICT companies therefore is to figure out what these technologies are that Japan would be investing in on an ongoing basis for reasons we have so far adduced, which is where the issue of process analysis comes in. In other words, it is crucial for these companies from a strategic perspective to understudy the country's health services and the issues they confront in other to know which specific technologies would be most appropriate to focus on offering the country. This exercise would also foster creativity and innovation as such companies would then be able to couple the raw technologies with value-added service offerings that would give them critical competitive advantage. Appreciating the nature, types, and extent of chronic noncommunicable diseases in the country for example, should be a good starting point for these companies, as the diseases that fall under this rubric offer immense potential for healthcare ICT monitoring and treatment both in the hospital and in particular outside the hospital. Could a software company that fully appreciates the need of the Japanese healthcare client in this regard not offer innovative products in collaboration with say a mobile phone manufacturer, local or foreign, and other healthcare ICT firms to tap this market, which is likely to continue to grow considering the fast rate of population aging in the country? The point here is that it is somewhat startling that many of these companies have essentially remained stuck in a monomodal mindset in an increasingly multimodal healthcare ICT economic climate. There is a need for these firms to move beyond simply developing software for medical billing and appointment scheduling, to exploiting the immense potential of multimedia convergence technologies for example, in order to shift healthcare ICT from an enabling to a constitutive mode, which the contemporary healthcare ICT not only yearns, but also would increasingly dem and. The persons that play computer games for example in Japan also fall ill, and some have asthma, diabetes, or heart diseases, and might not be there to play these games if they did not receive the appropriate treatment. In fact, it is even more amazing that it has not occurred to these software companies engaged in cut-throat competition in the game industry to offer their clients more sophisticated value propositions coupling the games with health-related products and services for example multimedia health promotion and disease prevention content, some even subscription-based? Could there not be some computer game enthusiasts interested to receive contextualized health information of their choice, or health message-bearing targeted computer games for say, the elderly to improve their cognitive integrity, for which incidentally there would likely be a huge market in countries such as Japan?

Population ageing in particular would continue to be a crucial driver of

healthcare ICT spending in Japan in the near future, as it increases pressure for increased spending on healthcare. A substantial reduction in medical fees and the start of a new insurance scheme for Japanese over 75 years should maintain health spending at about 5½% of GDP up to 2010₄. This spend ing containment predicates however, on slashing the demand for healthcare by preventing lifestyle-related diseases, the difficulties realizing such savings necessitating further reforms, including getting the private health sector more involved in health services delivery, including in managing hospitals and nursing homes. It is clear that improving the quality and efficiency of healthcare delivery is sine qua non to cost containment, which essentially is achieving the dual healthcare delivery objectives mentioned above. It is also clear that healthcare ICT plays a major role in achieving these goals, for example in actualizing the necessary disease prevention and health promotion programs that constitute the first step of the tripartite primary, secondary, and tertiary disease prevention approach. The technologies are also essential armaments in realizing the famed efficient operations of the private sector, hence would be essential to its success in running health services more efficiently and cost-effectively. Finally, the increased involvement of private companies in running the Japanese health systems would set in motion a chain reaction whose ultimate effect would be a more sophisticated healthcare stakeholder base, with clientele demand improved services. This would heighten competition among the private healthcare providers, which would stimulate investments in healthcare ICT, technologies that have the potential to broaden their service scope and value, and offer competitive advantage. In addition, the public would also increasingly invest in healthcare ICT products and services, for example, personal health records (PHR) systems that would give them access to and control over their health information, targeted and contextualized health information, and wireless monitoring devices, all of which an enterprising healthcare ICT firm could converge on a mobile device, for anywhere, anytime use. These issues would bear on other aspects of the Japanese economy, for example on whether or not the country's fiscal strengthening efforts, that is pegging government budget at 5% of the GDP, which would no doubt be a chore particularly because of increasing interest payments, would require added revenue, for example via increased taxes. The country's Ministry of Health, Labor and Welfare has a Statistics and Information Department, which implements and analyzes a variety of surveys to support policy planning, and plans and develop s information processing systems for promoting administrative informatization at the Ministry₆. Administrative informatization, whose goal is to apply information and communication technology in administration, promoted in the entire the government, under the "Basic Plan for Promoting Administrative Informatization", and includes efforts at paperless and more efficient clerical operations. The country has deployed networks and information systems in ministry and regional offices, including e-mails, Bulletin Board, and document management systems, and Kasumigaseki WAN and networks with local governments, for these purposes. Indeed, the overall goal was to realize e-government by the start of the twenty-first century. However, could one say the same of the country's health system, and if so, is there room for improvement in the applications of health information and communication technologies in the provision of qualitative health services, efficiently and cost-effectively? The Health Ministry's Health Policy Bureau plans and proposes policies for achieving a high quality and effective health system that could respond robustly to the health needs of its aging population, and of course of the rest of society, the changing disease structure and the increasingly suave demands of its peoples for higher quality health services. According to the Bureau, "It is our important task to establish a quality system to offer medical services that are at a level comparable to Japan's economic and living standards. In light of the above, efforts are being made for drastic reforms of various elements around medical services, aiming to realize 'high-quality' 'efficient' medical services for the new century." The bureau acknowledges the need of the public for health-related information and "promotes the disclosure of information necessary for patients' selection of medical institutions, through supporting the evaluation by third - party organizations of functions of hospitals". Finally, "The ministry strives to support these new medical technologies and promote the development of the drug and medical equipment industries in light of international competition, while implementing measures including the establishment of a system applying information processing and communication technologies that have shown marked progress in recent years." There is no doubt about the Health ministry's intention to encourage the utilization of information and communication technologies in several domains of the health system. However, there is equally none that it has much more to do in fostering the widespread implementation, and use of these technologies in the health system, in order to achieve the dual healthcare delivery objectives.

In fact, as far back as February of 1995, the Advanced Information and
Communications Society Promotion Headquarters, which the Prime Minster
headed, put together its Basic Policies for Promoting a Society of Advanced
Information and Communications, revised in November 1998. According to
these policies, government would promote the active utilization of information
and telecommunication technologies and the improvement of services in the
areas of health, medical care, and welfare closely linked to peoples lives[7]. The
goal was to realize a society where every citizen could enjoy the advantages of
ICT taking into cognizance the country s future society, which would have fewer
children and more seniors. Efforts that government has made include online
health information provision, including a health-information network system for
providing a variety of service-related and other information to the public, and for
standardized and secure information communication and sharing among
hospital healthcare professionals and between hospitals. It has also been
promoting the use of these technologies for care outside the hospitals and for
assisting the elderly and disabled to live relatively independent and fulfilling
lives. It has also since then be promoting the use of these technologies in other
domains indirectly health-related such as in administration and finance. The next
phase in the evolution of the use of healthcare information and communication
technologies in healthcare delivery would involve the "embedding" of these
technologies in day-to-day health service provision at all levels of service
delivery. In other words, these technologies would become integrated into a
comprehensive package of health service provision for each Japanese individual,
literally from "cradle to grave". The country has the technological infrastructure
for this to happen, and although it is one of the richest countries in the world,

314

nonetheless lacks the financial wherewithal not to make it happen. In other words, and as discussed above, for the long-term sustainability of the Japanese economy to materialize, it has to trim its budget, hence cannot afford not to take measures, including investing in the appropriate healthcare ICT and deploying them equally rationally for the delivery of qualitative health services to its peoples efficiently and cost-effectively, on fiscal discipline. To be sure, Japan has advanced technology manufacturers in areas such as electronics with electronics companies such as Sanyo, Sharp, Pioneer, Sony, and JVC, all known brands and some of the most active R&D activities in this sector. Japan is also prominent in the semiconductor markets worldwide, and in Robotics, among a host of high technology industries in which it features. Indeed, the country has a reputation for producing high quality, refined, and resilient, electronic products. Any foreign form contemplating competition on these companies turf must be ready to confront stiff competition. On the other hand, since the direction of healthcare ICT, implementation in the health industry is likely one that would use these technologies as simply enablers of functions, the success or otherwise of companies in the Japanese healthcare ICT markets would depend on the ability to differentiate via service offerings.

Thus, it would be important as noted earlier, for healthcare ICT firms to

understand the issues underlying health service provision in order to be able to compete effectively in the markets. This would be even more so as healthcare providers, particularly those in the private health sector would themselves, be seeking health information and communication technologies that could improve their value propositions to their clients, and offer them competitive advantage in both short and long-terms. Incidentally, Japan has a huge service sector, which contributes almost 75% to its overall economy, including Nippon Tel and Tel (NTT CoCoMo), the pre-eminent mobile phone operator in the country, with 56% share of Japan's mobile market emerging from NTT in 1991, to run mobile cellular operations. With revenues of US$45.183 Billion in 2005, and net income of US$6.972 Billion during the same year, among its products i-mode, a wireless Internet service, which enables cellular phone users to access mobile internet sites, is increasingly embraced not just in Japan, but also worldwide. Competing Japanese mobile operators are already out with similar mobile data services, EZweb s KDDI and J-sky s J-Phone, for examples, all jostling for the country s over 80 million subscribers as of June 2006. Vodafone has bought J-Phone including J-Sky, called it Vodafone Live!, and adapted J-Sky as Vodafone Live for Europe and elsewhere. The open standards-based i-mode has 46-8 million customers in Japan, and more than 5 million in other parts of the world as of the end of June 2006, its users with access to a variety of services such as e-mail, financial services, sports news, weather forecast, ticket booking, and games, served by an Eco-System including 4000 content partner companies. NTT DoCoMo oversees the content and operations of all official i-Mode sites, mostly commercial sites, which underscores the point made earlier regarding the seeming disinterest of healthcare ICT firms in offering health-related services to the consumers of a market that is, incidentally, potentially as large if not much larger than the ones that they currently serve. This dearth of health services is the more peculiar considering the availability or otherwise of such technologies as i-mode which could offer the health industry a range of services that the industry desperately needs. These issues again underline the need for healthcare ICT firms to understudy goings-on in the Japanese health sector and the critical issues and processes that need addressing and for which they could formulate profitable, long-term product/service mix strategies. In terms of ICT penetration, Japan has always lagged behind other East Asian countries such as South Korea, Hong Kong, Singapore, and Taiwan, under 60% penetration per population, but it is increasing. Interestingly, in 2001, the digital content market in Japan in 2001 was 48.5 billion Yen (US $400M), which included music delivery, online game, e-publishing and video streaming services, projected to increase to 550 billion Yen (US $5 billion) in 2006. The clientele is therefore not just there, but so is the purchasing capacity for health-related content in Japan. In fact, the Internet White Paper 2002 noted that 9.3% of the general Internet users have experience in buying commercial content, and 14.7 % of the broadband users have bought them, business software the most popular, 46% and 60% of regular and broadband users, respectively. Among regular and broadband users, 25% and 16%, respectively bough entertainment software, the next most popular, followed by music, which 23% and 15% of regular and broadband users respectively, bought. Indeed, surveys of Japanese consumers continue to show that IT products rank among the topmost products in the country, a trend that would likely continue with the increasing consumer confidence in the country. Urban population (percentage of total population) in Japan in 2000, and 2004, were 65% and 66%, respectively, according to the World Bank. Primary, secondary, tertiary school enrollment (percentage gross) in the same periods were 83% and 84%, respectively, Mobile subscribers (per 1,000 people), 526, 669, respectively, Population covered by mobile telephony (%), 99% for both years, Internet users (per 1,000 people), 600 and 606, respectively Personal computers (per 1,000 people) 359, and 429, respectively. There were 6.7 and 145.8 broadband subscribers (per 1,000 people) during the same periods respectively, and in contrast to these figures ICT, expenditure (percentage of GDP) fell from 8.4% to 7.4% in the same period.

These figures indicate that while the ICT sector is performing creditably

overall, more investments in ICT applications is not only required but also would likely happen considering the aforementioned reasons. Furthermore, this is even more likely with the launching of the country's national ICT policy via the e-Japan Strategy, directed from the Prime Minister's Office, itself an indication of the country's determination to rectify its sagging status in the global IT leadership, where it once held sway. The new strategy details the general structure and objectives for government 'e-policies', each government Ministry expected to come up with explicit legal and policy guidelines, which introduced in 2003 covered a variety of issues includ ing new laws on digital signatures, information privacy and confidentiality, commercial laws reforms, all aimed to be the propellant of e-commerce growth and the networked society. There is no doubt that developments in both the health and economic sectors in Japan are going to influence in profound ways the future of healthcare ICT investments in the country. Indeed, the environment is ripe for an increase in these investments in the near future. As with developments regarding global diffusion of ICT in general, access to ICT has not only increased significantly, albeit for the most part in terms of cellular mobile telephones and the Internet. Considering that a notable proportion of this growth not only occurred in emerging market economies, it did at a period characterized by a synchronized slump in the global economy and major belt-tightening in the technology sector[10]. There is no reason therefore why the same could not happen in Japan despite its intended fiscal discipline. In fact, it would be making this very effort at fiscal consolidation likelier investing in the technologies that could enable it achieve the dual healthcare delivery objectives of providing qualitative health services to its peoples at the same time curtailing its health spending.

References:

1. Available at: http://www.oecd.org/dataoecd/45/48/20431842.pdf
Accessed on July 21, 2006

2. Hillestad R, Bigelow J, Bower A, Girosi F, Meili R, Scoville R, and Taylor R Can Electronic Medical Record Systems Transform Healthcare? An Assessment of Potential Health Benefits, Savings, and Costs *Health Affairs*, Vol. 24, No. 5, pp. 1103-1117
Available at: http://www.rand.org/news/press.05/09.14.html
Accessed on July 22, 2006

3. Clinton Proposal Spotlights Healthcare Information Technology. Health Management *Technology*, Mar2004, Vol. 25 Issue 3, p8-8, 2/5p

4. Available at:
http://www.oecd.org/document/36/0,2340,en_2649_201185_37127588_1_1_1_1,00.
html
Accessed on July 22, 2006

5. Available at: http://news.bbc.co.uk/2/hi/middle_east/5207198.stm
Accessed on July 23, 2006

6. Available at: http://www.mhlw.go.jp/english/org/policy/p8-9.html

Accessed on July 23, 2006

7. Available at: http://www.mhlw.go.jp/english/wp/wp-hw/vol1/p2c7s2.html

Accessed on July 23, 2006

8. Available at: http://www.apdip.net/projects/dig-rev/info/jp/

Accessed on July 23, 2006

9. Available at: http://devdata.worldbank.org/ict/jpn_ict.pdf

Accessed on July 23, 2006

10. Available at:

http://www.weforum.org/pdf/Gcr/GITR_2003_2004/Progress_Chapter.pdf

Accessed on July 23, 2006

CONCLUSIONS

W e will not discuss North Korea in detail because of the lack of official records

from its government hence the dearth of information on what is really happening
in the country. Officially referred to as the Democratic People's Republic of
Korea, this extremely mountainous country has rich mineral resources but
production has declined, even stopped since 1990 in many mines, due to the
economic difficulties the country faced as aid declined from foreign sources, in
particular China. The country's infrastructure subsequently started falling apart
and its economy in decline, although its estimated potential oil reserves of 12
billion barrels in the seabed near Anju-ŭp, according to the North Korea
Petroleum Ministry, could turn its fortunes around in future. Its 23,113,019
peoples (2006 estimates) are ethnically homogenous, although differentially
located, mostly in the lowland plains, 61% living in urban centers. It has an
estimated literacy rate of about 99%, healthcare is free, and offered at people's
clinics all over the country, every citizen entitled to disability benefits and
retirement allowances. The country's centralized, or state-controlled, economy

stressed self-reliance, but depended heavily on Chinese and Russian aid, hence its downturn when aid ceased flowing resulting in catastrophic decline in its industrial, including agricultural base, and consequent widespread famine and a variety of health issues. With roughly 40% of the country's labor force engaged in agriculture, it is not difficult to see the magnitude of the ripple effect of the decline in this industry on the country's social and economic fabric. North Korea no longer trades exclusively with China, and other Communist countries. It bilateral trade in 2003 was $3.3 billion, exports in the same year slightly over $1 billion, it major trading partners, China (29.9 percent), South Korea (24.1 percent), and Japan (13.2 percent), its total imports, $2.1 billion, mainly from China (32.9 percent), Thailand (10.7 percent), and Japan (4.8 percent), during the same year. The figures were from the CIA Fact book. The country has indeed, taken a step further toward free trade, forming in 2002, the Kaesŏng Industrial Region, and other so-called Special Administrative Regions, including one in the northwestern city of Sinŭiju, close to the border with China. The zone has a rail link to Beijing, which has legal and economic autonomy, allowed free market operations, in the hope of fostering foreign trade and investments. With its economy stagnant and its military spending roughly a quarter of its GDP ($40 billion PPP in 2005), its health, education, and social services essentially free, questions about the quality and efficiency of its health services and their sustainability clearly loom large in the minds of many independent observers of the DPRK. This is even more so with food and other aid from the U.S, and other countries stalled due to lack of progress in the debacle consequent upon the country's nuclear weapons programs. Would the country therefore not need to explore the possibilities of implementing healthcare ICT to achieve the dual healthcare delivery objectives eventually, and what are the prospects of this happening? This question is pertinent considering that there was reportedly an increase in the number of mobile phones in Pyongyang, the country's capital, from just 3,000 in 2002 to 20,000 in 2004, when the government forbade their use. The country had 980,000 main lines in use in 2003, figures unavailable for Internet use and indeed, for other ICT use. There is therefore a potentially huge market in the country if only it would embrace the concepts that we have discussed thus far and opened up its economy to the world. In the meantime, healthcare ICT firms could explore business opportunities in the economic zones mentioned earlier, with perhaps the long-term view that more such zones would materialize, considering in particular that the country might be taking a cue from China regarding the approaches to market reforms. However, and as we have noted, it would be most appropriate for both the government of North Korea and prospective healthcare ICT firms to engage in process analyses of their intended markets. This in this case would in fact be relatively straightforward considering the likely massive need for a variety of healthcare information and communication technologies that would emerge with such analyses based on the status of ICT use in the country as a whole.

M acau, the first European settlement in the Far East, Macau became the

Macau Special Administrative Region (SAR) of China on 20 December 1999, pursuant to an agreement between China and Portugal on 13 April 1987 is the last in the geographic East Asia, we have not considered. China has spared Macao the former's socialist economic system under its 'one country, two systems' formula. Macao thus would enjoy some degree of autonomy in all issues safe foreign and defense affairs for the next half century. Macao has only 453,125 (July 2006 est.), 94.5% literacy rate, and a GDP of $10 billion (PPP) in 2004, which is growing at 2.8% (3rd Quarter 2005). Its revenues and expenditures were $3.16 billion and $3.16 billion respectively in FY05/06. Despite hit by the 1997-98 Asian financial crises and the global economic slump in 2001, its economy grew 10.1%, 14.2%, 28.6% in 2002, 2003, and 2004, respectively. It has a large number of visitors from mainland China, and a liberal economy that is attractive to foreign investors. The budget also returned to surplus since 2002, taxes on gambling casinos major revenue generators. Macao had 173,900 telephone lines in use, 432,400 mobile phone users, and 201,000 Internet users in 2004. Again, there are immense business opportunities for healthcare ICT firms in Macao, considering its liberalized economy. Like mainland China, its use of healthcare ICT is limited and a thorough analysis of its healthcare issues would likely reveal its areas of most needs for healthcare information and communications technologies, many of which would not likely be different from those of China in particular considering the similarities in the health problems they face.

The two regions that we have examined clearly have immense potential market opportunities for healthcare information and communications technologies. Exploiting this potential successfully, depends on the many factors that we discussed, and in particular, also on understanding fully the health issues of the country of interest to healthcare ICT vendors and operators, and of their non-health determinants. As we have noted, such an understanding, which requires commitment to process cycle analyses of these issues, would result in better appreciation of their underlying processes and more accurate determination of the healthcare information and communication technologies most appropriate to modifying and improving them. This exercise would also, conducted by government and its health authorities facilitate the achievement of the dual healthcare delivery objectives of delivering qualitative health services to its peoples efficiently and cost-effectively.

With healthcare funding increasingly under scrutiny, due to the ever-increasing health spending in many countries, and in some case, with questionable value for the money expended, and budgetary constraints, it is imperative for countries to explore ways to achieve these dual healthcare delivery goals. Healthcare information and communication technologies applied rationally for improving specific healthcare delivery processes hitherto determined subsequent upon thorough process cycle analyses could surely help achieve these goals. It is therefore imperative for health authorities in both Europe and East Asia to conduct these analyses, as by achieving the healthcare delivery objectives, they are not just maintaining the health of their peoples, but also contributing in no small measure the their country's sustainable economic growth.

It is undoubted that countries in both regions able to conceptualize their health services delivery this way would develop the required health projects and invest in the necessary healthcare ICT that would propel the countries forward toward achieving the dual objectives. With the link between health and the economy increasingly obvious, as is the global range of both, attention to the provision of qualitative and cost-effective health services is no longer an option, but rather a necessity. As this focus increases, so would be investments in healthcare information and communication technologies, and the opening up of markets for them on a considerable scale. This scenario would likely happen in both Europe and East Asia, and in particular in the latter, where the deployment of these technologies in healthcare delivery is still in the main rudimentary in some countries.

With the increasing focus on customer-focused health services, governments are also going to need to meet the expectations of an increasingly sophisticated healthcare clientele. This would mean over time the need for more varied value proposition, which the deployment of the appropriate healthcare information and communication technologies could no doubt help achieve. This in turn means that not only publicly funded, but also p rivately funded health systems would explore the possibilities that these technologies offer. Besides creating avenues for delivering better quality health services, which for private-sector services, could offer competitive advantage, hence higher prospects of profitability, and for public-sector services, the achievement of the dual healthcare delivery goals, the effects of these technologies on the overall economy in the long term would benefit all stakeholders.

Therefore, healthcare information and communications technologies are going to play an increasingly crucial role in healthcare delivery in the years ahead in both Europe and East Asia. Healthcare ICT vendors and others firms interested in offering their products and services in the regions could look forward to immense market opportunities for these technologies although they would also need to brace up for the equally intense competition in these markets, from both local and foreign firms. Such scenarios augur well for the individual residents of these regions. On the one hand, not only would they be receiving better quality healthcare, they would, less expensively, and more cost-effectively. On the other, and just as crucial, their countries would benefit overall as its improved health status robs off on economic growth and sustainability. The healthcare ICT vendors are therefore, not the only beneficiaries of the market openings. In fact, every healthcare stakeholder would be.

www.ingramcontent.com/pod-product-compliance
Lightning Source LLC
Chambersburg PA
CBHW031236050326
40690CB00007B/823